Legal Writing

Aspen Coursebook Series

Legal Writing

Fifth Edition

5E

Richard K. Neumann, Jr.
Professor of Law
Maurice A. Dean School of Law
Hofstra University

Sheila Simon
Assistant Professor of Law
Southern Illinois University

Suzianne D. Painter-Thorne
Professor of Law
Associate Dean for Strategic Initiatives
Mercer University School of Law

To contact Customer Service, e-mail customer.service@aspenpublishing.com, call 1-800-950-5259, or mail correspondence to:

Aspen Publishing
Attn: Order Department
PO Box 990
Frederick, MD 21705

Photo image: Jared Bowler

Printed in the United States of America.

1 2 3 4 5 6 7 8 9 0

ISBN 978-1-5438-5864-8

Library of Congress Cataloging-in-Publication Data application is in process.

About Aspen Publishing

Aspen Publishing is a leading provider of educational content and digital learning solutions to law schools in the U.S. and around the world. Aspen provides best-in-class solutions for legal education through authoritative textbooks, written by renowned authors, and breakthrough products such as Connected eBooks, Connected Quizzing, and PracticePerfect.

The Aspen Casebook Series (famously known among law faculty and students as the "red and black" casebooks) encompasses hundreds of highly regarded textbooks in more than eighty disciplines, from large enrollment courses, such as Torts and Contracts to emerging electives such as Sustainability and the Law of Policing. Study aids such as the *Examples & Explanations and the Emanuel Law Outlines* series, both highly popular collections, help law students master complex subject matter.

Major products, programs, and initiatives include:

- **Connected eBooks** are enhanced digital textbooks and study aids that come with a suite of online content and learning tools designed to maximize student success. Designed in collaboration with hundreds of faculty and students, the Connected eBook is a significant leap forward in the legal education learning tools available to students.
- **Connected Quizzing** is an easy-to-use formative assessment tool that tests law students' understanding and provides timely feedback to improve learning outcomes. Delivered through CasebookConnect.com, the learning platform already used by students to access their Aspen casebooks, Connected Quizzing is simple to implement and integrates seamlessly with law school course curricula.
- **PracticePerfect** is a visually engaging, interactive study aid to explain commonly encountered legal doctrines through easy-to-understand animated videos, illustrative examples, and numerous practice questions. Developed by a team of experts, PracticePerfect is the ideal study companion for today's law students.
- The **Aspen Learning Library** enables law schools to provide their students with access to the most popular study aids on the market across all of their courses. Available through an annual subscription, the online library consists of study aids in e-book, audio, and video formats with full text search, note-taking, and highlighting capabilities.
- Aspen's **Digital Bookshelf** is an institutional-level online education bookshelf, consolidating everything students and professors need to ensure success. This program ensures that every student has access to affordable course materials from day one.
- **Leading Edge** is a community centered on thinking differently about legal education and putting those thoughts into actionable strategies. At the core of the program is the Leading Edge Conference, an annual gathering of legal education thought leaders looking to pool ideas and identify promising directions of exploration.

for Church and Alex
RKN Jr

for Reilly and Brennan
SS

for Nate and for Oliver, who led me to teach
SDP-T

Summary of Contents

Contents

Chapter 3: More about Rules   17

Chapter 4: Analyzing a Statute   27

Chapter 5: Analyzing a Judicial Opinion   35

Chapter 6: Reading a Case for Issues, Rules, and Determinative Facts   43

Chapter 10: Working with Cases   79

2   The Process of Writing

Chapter 11: Getting to Know Yourself as a Writer   91

Chapter 12: Inside the Process of Writing   97

3   Office Memoranda

Organizing Analysis

Chapter 17: CREAC: A Formula for Structuring Proof of a Conclusion of Law   135

Chapter 18: Varying the Sequence and Depth of Rule Explanation and Rule Application   145

Chapter 19: Advanced CREAC: Organizing More Than One Issue   153

Contents

5 Working Effectively with Details

6   Informal Analytical Writing

Chapter 24: Advising and Counseling the Client   201

Chapter 25: Client Letters   205

Chapter 26: Electronic Communication   209

7   The Shift to Persuasion

Chapter 27: What Persuades a Court?   215

Contents

Chapter 28: Writing a Motion Memorandum   223

8   Telling the Client's Story

Chapter 29: The Statement of the Case in a Motion Memo or Appellate Brief   231

Chapter 30: Developing a Persuasive Story   235

Chapter 31: Telling the Story Persuasively   241

9 Making the Client's Arguments

Chapter 32: The Argument in a Motion Memo or Appellate Brief   251

Chapter 33: Point Headings and Subheadings   261

10 Appellate Briefs and Oral Argument

Chapter 38: Making Policy Arguments   305

Chapter 39: Oral Argument   309

Appendices 319

Index   357

Acknowledgments

From Richard K. Neumann, Jr:

Thank you to J. Lyn Entrikin, our third-edition co-author, for her many contributions to the book. For advice, thank you to Anne Kringel, Coleen Barger, Mary Beth Beazley, Robin Boyle, Ralph Brill, Jen Gundlach, Derek Kiernan-Johnson, Amy Langenfeld, Jan Levine, Pam Lysaght, Terry Pollman, Ruth Anne Robbins, Amy Stein, Judy Stinson, and Ed Telfeyan. For research assistance and suggestions, thanks to Elizabeth Brehm, Raf Cheema, Jennifer Garber, Rachael Ringer, Michelle Gordon, Caitlin Locurto, Samuel Lui, Nina Ovrutsky, Laura Schaefer, Matt Weinick, and Frances Zemel. For suggestions, thanks to Barbara Dillon, Alex Fiore, Francis Forde, Angelina Ibragimov, Felicia Leo, Alex Leonard, Danielle Manor, Gariel Nahoum, Jody-Ann Tyrell, and Jason Weber. And for sharing their thoughts about professional use of email, we are grateful to the following members of the bar: Elizabeth Brehm, Heather Canning, Mirel Fisch, Evgeny Krasnov, Adam Kahn, Melissa Manna, Ronald Meister, Madelyn Mostiller, and Jane Sovern.

Church and Alex have taught me much about how to learn and about how textbooks can become both lighter and deeper. At the keyboard I have often wondered what kind of book they might want to learn from, whatever they might study.

From Sheila Simon:

Thank you to Susan Williams and Ramon Escapa, who contributed long and often tedious hours to this book. Jayme McCarroll and Lynda Killoran are the stars who turned scripts into moving images for the book's website. Thanks to many people who gave ideas and energy, including Peter Alexander, Levi Burkett, Delio Calzolari, Amy Campbell, Bruce Ching, Laura Cox, Brannon Denning, Andrea Jones, Elizabeth Kee, Hannah Kelley, Sue Liemer, Melissa Marlow, Matt Rokusek, Hollee Temple, Tim Ting, and Melissa Weresh. Thanks also to the many students who allowed me to consider using their writing, particularly Elizabeth Gastélum, Nate Bailey, Joanne Olson, Caroline Borden, Berta Brazdeikyte, Kasey Farris, Morgan Campbell. Special thanks to the parents of Andrew Range. I am grateful to Richard Neumann for the opportunity to work with him. I have learned from Richard far more than I have contributed to this book.

Thanks to my husband, Perry Knop, for his constant encouragement. And our daughters, Reilly and Brennan Knop, are my best source of learning about teaching.

From Suzianne D. Painter-Thorne:

Thank you Richard K. Neumann, Jr., and Sheila Simon for inviting me to work with you on this book. I could not have asked for better coauthors, and I am grateful for such a wonderful opportunity and writing experience. Thank you to my students, who have all helped me in one way or another become better at explaining writing. Thanks also to my many colleagues at Mercer Law and beyond who at some point provided advice and encouragement that deepened my understanding of teaching and of writing, particularly Linda Berger, Latisha Nixon-Jones, Cathren Page, David Ritchie, Jennifer Sheppard, Karen J. Sneddon, and Pamela Wilkins. Special appreciation goes to the late Honorable Harry Pregerson, who, through good humor, keen mind, and kind example, made me a better person and taught me more about being a lawyer—and more about writing—than anyone. "Short declarative sentences." Yes, Judge. I will try harder. We all miss you.

Thanks to my husband, Nathan, for his seemingly limitless support. I promise not to push the limit. Finally, thanks to Oliver, who revealed my patience and taught me that I could teach.

From Richard, Sheila, and Suzianne:

At Aspen and Wolters Kluwer, we are grateful to Dana Wilson for her extraordinary skill and insight while managing us and the book through many editorial difficulties in its early editions; to George Serafin for suggesting the book's concept; and to Carol McGeehan and Rick Mixter for their help in brainstorming its possibilities.

We are also grateful to the anonymous reviewers who read drafts of the manuscript and subsequent editions for Wolters Kluwer and made many valuable suggestions. (It really is anonymous; you know who you are. But we don't.)

The authors wish to acknowledge the following source for materials reprinted in this edition:

CALVIN AND HOBBES © Watterson. Reprinted with permission of Andrews McMeel Syndication. All rights reserved.

1 Writing and Professional Work

§ 1.1 Writing as a Professional

Becoming a professional is a long and gradual process. It begins the first time students open a law school textbook and continues for many years to come.

In school, students write to satisfy requirements such as producing a term paper or demonstrating knowledge in an exam. But professional work is different. Lawyers write to *make things happen*. A lawyer writes an appellate brief, for example, to persuade a court to rule in favor of the lawyer's client. If the lawyer succeeds, the client wins. Clients hire lawyers to *get results*.

Writing is so essential to the practice of law that a good writer has an enormous advantage throughout her legal career. Law firm hiring partners often say that the two most important factors in deciding whether to hire a job applicant are the quality of the applicant's writing sample and the extent to which the applicant conveys professionalism in an interview. A lawyer can build a reputation on writing. What you *say* can fade in memory. But what you *write* will always be there as an example of your work.

Law firm associates who write clear and thorough office memos tend to be given more responsibility. Transactional lawyers are measured in part by the quality of the contracts they write, and estate-planning lawyers are measured by how well they write wills and trusts. In a trial court, a lawyer who writes persuasive pleadings and motion memos has credibility. Appellate courts and research services routinely put lawyers' appellate briefs online, where everyone can see how well, or not so well, a lawyer writes. Sometimes judges comment on how helpful or unhelpful a lawyer's brief was. And a judge's own reputation rests on the clarity of opinions the judge writes when deciding cases.

To be a lawyer is to be a writer. In the law school course for which you are reading this book, you will learn to be a lawyer who writes well.

§ 1.2   A Professional Audience

Your audience is all the people who read the documents you write: supervising lawyers as well as judges, opposing counsel, and other lawyers outside your law firm or organization. They all share three characteristics.

First, the typical reader must make a decision and will read your document to find the material necessary for that decision. Your reader wants and needs your help. The more helpful you are, the better lawyer you are. If you're not helpful, you aren't doing a good job of lawyering.

Second, your typical reader is a busy person who must read quickly and doesn't have time to read twice. Unlike school, your reader is not paid to read your writing. Thus, your writing must communicate so clearly and concisely that your reader quickly understands all your analyses. Your writing must be *efficient* for the reader.

Third, the typical legal reader is skeptical by nature and for good reason. This skepticism is not limited to opposing counsel. Badly made decisions harm people. Judges and your supervising attorney learned long ago to make decisions only if they are based on a foundation of solid reasoning from accurate analysis of law and facts. Whether they're an opposing counsel, judge, or supervising attorney, each reader is inclined to look for gaps or weaknesses in your analysis. If the reader can't find any, you have done a good job. But if the reader does find gaps or weaknesses, you won't be believed. Your readers aren't being unkind when they do this. Skepticism helps them make better decisions.

You'll be a better writer if, while writing, you think frequently about your reader's needs and sensibilities. This is called *audience sense*.

§ 1.3   Memos and Briefs

An *office memorandum* analyzes a legal issue objectively. It answers questions about how the law treats certain facts. The reader—your primary audience—will often be a supervising lawyer, such as a partner in a law firm.

A lawyer writes a *motion memorandum*, also called a *trial brief*, to persuade a trial court to decide an issue in favor of the lawyer's client. A lawsuit starts in a trial court, and the memo's audience is the trial judge.

A lawyer writes an *appellate brief* to persuade an appellate court to affirm or reverse the decision of a lower court. An appellate brief's audience is all the judges who will decide the appeal.

§ 1.4   Predictive Writing and Persuasive Writing

In an office memo, you *predict* objectively how a court would decide a legal issue on which you are writing. In a motion memo or appellate brief, you try to *persuade* the court to make a decision favorable to your client.

Predicting: Suppose your client runs a website from which ringtones can be downloaded onto cell phones. Your client asks, "If we copy the ringtones sold by the telephone company, and if we then sell them for a lower price, will we get into trouble?" Because you're learning to think precisely about the law, your mind will translate "will we get into trouble?" into questions like these:

- Does the phone company own a copyright or have some other property interest in its ringtones?
- If the answer is yes, would a court order the client to pay damages to the phone company if the client copies the company's ringtones?

Other issues could grow out of the facts, but these two illustrate predictive thinking.

Persuading: Suppose the client does copy the phone company's ringtones and the phone company sues. In the trial court, you might ask the judge to dismiss the phone company's case. If you lose at trial, you might appeal to a higher court, asking that the outcome in the trial court be reversed. In both situations, you'll try to persuade a judge or judges to decide in favor of your client. You'll do so by telling the client's story in a compelling way and by making logical arguments to support your position.

§ 1.5   How to Use This Book

Different people learn differently, and we have designed the book to accommodate as many learning styles as possible.

Although we can't sit with you individually and talk, we try to come as close to that as we can in a book. Therefore, we have also written the book in an informal style. We try to explain what you need to know without creating distance between you and the book.

When you write memoranda and briefs in this course, **please do *not* imitate this book's informality**. Memoranda and briefs are formal documents. For example, in this book we sometimes use contractions (two words merged into one with an apostrophe), but **contractions do not belong in formal documents**. And we use italics and dashes more than you should. In formal memoranda and briefs, italics and dashes have a place for emphasis, but not often.

On the other hand, we have tried to write the book in a style that illustrates some of the most important features of legal writing—clarity, precision, conciseness, and vividness. When you find those characteristics in any writing, they are worth imitating.

Part 1

Legal Rules and Their Sources

2 Inside a Rule of Law

§ 2.1 The Inner Structure of a Rule

A rule is a formula for making a decision. For example: "A person who drives a motor vehicle at a speed greater than a posted speed limit is guilty of speeding." Here's how this rule would look as a formula:

$$\text{drives + motor vehicle + faster than a posted speed limit}$$
$$= \text{guilty of speeding}$$

Suppose that you receive a speeding ticket and appear in court to contest it. The police officer would testify, and you would testify. If other people saw what happened, they might testify.

Listening to the testimony, the judge would be interested in three things. Were you driving something? Was it a motor vehicle (not a bicycle or a glider)? And were you traveling faster than the speed limit posted by the side of the road? That's because the judge will decide your case exactly according to the speeding rule's formula.

Most rules have three components:

1. **A test.** In the speeding example, the test is *driving a motor vehicle faster than a posted speed limit*. A test is a list of elements or factors.
2. **A result that occurs when the test is satisfied.** In the speeding example, the result is *guilty of speeding*.
3. **A causal term that determines whether the result is mandatory, prohibitory, discretionary, or declaratory.** (We'll explain these in a moment.) In the speeding example, the result is declaratory: You are declared guilty.

Some rules also have a fourth component:

> **4. One or more exceptions that, if satisfied, would prevent the result, even if the test has been satisfied.** For example, if the rule above contained the words "unless the motorist reasonably believes it necessary to exceed the speed limit in order to prevent injury to a person or substantial damage to property," that would be an exception. Often an exception is expressed in a dependent clause beginning with *unless* or *except*.

§ 2.2   Two Types of Tests

A test is based on either elements or factors.

Elements Tests. An elements test is satisfied only if *all* the items in the list are satisfied.

Let's return to the speeding rule's formula. To figure out whether you're guilty, compare each of the phrases in the first line to the facts. You're guilty if you were behind the wheel and operating the controls (*drives*), the thing you were driving was a car (*motor vehicle*), and you were driving perhaps 60 miles per hour when you passed a sign by the side of the road that said "Speed Limit 45" (*faster than a posted speed limit*).

But you aren't guilty if you were in the passenger seat (*not driving*) regardless of how fast the car traveled. An elements test is satisfied only if *every* element is present in the facts.

Factors Tests. Factors are criteria that function as guidelines for making a decision.

In a given set of facts, some factors might tilt in favor of enforcing the rule, and other factors might tilt against enforcing it. In applying a factors test, a court weighs all the factors together, which is why some factors tests are also called balancing tests. The test is satisfied if the factors, taken as a whole, tilt in the direction of enforcing the rule.

Factors usually don't have equal weight. In a five-factor test, for example, the factors wouldn't be worth 20% each. Suppose that a five-factor test is applied to a hypothetical set of facts, and the results look like this: Factors 1 and 2 might tilt slightly against enforcing the rule. Factors 3 and 4 might not matter because no facts are relevant to them in this particular case. Factor 5 might tilt overwhelmingly in favor of enforcing the rule.

Looking at those factors as a group, Factor 5 would probably be decisive. Factors 1 and 2 tilt in the other direction, but only slightly so. And Factors 3 and 4 don't matter.

Comparing Elements Tests and Factors Tests. Elements tests are rigid. *Every* element is essential, and *every* element must be satisfied. If any element—even just one of them—isn't satisfied, the whole test isn't satisfied, and a court will refuse to enforce the rule. Most of the rules you will encounter in the first year of law school have elements tests. For example, suppose your client is being sued for negligence. To prevail, a plaintiff would have to prove that (1) your client owed a legal duty; (2) your client breached that duty; (3) the plaintiff suffered an injury; and (4) that the breach caused the plaintiff's injury. If plaintiff is unable to prove any of these elements, their claim will fail.

A factors test is flexible. Usually none of the individual factors is essential. Some might tilt in favor of enforcing the rule, and some might tilt against. A court weighs them as a group. If those that tilt in favor of enforcing a rule outweigh those that tilt against, a court will enforce the rule. If the opposite is true, a court won't enforce it.

§ 2.3   Four Types of Causal Terms

A **mandatory rule** requires someone to act and might be expressed in words like "shall" or "must" in the causal term. "Shall" means "has a legal duty to." "The court shall grant the motion" means the court has a legal duty to grant it.

A **prohibitory rule** forbids someone to act and is generally expressed by the words "may not" or "shall not" in the causal term.

A **discretionary rule** gives someone the power or authority to do something. That person has discretion to act but is not required to do so. You might see words like "may" or "has the authority to" in the causal term.

A **declaratory rule** simply states (declares) that something is true. That might not seem like much of a rule, but the consequences of the declaration can be serious. The speeding rule we've been discussing is declaratory: "A person who drives a motor vehicle at a speed greater than a posted speed limit is guilty of speeding." If all the elements of that declaration are satisfied, other rules are activated. If you're speeding, a police officer can give you a ticket because another discretionary rule elsewhere in the law gives police the authority to do that. A court can sentence you to a fine because another discretionary rule gives courts power to impose penalties for speeding. And in many states, a mandatory rule requires the motor vehicle department to impose points on your driver's license.

A declaratory rule places a label on a set of facts (the elements or factors). The rule's power is what that label permits or requires people to do (the police officer to give you a ticket, and so on). Often the declaration is expressed by the word "is" or "means" in the causal term. But other words might be used there instead. Look at what the rule *does*. If it simply states that something is true, it's declaratory. If it does more than that, it's another kind of rule.

"Shall" and "shall not" can be confusing if you aren't careful. Legislatures and lawyers are sometimes careless with these words and use them just for emphasis. When you see them in a statute, ask yourself whether the sentence in which they occur requires someone to act (a mandatory rule) or forbids them to act (a prohibitory rule). If the sentence neither requires conduct nor forbids it, it might create a discretionary or declaratory rule. Again, you must look at what the rule *does*.

Here are examples illustrating the four types of rules:

mandatory   A person driving a motor vehicle *shall* stop at a stop sign or a red traffic light.

prohibitory   A person *shall not* drive a motor vehicle unless licensed to do so by the Department of Motor Vehicles.

discretionary A person driving a motor vehicle *may* turn right after coming to a complete stop at a red traffic signal and yielding the right-of-way to pedestrians and other motor vehicles, unless a sign erected by the highway department prohibits doing so.

declaratory   A person who violates any section of the Vehicle Code is guilty of an infraction.

§ 2.4   Analyzing a Rule to Figure Out What It Means

Analyzing a rule is a three-step process.

§ 2.4.1   *Step 1: Break Down the Rule into Its Parts*

Take apart the rule by diagramming it. List and number the elements or factors in the test. Identify the causal term and the result. If there's an exception, identify it, and if the exception has more than one element or factor, list and number them as well.

In Step 1, *you don't care what the words mean.* You want to know only the rule's *structure.* You're breaking down the rule into parts small enough that you can understand each one. Let's take the discretionary rule in § 2.3 and run it through Step 1. Here is the rule diagrammed:

> **Elements in the Test:**
> If
> (1) a person driving a motor vehicle
> (2) comes to a complete stop
> (3) at a red traffic signal and
> (4) yields the right-of-way to pedestrians and other motor vehicles,

> **Causal Term:**
> the driver may

> **Result:**
> turn right

> **Exception:**
> unless a sign erected by the highway department prohibits doing so.

You don't need to lay out the rule exactly this way. You can use any method of diagramming that breaks up the rule so you can understand it. The point is to break up the rule visually so that it's no longer a blur of words and you can *see separately* the elements or factors in the test, the causal term, the result, and any exception.

When can you combine the causal term and result? You can do it whenever that wouldn't confuse you. If you can understand the following, you can combine them, at least with this rule:

> **Causal Term and Result:**
> the driver may turn right

§ 2.4.2 *Step 2:* Look at Each Part Separately

Many rules seem baffling at first. Step 1 breaks the rule down into smaller parts. In Step 2, look at each of those parts separately to figure out what each means. Examine the details. Figure out the meaning of each element or factor, the causal term, the result, and any exception. If you aren't certain what a word means, look it up in a legal dictionary. Because you're looking at smaller parts now, the figuring out becomes easier.

Decide now what kind of rule you have. Is it an elements rule or a factors rule? Is it mandatory, prohibitory, discretionary, or declaratory?

§ 2.4.3   *Step 3:* Put the Rule Back Together in a Way That Helps You Use It

Sometimes that means rearranging the rule so that it's easier to understand. For example, when you first read the rule, if an exception came at the beginning and the elements came last, rearrange the rule so the elements come earlier and the exception last. It will be easier to understand that way.

For many elements rules—though not all of them—the rule's inner logic works like this:

What events or circumstances set the rule into operation?
(These are the elements or factors.)

When all the elements are present, what happens?
(The causal term and the result supply the answer.)

Even if all the elements are present, could anything else prevent the result?
(An exception, if the rule has any.)

Usually, you can put the rule back together by creating a flowchart and trying out the rule on some hypothetical facts to see how it works. A flowchart is essentially a list of questions. You'll be able to make a flowchart because of the diagramming you did earlier in Step 1, which not only breaks the rule down so that it can be understood, but also permits putting it back together so that it's easier to apply. The flowchart below comes straight out of the diagram in Step 1 above.

Elements

1. Were you driving a motor vehicle?
2. Did you come to a complete stop?
3. Did you do that at a red traffic signal?
4. Did you yield the right-of-way to pedestrians and other motor vehicles?

Exception

Did a sign erected by the highway department prohibit turning right on a red light?

Causal Term and Result

(if all the elements questions are answered "yes" and if the exception question is answered "no"—)
You may turn right.

Step 3 helps you add up everything to see what happens when the rule is applied to a given set of facts.

Assume that you're being tried in traffic court for making an illegal turn at a red light. The police officer testifies that you were driving a car (*element #1 satisfied*) and that this happened at a red traffic light (*element #3 satisfied*). You're acting as your own attorney. On cross-examination, you ask the police officer the following:

Q: Did I come to a complete stop before turning right?
A: Yes. (*element #2 satisfied*)
Q: Did any pedestrians have a "walk" signal?
A: No. (*beginning element #4*)
Q: Did any approaching cars have a green light?
A: No. (*element #4 satisfied*)
Q: Did a sign at this intersection prohibit right-turn-on-red?
A: No. (*exception does not apply*)

A few minutes later, this happens:

You: Your Honor, the evidence satisfies all the elements in the test that gives me discretion to turn right on a red light, and the evidence doesn't substantiate the exception to that rule. Therefore I was legally permitted to turn right.
Judge: Not guilty. Charge dismissed.
    (*leans over and speaks softly*) Nice job in your first trial.

§ 2.4.4   The Three Steps Summarized

Here are the steps (explained above) in analyzing a rule:

Step 1 Break the rule down into its parts (*§ 2.4.1*).

Step 2 Look at each of those parts separately (*§ 2.4.2*).

Step 3 Put the rule back together in a way that helps you use it (*§ 2.4.3*).

Exercise 2-A. Four Rules for Law School Exams

Consider the following rules:

The compelling circumstances rule	Compelling circumstances include serious illness or an emergency in which the student's or a family member's health or property is endangered, but do not include nervousness, fatigue, oversleeping, or forgetting an examination's time or place.
The excused exam rule	The dean of students may excuse a student from taking an examination at the scheduled time and place if the student or someone acting on the student's behalf asserts that compelling circumstances prevent the student from functioning effectively during the exam, and if the dean of students receives evidence documenting that compelling circumstances exist.
The makeup exam rule	The registrar shall schedule a makeup examination for an appropriate date and time, considering both the student's compelling circumstances and the school's need to compute final grades for all students in a timely manner.
The electronic devices rule	A student is not permitted to have any electronic device in the exam room other than a laptop computer on which the school's information technology department has installed exam software.

Part 1. For each rule, label the test, the causal term, and the result. If the rule has an exception, label that as well. You might find this easier if you use different color inks or highlighters.

Part 2. For each rule, decide whether it is mandatory, prohibitory, discretionary, or declaratory.

Part 3. For each rule, decide whether the test is based on elements or factors.

Exercise 2-B. A Rule on Late Papers

Below is a rule that appears in a professor's syllabus—not *your* professor's syllabus.

If a student submits a paper after the deadline, the student's grade on that paper will be reduced 5% for every hour the paper is late unless the student submits written proof that the student or a member of the student's family had been hospitalized or otherwise gravely at risk within 24 hours before the deadline.

Use the three-step process in § 2.4 to analyze the rule. Identify any parts of it that need further definition. What questions would you ask of this professor to make sure you understand the full meaning of each part of the rule?

3   More about Rules

§ 3.1   Remedies, Causes of Action, and Affirmative Defenses

Most of the rules you will study in law school define causes of action or affirmative defenses, which together determine whether a party can get a remedy.

A plaintiff sues to get a *remedy*. A remedy (also called *relief*) is what the law can do to solve a problem. The most common remedy is damages—money, paid by the parties responsible for causing harm, to compensate the party that suffered the loss. But damages aren't the only remedy. Sometimes a court will issue an injunction that doesn't involve paying money. An injunction is a court order requiring that a party do something (like clean up after a toxic spill) or requiring a party to stop (enjoin) doing something (like polluting a river). Other times a court might declare the rights of the parties without awarding damages or requiring that any action be taken.

A harm the law will remedy is called a *cause of action* or a *claim*. If a plaintiff can't prove a cause of action, the plaintiff won't get a remedy. Even if a plaintiff does prove a cause of action, a court won't order a remedy if the defendant proves an *affirmative defense*.

For example, when a plaintiff proves that a defendant intentionally confined him and that the defendant was not a law enforcement officer acting within the scope of an authority to arrest, the plaintiff has proved a cause of action called *false imprisonment*. Here is the rule:

False imprisonment consists of (1) a confinement (2) of the plaintiff (3) by the defendant (4) intentionally (5) where the defendant is not a sworn law enforcement officer acting within that authority.

But if the defendant can prove that she caught the plaintiff shoplifting in her store and restrained him only until the police arrived, she might have an affirmative defense called a *shopkeeper's privilege*. When a defendant proves all the elements of a shopkeeper's privilege, a court will not award the plaintiff damages, even if he has proved false imprisonment. Here is the rule:

> A shopkeeper or a shopkeeper's employee is not liable for false imprisonment when (1) the shopkeeper or shopkeeper's employee (2) has reasonable cause to believe that (3) the plaintiff (4) has shoplifted (5) in the shopkeeper's place of business and (6) the confinement occurs in a reasonable manner, for a reasonable time, and only to the extent needed to detain the plaintiff for law enforcement purposes.

§ 3.2   Where Rules Come From (Sources of Law)

Our legal system has two primary sources of law: statutes and case law.

§ 3.2.1   Statutes

Legislatures create rules of law by enacting statutes such as the Freedom of Information Act, which gives you the right to read and copy certain government documents. The federal legislature—Congress—enacts federal statutes. Each state has a legislature of its own to enact state statutes. Within each state, counties and municipalities can enact local ordinances.

In addition, some rules of law are found in materials that resemble statutes but weren't enacted by legislatures. Statute-like provisions include constitutions, administrative regulations, and court rules. Administrative regulations are issued by government agencies, and court rules are adopted usually, but not always, by courts.

§ 3.2.2   Case Law

American law is derived from English law. In England, courts existed before legislatures gained the power to make law. Without legislation, those courts not only enforced law but also created the law they were enforcing. The main tool English courts used in this process was a rule called *stare decisis*, Latin for "let stand that which has been decided," or, more loosely, "follow the rules courts have followed in the past." A past court decision is a *precedent*, which later courts, within limits, are required to take into account. Courts record their decisions in judicial opinions. Lawyers use the words *cases*, *case law*, *decisions*, *opinions*, and *precedents* interchangeably to refer to these decisions and to the opinions that explain them. This judge-made law is called common law.

In modern American law, the common law continues to exist to the extent it hasn't been superseded by legislation. Most of what you'll study in the course on Torts, for example, is common law because legislatures have enacted only a few statutes on the subject. For a common law issue, the rules come exclusively from case law. Courts, having created the common law, can change it and periodically do, in decisions that enforce the law as changed.

In addition, many statutes have ambiguities, and often we don't know what a statute means until the courts interpret it—through judicial decisions applying the statute to specific facts. If the statute is unclear, we must read the case law to find out what it means. By interpreting the statute, courts essentially finish the process of law creation that the legislature started by enacting the statute in the first place.

Thus, courts make law in two ways. First, they created the common law centuries ago and sometimes change it today. Second, when they interpret statutes, they add meaning to what the legislature has enacted.

Each state has its own courts enforcing that state's law, and in addition the federal government has courts throughout the country enforcing federal law. Federal courts include general trial courts (the United States District Courts), intermediate appellate courts (the United States Courts of Appeals), and a final appellate court (the United States Supreme Court). The Courts of Appeals are divided into thirteen Circuits.

Most large and medium-sized states have a similar structure: a general trial court, an intermediate appellate court, and a final appellate court. Smaller states might not have an intermediate appellate court. Both federal and state systems also include specialized courts, such as the United States Tax Court or a state's family court. Court names differ from state to state.

§ 3.3   Some Questions about Rules

1. Must the elements or factors always be stated before the rest of the rule? No. If you have a simple causal term and result together with a complicated test listing many elements or factors, you can put the test last. For example:

> Common law burglary is committed by breaking and entering the dwelling of another in the nighttime with intent to commit a felony therein.[1]

If the elements were listed first, this rule would be a lot harder to understand.

---

1. This was the crime at common law. Because of the way its elements are divided, it does a good job of illustrating several different things about rule structure. But the definition of burglary in a modern criminal code will differ.

2. If a rule has lots of elements or factors, or if they are complicated or ambiguous, how can you make it clear where one ends and the next begins? You can insert a number before each element or factor:

> Common law burglary is committed by (1) breaking and (2) entering (3) the dwelling (4) of another (5) in the nighttime (6) with intent to commit a felony therein.

3. With an elements rule, how can you tell what the elements are? Think of each element as a separate fact, the absence of which would prevent the rule's operation. If you can think of a scenario that has a realistic chance of occurring in real life and in which only *part* of the element might be true, then you actually have two or more elements in place of what you thought was only one element.

For example, is "the dwelling of another" one element or two? A person might be guilty of some other crime, but he is not guilty of common law burglary when he breaks and enters the restaurant of another, even in the nighttime and with intent to commit a felony therein. The same is true when he breaks and enters his own dwelling. In both of these scenarios, part of "the dwelling of another" is present and part is missing. "The dwelling of another" thus includes two elements: the nature of the building (a residence) and the identity of its resident (a person other than the defendant).

Often you won't know the number of elements in a rule until you have consulted the judicial decisions that interpret it. Is "breaking and entering" one element or two? The cases define "breaking" in this sense as the creation of a gap in a building's protective enclosure, such as by opening a door, even when the door was left unlocked and the building was thus not damaged. The cases further define "entering" for this purpose as placing inside the dwelling any part of oneself or any object under one's control, such as a crowbar. Can a person "break" without "entering"? Yes. If you open a window by pushing it up from outside the building, and if, before you do anything else, the police appear and arrest you, you "broke" by opening the window, but you didn't enter. "Breaking" and "entering" are therefore two elements. But to know that, you must read the judicial decisions that define these terms.

4. With a factors rule, how can you tell what the factors are? When a court uses a factors test, the court will typically list them and sometimes explain them. For example, the Sixth Amendment to the U.S. Constitution creates a right to a speedy trial: "In all criminal prosecutions, the accused shall enjoy the right to a speedy and public trial . . . ." But the Amendment provides no criteria for judging whether a trial has been prompt enough. The Supreme Court developed a test in *Barker v. Wingo:*[2]

---

2. 407 U.S. 514, 530–32 (1972).

We . . . identify . . . [four] factors which courts should assess in determining whether a particular defendant has been deprived of his right [to a speedy trial] . . . : Length of delay, the reason for the delay, the defendant's assertion of his right, and prejudice to the defendant.

The length of the delay is to some extent a triggering mechanism. Until there is some delay which is presumptively prejudicial, there is no necessity for inquiry into the other factors that go into the balance. . . . [T]he length of delay that will provoke such an inquiry is necessarily dependent upon the peculiar circumstances of the case. To take but one example, the delay that can be tolerated for an ordinary street crime is considerably less than for a serious, complex conspiracy charge.

Closely related to length of delay is the reason the government assigns to justify the delay. Here, too, different weights should be assigned to different reasons. A deliberate attempt to delay the trial in order to hamper the defense should be weighted heavily against the government. A more neutral reason such as negligence or overcrowded courts should be weighted less heavily but nevertheless should be considered since the ultimate responsibility for such circumstances must rest with the government rather than with the defendant. Finally, a valid reason, such as a missing witness, should serve to justify appropriate delay.

. . . Whether and how a defendant asserts his right is closely related to the other factors we have mentioned. . . . The more serious the deprivation, the more likely a defendant is to complain. . . .

A fourth factor is prejudice to the defendant. . . . If witnesses die or disappear during a delay, the prejudice is obvious. There is also prejudice if defense witnesses are unable to recall accurately events of the distant past. Loss of memory, however, is not always reflected in the record because what has been forgotten can rarely be shown.

If the test is in a statute, the factors will be listed there. For example, this is part of an Illinois statute that guides a court's discretion in deciding who should receive custody of a child:

In determining the child's best interests for purposes of allocating parenting time, the court shall consider all relevant factors, including, without limitation, the following:

(1) the wishes of each parent seeking parenting time;

(2) the wishes of the child, taking into account the child's maturity and ability to express reasoned and independent preferences as to parenting time;

(3) the amount of time each parent spent performing caretaking functions with respect to the child in the 24 months preceding the filing of any petition for allocation of parental responsibilities or, if the child is under 2 years of age, since the child's birth;

(4) any prior agreement or course of conduct between the parents relating to caretaking functions with respect to the child;

(5) the interaction and interrelationship of the child with his or her parents and siblings and with any other person who may significantly affect the child's best interests;

(6) the child's adjustment to his or her home, school, and community;

(7) the mental and physical health of all individuals involved;

(8) the child's needs;

(9) the distance between the parents' residences, the cost and difficulty of transporting the child, each parent's and the child's daily schedules, and the ability of the parents to cooperate in the arrangement;

(10) whether a restriction on parenting time is appropriate;

(11) the physical violence or threat of physical violence by the child's parent directed against the child or other member of the child's household; . . . [3]

5. What if you read a rule that doesn't specify *who* has a legal duty or is prohibited from doing something or has discretion to act? For example:

A motion for a new trial must be filed no later than 28 days after the entry of judgment.[4]

"Shall" means "has a legal duty to." Here, someone has a legal duty to file this kind of motion "no later than 28 days after the entry of judgment." Who has the duty? The rule doesn't say. You must figure it out from the context. A judgment is the document that terminates a lawsuit, for example after a trial. If the losing party wants a new trial, she has a legal duty to file a motion for one no later than 28 days after entry of judgment.

6. When you find the word *or* in a list of elements, what does it mean? It usually means that an element can be satisfied in more than one way. Here's an example:

A person shall not drive or park on a public street a motor vehicle to which license plates issued by a government motor vehicle department are not attached.

Here it is again, with *or* underlined and the elements enumerated:

A person shall not (1) drive <u>or</u> park (2) on a public street (3) a motor vehicle (4) to which license plates issued by a government motor vehicle department are not attached.

---

3. 750 Ill. Comp. Stat. Ann. §5/602.7 (LexisNexis 2018).

4. Fed. R. Crim. P. 59(b).

The first element can be satisfied by doing *either* of two acts: driving on a public street or parking on a public street. It isn't necessary to do both. One is enough. Why would a rule be created this way?

Suppose a police officer found a parked car without license plates and a person nearby with keys to the car. The officer didn't see the person drive the car and therefore can't issue a citation for driving a motor vehicle without license plates. But it's a fair inference that the person parked the car, and the officer can reasonably issue a citation for that. A legislature enacting this statute would want to stop people from *driving* motor vehicles without license plates. It wouldn't care much about parking them. Penalizing parking is a way of indirectly penalizing driving in situations where the police don't have eyewitness evidence that the car was driven without license plates.

Thus you can violate this rule in either of two ways. You can drive a motor vehicle without license plates on a public street. Or you can park it on a public street. The *or* creates alternative ways of satisfying the first element.

Exercise 3-A. Nansen and Byrd

Part 1. With the aid of §§ 16 and 221(a) of the Criminal Code (below), outline the rule in § 220 into a list of elements and exceptions. Annotate the list by adding definitions for the elements and for any exceptions you might come across.

> #### Criminal Code § 16
> When a term describing a kind of intent or knowledge appears in a statute defining a crime, that term applies to every element of the crime unless the definition of the crime clearly indicates that the term is meant to apply only to certain elements and not to others.

> #### Criminal Code § 220
> A person is guilty of criminal sale of a controlled substance when he knowingly sells any quantity of a controlled substance.

> #### Criminal Code § 221(a)
> As used in section 220, "sell" means to exchange for goods or money, to give, or to offer or agree to do the same, except where the seller is a licensed physician dispensing the controlled substance pursuant to a permit issued by the Drug Enforcement Commission or where the seller is a licensed pharmacist dispensing the controlled substance as directed by a prescription issued by a licensed physician pursuant to a permit issued by the Drug Enforcement Commission.

Part 2. You have interviewed Nansen, who lives with Byrd. Neither is a licensed physician nor a licensed pharmacist. At about noon on July 15, both were arrested and charged with criminal sale of a controlled substance. Nansen has told you the following:

> Byrd keeps a supply of cocaine in our apartment. He had been out of town for a month, and I had used up his stash while he was gone. I knew that was going to bend Byrd completely out of shape, but I thought I was going to get away with it. I had replaced it all with plaster. When you grind plaster down real fine, it looks like coke. For other reasons, I had decided to go to Alaska on an afternoon flight on July 15 and not come back. Byrd was supposed to get back into town on July 16, and by the time he figured out what had happened, I would be in the Tongass Forest.
>
> But on the morning of the 15th, Byrd opened the door of the apartment and walked in, saying he had decided to come back a day early. I hadn't started packing yet—I wouldn't have much to pack anyway—but I didn't know how I was going to pack with Byrd standing around because of all the explaining I'd have to do. I also didn't want Byrd hanging around the apartment and working up an urge for some cocaine that wasn't there. So I said, "Let's go hang out on the street."
>
> We had been on the sidewalk about ten or fifteen minutes when a guy came up to us and started talking. He was dressed a little too well to be a regular street person, but he looked kind of desperate. I figured he was looking to buy some drugs. Then I realized that that was the solution to at least some of my problems. I took Byrd aside and said, "This guy looks like he's ready to buy big. What do you think he'd pay for your stash?" Byrd looked reluctant, so I turned to the guy and said, "We can sell you about three ounces of coke, but we have to have a thousand for it." When the guy said, "Yeah," Byrd said, "Wait here" and ran inside the apartment building. A thousand was far more than the stuff was worth.
>
> Byrd walked out onto the stoop with the whole stash in his hand in the zip-lock bag he kept it in, and while he was walking down the steps, about ten feet away from me and the guy who wanted to buy, two uniforms appeared out of nowhere and arrested Byrd and me.

The "guy" turned out to be Officer D'Asconni, an undercover police officer who will testify to the conversation Nansen has described. The police laboratory reports that the bag contained 2.8 ounces of plaster and 0.007 ounces of cocaine. When you told Nansen about the laboratory report, he said the following:

> I didn't think there was any coke in that bag. What they found must have been residue. I had used up every last bit of Byrd's stuff. I clearly remember looking at that empty bag after I had used it all and wondering how much plaster to put in it so that it would at least look like the coke Byrd had left behind. I certainly didn't see any point in scrubbing the bag with cleanser before I put the plaster in it.

Part 3. Will Nansen or Byrd be convicted of criminal sale of a controlled substance?

> **Criminal Code § 221(b)**
> As used in section 220, "controlled substance" includes any of the following: . . . cocaine . . . .

> **Criminal Code § 10**
> No person may be convicted of a crime except on evidence proving guilt beyond a reasonable doubt.

Using your annotated outline of elements, decide whether each element can be proved beyond a reasonable doubt and whether any exceptions are satisfied. Then predict whether Nansen or Byrd will be convicted.

4 Analyzing a Statute

Elizabeth: Wait! You have to take me to shore. According to the Code of the Order of the Brethren. . . .

Captain Barbossa: First, your return to shore was not part of our negotiations nor our agreement so I "must" do nothing. And secondly, you must be a pirate for the pirate's code to apply and you're not. And thirdly, the code is more what you'd call "guidelines" than actual rules. Welcome aboard the Black Pearl, Miss Turner.

—Pirates of the Caribbean: The Curse of the Black Pearl

§ 4.1 A Statute's Structure

Statutes are groups of legal rules. Unlike most other things you have read, a statute does not describe or explain anything. It has no story or characters. Almost every word in a statute is part of a legal rule. And most of the rules in statutes are written in an abstract way because they are drafted to apply to many people and different sets of circumstances. Further, statutes are written by a legislative body attempting to articulate rules that would appeal to the largest number of legislators to get the votes needed, as legislators often say "to pass the damn thing." Consequently, statutes can be difficult to understand without some analysis.

§ 4.2 Outlining a Statute

Lawyers deal with statutes and rules of one kind or another almost every day. While many law school courses focus primarily on common law and case analysis, you might be surprised by how often statutes and rules come into play in solving your clients' legal problems. For instance, many of the cases you read center on a court's analysis of a particular statute.

A statute makes much more sense once you look for the individual rules and outline the statute to separate it into its parts. Outlining a statute helps you break it down into its separate rules to figure out how each of them operates and how they work together.

§ 4.2.1   *Step 1:* Decide How Many Legal Rules Are in the Statute

As Chapter 2 explains, every legal rule is one of the following: mandatory, prohibitory, discretionary, or declaratory. A statute contains one or a combination of these types of rules.

In Step 1, don't worry about what the words actually mean. That comes later in Step 2. Instead, just try to separate one rule from another and list each rule within the statute separately.

For example, how many rules are in the following statute?

> (a) Any person having an interest in land including the structures, buildings, and equipment attached to the land, including without limitation, wetlands, rivers, streams, ponds, lakes, and other bodies of water, who lawfully permits the public to use such land for recreational, conservation, scientific, educational, environmental, ecological, research, religious, or charitable purposes without imposing a charge or fee therefor, or who leases such land for said purposes to the commonwealth or any political subdivision thereof or to any nonprofit corporation, trust or association, shall not be liable for personal injuries or property damage sustained by such members of the public, including without limitation a minor, while on said land in the absence of wilful, wanton, or reckless conduct by such person.[1]

You can bring order to the sea of words by using a step-by-step, analytical approach. Break down the statute by looking at what it is mandating, prohibiting, permitting, and/or declaring. That list will lead you into the individual rules within the statute. Once the rule is broken down, it becomes more clear that the statute quoted above has one very complicated rule, which includes one exception.

The rule declares that owners of land, wetlands, and improvements are immune from civil liability to members of the public, including minors, for personal injury or property damage that occurs on the land. The rule applies in only two sets of circumstances: (1) when the owner allows the public to use the property for certain

---

1. Mass. Gen. Laws Ann. ch. 21, § 17C (West 2010).

purposes at no charge, or (2) when the owner leases the property to a state[2] or local government, or to a nonprofit corporation, for one of the same purposes. Even if all of the rule's elements are met, the statute excludes certain kinds of conduct by the property owner that injures a member of the public on the land.

§ 4.2.2   *Step 2: Analyze Each Rule to Determine What It Means*

For each rule you have identified in the statute, use the method explained in Chapter 2 to take the rule apart to determine what it means. First, break the rule down into its parts (see § 2.4.1). Second, look at each of those small parts separately (§ 2.4.2). And third, put the rule back together in a way that helps you use it (§ 2.4.3).

From the example above, you have only one rule, but it has a complicated structure. To reveal the rule's structure, look for the connecting words between each subpart of the rule and underline them. When you use this process to analyze the statute quoted in § 4.2.1, here's the outline you end up with. The connectors are underlined.

Elements

1. any person having an interest in land, <u>including</u>:[3]
   (a) attached structures, buildings, and equipment, <u>and</u>
   (b) wetlands, rivers, streams, ponds, lakes, and other bodies of water
2. who does <u>one</u> of the following:
   (a) lawfully permits the public to use the property without charge or fee <u>or</u>
   (b) leases the property to
      (i) the commonwealth or any political subdivision, <u>or</u>
      (ii) a nonprofit corporation, trust, or association
3. for <u>one</u> of the following purposes:
   (a) recreational,
   (b) conservation,
   (c) scientific,
   (d) educational,
   (e) environmental,

---

2. The statute's language refers to "commonwealth," the term used in Kentucky, Massachusetts, Pennsylvania, and Virginia law when referring to the state itself. The other states refer to their governments by the more familiar term "state" government.

3. The first part of the statute applies to any person who has "an interest in land including the structures, buildings, and equipment attached to the land, including without limitation, wetlands, rivers, streams, ponds, lakes, and other bodies of water." From the first part of this wording, we know the person must have an interest in *land*. The rest of the wording following "including" simply *defines* exactly what the statute means by the term *land*. This is an example of an *inclusive* definition that gives a non-exhaustive list of examples. In this case, *land* is defined broadly to include any improvements ("structures, buildings, and equipment attached"), and any marshes, streams, and bodies of water on the land ("wetlands, rivers, streams, ponds, lakes, and other bodies of water"). This second element's two subparts are joined together with the word "and" to illustrate that the statutory term "land" has a more general meaning than a reader might otherwise give it.

(f) ecological,
(g) research,
(h) religious, <u>or</u>
(i) charitable

Causal term

shall not

Result

be liable for personal injuries or property damage sustained by such members of the public (including minors) while on said land

Exception

in the absence of wilful, wanton, or reckless conduct by such person

Now look at the rule to see what it *does*. Although the causal term includes "shall not," this rule is a *declaration* that under certain circumstances, a landowner isn't liable for personal injuries or property damage to those whom she allows to use the property for certain purposes listed in the statute.

The rule's elements require that for the owner to be absolved of liability, the property must be used for certain purposes (recreational, conservation, scientific, educational, environmental, ecological, research, religious, or charitable), and only if the land is open to the public at no charge, or if it is leased to nonprofit corporations, trusts, or associations for one of those purposes. Conversely, if the land is used for some other purpose, or if it is leased to a private individual or a for-profit corporation, the statute does not protect the landowner from civil liability for injuries or property damage, even if a user is on the owner's land for one of the purposes listed in the rule.

The *exception* means that even if all the elements of the declaration are satisfied, the statute does not prevent civil liability by the landowner if her wilful, wanton, or reckless conduct causes harm to a member of the public. In other words, if the landowner's bad conduct (worse than simple negligence) causes the injury, she cannot avoid liability.

Now, let's apply the statute to a set of specific facts.

Suppose your client owns 160 acres of farmland surrounding a farm pond. This landowner allows children to swim in the pond for free whenever they wish. A neighbor's eight-year-old son drowns one afternoon while swimming in the pond without adult supervision. Is the landowner liable to the child's parents for wrongful death?

Applying the rules in the statute as outlined, we can conclude that the four elements of the declaration are met: The client *owns an interest in land* together with the farm *pond* (element 1). The landowner allows members of the *public*, including *minors*, to use the property *without charge* (element 2(a)) for swimming, which is a *recreational purpose* (element 3(a)). Without more, we can apply the causal term and the result to predict that the client will not be liable.

But wait. There's more. The statute includes an exception if the landowner's "wilful, wanton, or reckless conduct" caused the child's injury. As far as we know from the facts given in the hypothetical, the owner's *conduct* had nothing to do with the child's drowning. While the child's parents might argue that the owner was *reckless* by not supervising the swimming children, you might consider arguing that your client's failure to act was not reckless *conduct*. The outcome will turn on how the court interprets the statutory word *conduct*.

What do the terms "wilful, wanton, or reckless conduct" mean? To find out, you would look for definitions elsewhere in the statute as well as in any cases in your jurisdiction that have interpreted the words in the statute.

§ 4.2.3   The Two Steps Summarized

Here are the two steps (explained above) in outlining a statute:

Step 1   Decide how many legal rules are in the statute (§ 4.2.1).

Step 2   Analyze each rule in the statute to figure out what it means (§ 4.2.2):
    (a)   Break the rule down into its parts (§ 2.4.1).
    (b)   Look at each of the parts separately to figure out what it does (§ 2.4.2).
    (c)   Put the rule back together in a way that helps you use it (§ 2.4.3).

Exercise 4-A. Outlining U.C.C. § 2-302(1) on Unconscionability

Outline Uniform Commercial Code § 2-302(1), which appears below.

If the court as a matter of law finds the contract or any term of the contract to have been unconscionable at the time it was made the court may refuse to enforce the contract, or it may enforce the remainder of the contract without the unconscionable clause, or it may so limit the application of any unconscionable clause as to avoid any unconscionable result.

Exercise 4-B. Outlining a Dram Shop Liability Statute

Outline the Arkansas dram shop liability statutes, which appear below.

Ark. Code Ann. § 16-126-103. In cases where it has been proven that an alcoholic beverage retailer knowingly sold alcoholic beverages to a minor or sold under circumstances where such retailer reasonably should have known such purchaser was a minor, a civil jury may determine whether or not such knowing sale constituted the proximate cause of any injury to such minor, or to a third person, caused by such minor.

Ark. Code Ann. § 16-126-104. In cases where it has been proven that an alcoholic beverage retailer knowingly sold alcoholic beverages to a person who was clearly intoxicated at the time of such sale or sold under circumstances where the retailer reasonably should have known the person was clearly intoxicated at the time of the sale, a civil jury may determine whether or not the sale constitutes a proximate cause of any subsequent injury to other persons. For purposes of this section, a person is considered clearly intoxicated when the person is so obviously intoxicated to the extent that, at the time of such sale, he presents a clear danger to others. It shall be an affirmative defense to civil liability under this section that an alcoholic beverage retailer had a reasonable belief that the person was not clearly intoxicated at the time of such sale or that the person would not be operating a motor vehicle while in the impaired state.

Ark. Code Ann. § 16-126-105. Except in the knowing sale of alcohol to a minor or to a clearly intoxicated person, the General Assembly hereby finds and declares that the consumption of any alcoholic beverage, rather than the furnishing of any alcoholic beverage, is the proximate cause of injuries or property damage inflicted upon persons or property by a legally intoxicated person.

Exercise 4-C. Applying a Dram Shop Liability Statute

After outlining the statute in Exercise 4-B, use your outline to predict the outcome of the following case:

Joe Atkinson played basketball for his high school team. Even at the young age of sixteen, he was 6'4". College basketball scouts had already offered him scholarships to play basketball, so he owned several college sweatshirts and baseball caps bearing college logos.

On the day of the accident, Joe rode his bike to a retail liquor store. Wearing a sweatshirt bearing the name of the local university, he went inside and paid cash for a six-pack of beer and a bottle of Mogen David 20/20 wine. The liquor store cashier did not ask Joe for identification before ringing up the sale.

In the parking lot behind the liquor store, Joe drank half the bottle of MD 20/20 and strapped the paper bag holding the six-pack onto the back of his bike.

A few minutes later, on his way to a friend's house, he rode into an intersection against a red light. A motorcycle traveling through the intersection on a green light collided with his bike, knocking both Joe and the six-pack off the bike and onto the pavement. Joe was thrown from the bike, sustaining severe injuries. The six-pack was unhurt.

Is the liquor store liable to Joe for his injuries? Does the store have any affirmative defense? If the case goes to trial, will the jury have discretion to decide whether the liquor store's sale of beer and wine to Joe was the proximate cause of his injuries? Using your outline, explain your answers.

5 Analyzing a Judicial Opinion

§ 5.1 The Contents of a Judicial Opinion

When law professors refer to "a case," they mean a judicial opinion through which a court announces and explains a decision. A judicial opinion can include up to ten ingredients:

1. the case name and citation
2. the factual story (what happened before the lawsuit began)
3. the procedural story (what happened during the lawsuit)
4. the issue or issues to be decided by the court
5. the arguments made by each side
6. the court's holding on each issue
7. the rule or rules of law the court enforces through each holding
8. the court's reasoning
9. dicta
10. the remedy the court granted or denied

Most opinions don't include all these things, but a typical opinion has most of them.

Learning to read and analyze cases is one of the primary skills you will learn in the first year of law school. Developing that skill is easier if you identify and label each of its ingredients as you read. Identifying and labeling the ingredients breaks the opinion down into smaller chunks that you can more easily understand. It also helps you see how the parts are related to each other and produce the court's decision.

The *case name* is made up of the names of the plaintiff and defendant separated by "v." (That's how lawyers abbreviate "versus.") The citation is the volume, publication, and page where the opinion can be found, together with the date.

Opinions often begin with the *factual story*. It describes what the parties and other people did before the lawsuit began.

The court will next describe the *procedural story*, which lawyers often call the *procedural history*. After the lawsuit or prosecution began, what did the lawyers and judges do? Examples are motions, trial, judgment, and appeal. Although a court might ascribe a procedural action to a party ("The defendant moved to dismiss . . ."), that's really what the party's lawyer did.

A court might also set out, or at least imply, the *issue or issues* to be decided and the *arguments* made by each side. An issue is a question the court must answer because the parties disagree about it. When a court expressly states the issue, it might begin a sentence with words like "This appeal requires us to decide whether . . ." or "The parties raise an issue of . . . ." When a court implies the issue, it will describe the arguments made by each party; the implied issue is then the question of which party is right. Some cases involve only one issue. Other cases involve multiple issues.

For each issue, the court will state its *holding*, which is essentially the court's answer to the question posed in the issue. In support of its holding, the court will state the *rule or rules of law* it is enforcing. Sometimes resolving an issue involves only one rule. Sometimes several rules are needed. When that happens, some rules are subsidiaries of other rules. A subsidiary rule expands on part of a more general rule. A subsidiary rule adds specificity to a general rule.

Suppose that a lawyer has been sued by a former client, who alleges that the lawyer committed malpractice by giving the client bad advice. Suppose also that at trial the jury returned a verdict in favor of the client (the plaintiff), and that the lawyer (the defendant) moved for a new trial, arguing that the jury's verdict was against the weight of the evidence. The trial court denied the motion, and the lawyer appealed. When you read the appellate court's opinion, you might see sentences like the ones in the right-hand column below. The left-hand column tells you what kinds of sentences they are.

issue	We must decide whether the client produced enough evidence of malpractice to justify the jury's verdict.
general rule on lawyer malpractice	To prevail on a claim for legal malpractice, the client must prove that the lawyer failed to exercise ordinary professional care, skill, and diligence.
subsidiary rule on a specific duty	Among other things, a lawyer is required to know the law and to research the relevant statutes and case law, to the extent necessary, before giving advice to a client.
holding	The trial court correctly denied the lawyer's motion for a new trial. The evidence shows that the lawyer failed to perform the legal research that an ordinarily prudent attorney would do before rendering legal advice in a case of this nature.

The general rule applies to all malpractice claims. Lawyers' work can be divided into many categories, such as examining witnesses at trial, negotiating settlements, writing pleadings, and advising clients. How does the general rule govern advising clients? The subsidiary rule provides the specifics.

The *reasoning*—often called the rationale—is the court's analysis of the law and how it applies to the facts. The reasoning often discusses or hints at the *policy* behind the rules the court enforces. A rule's policy is its purpose—what the law is trying to accomplish through the rule.

Somewhere in the opinion the court might place some *dicta*, which is discussion not necessary to support a holding and therefore not part of binding precedent. The full term is *obiter dicta*, which is Latin for "words said along the way." Think of it as side chat—something a court says that might be interesting but isn't necessary to prove that the holding is right.

An opinion usually ends with the *relief granted or denied*. If the opinion is the decision of an appellate court, the relief may be an affirmance or a reversal of the lower court's decision. If the opinion is from a trial court, the relief is most commonly the granting or denial of a motion.

In an appellate court, several judges will decide together. An appellate court's decision is announced in the *court's opinion* or the *majority opinion*. If one of the judges doesn't agree with some aspect of the decision, that judge might write a *concurrence* or a *dissent*. A concurring judge agrees with the result the majority reached but would have used different reasoning to get there. A dissenting judge thinks the court reached the wrong result. Concurrences and dissents aren't binding precedent. Only the court's majority opinion has that authority.

§ 5.2   Reading Aggressively in Law School

Most people read passively most of the time—breezing through paragraphs, understanding some or most of what appears on the page, and guessing about the rest. You cannot succeed in law school by skimming or reading passively. Lawyers—and successful law students—read *aggressively*.

In college, most of your reading was in textbooks written to explain things to you. You were the audience. Law school is different. Judicial opinions and statutes are most of what you'll read as a law student. A judge writing a judicial opinion doesn't wonder, "How should I write this opinion so a first-year law student can easily understand it?" A judge instead writes primarily for a professional audience of lawyers and other judges—who quickly understand legal wording and concepts that might baffle law students.

Several studies have shown that an important part of success in the first year of law school is learning to read analytically, the way experienced lawyers do.[1] Experienced lawyers don't glide from one sentence to the next, waiting for meaning to jump off the page. Instead, they read aggressively, dissecting the opinion as they go through it.

Aggressive reading is pulling apart, in your mind, what appears on the page so you can wring meaning out of it. Consciously or unconsciously, aggressive readers engage in silent dialogs with themselves about what they are reading. They ask themselves questions, which they then try to answer. For example:

"Why is the judge emphasizing that fact?"
(A passive reader isn't curious.)

"What's preventing me from understanding that paragraph?"
(A passive reader ignores the paragraph without trying to figure it out.)

"What does that phrase mean? How can I find out?"
(A passive reader just skims over the phrase.)

Who's in charge—the reader or the page? For a passive reader, the page is in charge because the passive reader lets words hide their meaning. An aggressive reader refuses to allow words to do that. An aggressive reader interrogates until the words give up and confess what they mean.

Aggressive reading is one of the most important skills for success in law school. You can start by aggressively carving up judicial opinions, looking for the ingredients listed at the beginning of this chapter, and marking each ingredient using highlighters or handwritten notes in the margin. Experienced lawyers identify the ingredients quickly and almost unconsciously—instantly recognizing, for example, where the factual story ends and the procedural story begins. Your goal is to become that efficient.

While much of the opinions you will read are available in an e-reader or online form, don't fall into the trap of using your computer's or device's "search" feature to hunt for words you think matter in the opinion. Doing so might seem more efficient, but it opens up the possibility of missing what the court believed was important, leading you to misunderstand the court's reasoning and the lesson from the case. Just as important, it denies you the opportunity to engage with the text and to develop skills necessary to your success as a student and as a lawyer. Further, because e-readers encourage skimming, a better practice, at least while you are learning to read cases, is to read a printed copy of the opinion (a pdf on a tablet using a stylus in lieu of a pen or highlighter is a good substitute). Either will allow you to mark up the page with your observations, so you can read more aggressively.

---

1. *See* Ruth Ann McKinney, Reading Like a Lawyer: Time-Saving Strategies for Reading Law Like an Expert (2d ed. 2012); *see also* Leah M. Christensen, *Legal Reading and Success in Law School: An Empirical Study*, 30 Seattle U. L. Rev. 603 (2007); Laurel Currie Oates, *Beating the Odds: Reading Strategies of Law Students Admitted Through Alternative Admissions Programs*, 83 Iowa L. Rev. 139 (1997).

Words are a lawyer's stock in trade. Architecture is a sight profession, few words and much drawing. Engineering is a numbers profession, few words and much math. But *law is all words*: reading, writing, talking, and listening. Lawyers must be extraordinarily precise with language. If a word or phrase is new to you or is used in an unusual way, find out what it means. Don't guess.

Use a *legal dictionary* to look up words and phrases that seem like lawyer-talk. But don't stop there. Look up any word or phrase that seems to be used in an unusual way. A *term of art* is a word or phrase that has a special meaning in a profession. Some legal terms of art obviously have a special meaning to lawyers, such as *parol evidence*, *habeas corpus*, and *res ipsa loquitur*. But others are deceptive. They're words you've seen many times before, but they mean something different in the law. Examples are *consideration*, *representation*, *condition*, *performance*, *avoidance*, and *remedy*. Look up in a law dictionary *any word or phrase that seems to be used in an unusual way*.

If you're not sure what a word means and if it isn't in a law dictionary, look it up in a *general dictionary*. If you don't have a general dictionary in book form, use a website like Merriam-Webster Online. Bookmark a general dictionary website in your browser or download a general dictionary app into your phone.

Exercise 5-A. Analyzing a Judicial Opinion

Read *Conti v. ASPCA*, reprinted below, and find each of the judicial opinion ingredients as they occur (if they do) in this court's decision. Mark up the text generously, with highlighting and margin notes, so you can discuss your analysis in class. Look up every unfamiliar word in a legal dictionary, as well as every familiar word that is used in an unfamiliar way.

Conti v. ASPCA
353 N.Y.S.2d 288 (N.Y. City Civ. Ct. 1974)

RODELL, J.

Chester is a parrot. He is fourteen inches tall, with a green coat, yellow head and an orange streak on his wings. Red splashes cover his left shoulder. Chester is a show parrot, used by the defendant ASPCA in various educational exhibitions presented to groups of children.

On June 28, 1973, during an exhibition in Kings Point, New York, Chester flew the coop and found refuge in the tallest tree he could find. For seven hours the defendant sought to retrieve Chester. Ladders proved to be too short. Offers of food were steadfastly ignored. With the approach of darkness, search efforts were discontinued. A return to the area on the next morning revealed that Chester was gone.

On July 5, 1973 the plaintiff, who resides in Belle Harbor, Queens County, had occasion to see a green-hued parrot with a yellow head and red splashes seated in his backyard. His offer of food was eagerly accepted by the bird. This was repeated on three occasions each day for a period of two weeks. This display of human kindness was rewarded by the parrot's finally entering the plaintiff's home, where he was placed in a cage.

The next day, the plaintiff phoned the defendant ASPCA and requested advice as to the care of a parrot he had found. Thereupon the defendant sent two representatives to the plaintiff's home. Upon examination, they claimed that it was the missing parrot, Chester, and removed it from the plaintiff's home.

Upon refusal of the defendant ASPCA to return the bird, the plaintiff now brings this action in replevin.

[If the parrot] is in fact Chester, who is entitled to its ownership?

The plaintiff presented witnesses who testified that a parrot similar to the one in question was seen in the neighborhood prior to July 5, 1973. He further contended that a parrot could not fly the distance between Kings Point and Belle Harbor in so short a period of time, and therefore the bird in question was not in fact Chester.

The representatives of the defendant ASPCA were categorical in their testimony that the parrot was indeed Chester, that he was unique because of his size, color and habits. They claimed that Chester said "hello" and could dangle by his legs. During the entire trial the court had the parrot under close scrutiny, but at no time did it exhibit any of these characteristics. The court called upon the parrot to indicate by name or other mannerism an affinity to either of the claimed owners. Alas, the parrot stood mute.

Upon all the credible evidence the court does find as a fact that the parrot in question is indeed Chester and is the same parrot which escaped from the possession of the ASPCA on June 28, 1973.

The court must now deal with the plaintiff's position, that the ownership of the defendant was a qualified one and upon the parrot's escape, ownership passed to the first individual who captured it and placed it under his control.

The law is well settled that the true owner of lost property is entitled to the return thereof as against any person finding same.

This general rule is not applicable when the property lost is an animal. In such cases the court must inquire as to whether the animal was domesticated or ferae naturae (wild).

Where an animal is wild, its owner can only acquire a qualified right of property which is wholly lost when it escapes from its captor with no intention of returning.

Thus in *Mullett v. Bradley* (24 Misc. 695) an untrained and undomesticated sea lion escaped after being shipped from the west to the east coast. The sea lion escaped and was again captured in a fish pond off the New Jersey coast. The original owner sued the finder for its return. The court held that the sea lion was a wild animal (ferae naturae), and when it returned to its wild state, the original owner's property rights were extinguished.

In *Amory v. Flyn* (10 Johns. 102) plaintiff sought to recover geese of the wild variety which had strayed from the owner. In granting judgment to the plaintiff, the court pointed out that the geese had been tamed by the plaintiff and therefore were unable to regain their natural liberty. . . .

The court finds that Chester was a domesticated animal, subject to training and discipline. Thus the rule of ferae naturae does not prevail and the defendant as true owner is entitled to regain possession.

The court wishes to commend the plaintiff for his acts of kindness and compassion to the parrot during the period that it was lost and was gratified to receive the defendant's assurance that the first parrot available would be offered to the plaintiff for adoption.

Judgment for defendant dismissing the complaint without costs.

Exercise 5-B. Distinguishing Holdings, Dicta, Rules, and Reasoning

In a New Jersey case,[2] a truck driver sent text messages back and forth to a friend while he was driving home from work. Distracted by the text messages, he swerved across the center line and collided with an oncoming motorcycle, seriously injuring the motorcyclist, who sued both the truck driver and his friend for negligence. One of the legal issues was whether the sender of a text, here the friend, could be held liable to the injured motorcyclist when the text message distracted the truck driver and led him to collide with another vehicle.

The trial court granted summary judgment for the sender of the text, and the plaintiff motorcyclist appealed. The parties disagreed about whether a "remote texter" like the friend owed a legal duty to a third-party driver or occupant of a motor vehicle if the texter knew that the recipient truck driver would most likely read the text message while driving.

The following passages are edited from the appellate court's opinion. Determine whether each passage is a *holding*, *dicta*, a *legal rule*, or *legal reasoning*. Be prepared to explain your answers in class.

1. Whether a duty of care exists is generally a matter for a court to decide, not a jury.
2. A passenger who distracts a driver can be held liable for the passenger's own negligence in causing an accident. In other words, a passenger in a motor vehicle has a duty "not to interfere with the driver's operations."
3. The public interest requires fair measures to deter dangerous texting while driving.

---

2. *Kubert v. Best*, 75 A.3d 1214 (N.J. Super. Ct. App. Div. 2013).

4. Because the necessary evidence to prove breach of the remote texter's duty to the plaintiff is absent in this record, the trial court properly granted summary judgment for defendant.

5. In New Jersey, the use of a wireless telephone or electronic communication device by an operator of a moving motor vehicle on a public road or highway violates the Traffic Code, unless the telephone is a hands-free wireless telephone, or the electronic communication device is used hands-free.

6. One does not actually have to be the person who threw a rock to be liable for injury caused by the rock.

7. In a lawsuit alleging that a defendant is liable to a plaintiff because of the defendant's negligent conduct, the plaintiff must prove four things: (1) that the defendant owed a duty of care to the plaintiff, (2) that the defendant breached that duty, (3) that the breach was a proximate cause of the plaintiff's injuries, and (4) that the plaintiff suffered actual compensable injuries as a result. The plaintiff bears the burden of proving each of these four "core elements" of a negligence claim.

8. A person should not be held liable for sending a wireless transmission simply because some recipient might use his cell phone unlawfully and become distracted while driving. Whether by text, email, Twitter, or other means, the mere sending of a wireless transmission that unidentified drivers may receive and view is not enough to impose liability.

9. The sender of a text message can potentially be liable if an accident is caused by texting, but only if the sender knew or had special reason to know that the recipient would view the text while driving and thus be distracted.

10. The New Jersey public has learned the dangers of drinking and driving through a sustained campaign and enhanced criminal penalties and civil liability.

Reading a Case for Issues, Rules, and Determinative Facts

§ 6.1 How to Identify Issues, Rules, and Determinative Facts

Many facts are mentioned in an opinion just to provide background, continuity, or what journalists call "human interest." Other facts might be related to the court's thinking but aren't crucial. The most important facts are the ones that *caused* the court to come to its decision.

This last group—the *essential* or *determinative facts*—are essential to the court's decision because they determined the outcome. If they had been different, the decision would have been different. They lead to the rule of the case—the rule of law for which the case stands as precedent. Discovering that rule is the most important goal of reading cases. When several issues are raised together in a case, the court must make several rulings, and an opinion may thus stand for several different rules.

The determinative facts can be identified by asking the following: *If a particular fact had not happened, or if it had happened differently, would the court have made a different decision?* If so, it is one of the determinative facts. This can be illustrated with a decision that has nothing to do with law.

Suppose you're looking for a place to live now that you're attending law school. A rental agent has just shown you an apartment. The following are true:

A. The apartment is located half a mile from the law school.

B. It's a studio apartment (one room plus a kitchenette and bathroom).

C. The building appears to be well maintained and safe.

D. The apartment is at the corner of the building, and windows on two sides provide ample light and ventilation.

E. It's on the third floor, away from the street, and the neighbors don't seem to be disagreeable.

F. The rent is $975 per month, furnished.

G. You have a widowed aunt, with whom you get along well and who lives alone in a house 45 minutes by bus from the law school. She has offered to let you use the second floor of her house during the school year. The house and neighborhood are safe and quiet, and the living arrangements would be satisfactory to you.

H. You have taken out loans to go to law school.

I. You don't have access to a car.

J. Reliable local people have told you that you probably can't find an apartment that is better, cheaper, or more convenient than the one you have just inspected.

Which facts are *essential* to your decision? For example, if the apartment had been two miles from the law school (rather than a half-mile), would your decision have been different? If the answer is no, fact A couldn't be determinative. It might be part of the factual mosaic and might explain why you looked at the apartment in the first place, but you wouldn't base your decision on it.

The determinative facts, the issue, the holding, and the rule all depend on each other. In the apartment hypothetical, for example, if the issue were different—say, "How should I respond to an offer to join the American Automobile Association?"—the selection of determinative facts would also change. In fact, the only determinative one would be fact I: "You don't have access to a car."

Often a court won't explicitly state the issue, the holding, or the rule for which the case stands as precedent. And courts don't usually label the determinative facts as such. Whenever a court gives less than a full explanation, you must use what is explicitly stated to pin down what is only implied.

If the court states the issue but doesn't identify the rule or specify which facts are determinative, you might discover the rule and the determinative facts by answering the following questions:

Who is suing whom over what series of events and to get what relief?
What issue does the court say it intends to decide?
How does the court decide that issue?
On what facts does the court seem to rely in making that decision?
What rule does the court enforce?

Facts from a case can often be reformulated to be more general than the court described them. In the apartment hypothetical, for example, a generalized reformulation of fact G might be the following:

You have a rent-free alternative to the apartment, but the alternative would require 45 minutes of travel each way to school plus the expense of public transportation.

A generalized version of the facts can supply a guide to deciding later cases where the factual details are similar but not identical. For example, suppose a later case involves a person who is a member of the clergy in a religious organization that has given her a leave of absence to attend law school. Assume that she may continue to live rent-free in the satisfactory quarters the religious organization has provided, but getting to the law school would require walking for 15 minutes and then riding a subway for 30 minutes, at the same cost as a bus ride. Isn't this really the same situation as the aunt's house, but with different details? The generalized reformulation covers *both* sets of facts.

§ 6.2   Formulating a Narrow, Middling, or Broad Rule

When a court doesn't state a rule of the case, you might be able to formulate the rule by converting the determinative facts into elements of a rule. Often you can interpret the determinative facts narrowly (specifically) or broadly (generically). Notice how different formulations of a rule can be extracted from the apartment example. If the student decides to stay with the aunt, a narrow rule formulation might be the following:

> A law student who has a choice between renting an apartment and living in the second floor of an aunt's house should choose the latter when the student has had to borrow money to go to law school and when the apartment's rent is $945 per month but the aunt's second floor costs nothing except for bus fares.

Because this rule is limited to the specific facts in the hypothetical, it can directly govern only a tiny number of future decisions, if any at all. For example, it won't directly govern the member of the clergy described above.

Although the clergy member might be able to reason by analogy from the narrow rule, she would not be directly governed by it. Analogy is indirect. A broader rule would directly govern *both* situations:

> A student on a tight budget shouldn't pay rent when a nearly free alternative is available.

An even more general formulation would govern an even wider circle of applications:

> A person with limited funds shouldn't lease property when there is a satisfactory and nearly free alternative.

The following, however, is so broad as to be meaningless:

A person shouldn't spend money unnecessarily.

Exercise 6-A. Isolating Determinative Facts and Formulating a Rule

Part 1. Reread *Conti v. ASPCA* (Exercise 5-A in Chapter 5). Identify the determinative facts, and summarize them in one paragraph.

Part 2. After identifying the determinative facts, write a narrow version of the *Conti* rule. Then write a broad version of it.

Exercise 6-B. The Cow and the Swimming Pool

A farmer's swimming pool was damaged when one of his cows, a 300-pound heifer—which everyone describes as an ordinary and gentle cow accustomed to life outside a barn—strayed from the pasture where she was grazing. She wandered into the farmer's unfenced yard and stepped on the canvas cover over the farmer's swimming pool. The cow fell through, damaging the pool cover and the pool itself. The farmer filed a claim under his homeowner's insurance policy, seeking reimbursement for the repair costs. The insurer denied the claim and cited the following provision from the insurance policy, particularly the words underlined below:

This policy does not insure against loss from wear and tear; marring or scratchings; deterioration; inherent vice; latent defect; mechanical breakdown; rust; mold; wet or dry rot; contamination; smog; smoke from agricultural smudging or industrial operations; settling, cracking, shrinkage, bulging or expansion of pavements, patios, foundations, walls, floor, roofs or ceilings; birds, vermin, rodents, insects or <u>domestic animals</u> . . . .[1]

Part 1. Assume you represent the farmer in a suit against the insurer. You will argue that the exclusion does not apply here. Formulate a rule from *Conti v. ASPCA* (Exercise 5-A in Chapter 5) that supports that argument.

Part 2. Now assume you are on the other side of the case, representing the insurer. Formulate a rule from *Conti v. ASPCA* that supports an argument that the policy does exclude coverage in the farmer's case.

---

1. *Smith v. State Farm Fire & Cas. Co.*, 381 So. 2d 913, 914 (La. Ct. App. 1980).

Policy and Why Courts Care About It

In the Bookstore

Time: August.
Place: the campus bookstore.
Student approaches the cashier counter, carrying a big pile of books.
Behind the counter stands a store clerk.

Student: I'd like to return these books.

Clerk: Do you have a receipt?

Student: No.

Clerk: *[points to sign]* The rule is *[reading sign aloud]* "No returns without a receipt."

Student: *[frustrated]* But I just bought them.

Clerk: *[looks at sign]* It doesn't say, "except when you just bought them."

Student: But I just bought them.

Clerk: Maybe I should rephrase the rule: "If you have a receipt, you may return the books. You don't have a receipt, so you may not return the books." Sorry.

Student: Look, I bought them half an hour ago. When I got back to my dorm room, there was an email from the registrar saying they switched me into a different section, where the professors are different, and those professors assigned different books. I don't have any choice in this. I'm a first-year law student, and all the courses are required. They assign me to a section. I need completely different books for five courses.

Clerk: *[in a snide tone]* Did your dog eat your receipt?

Student: No. I just can't find it. Don't you ever lose things?

Clerk: Not within a half hour. A rule's a rule. Sorry.

Student: But every rule has a purpose. What's the purpose of this rule?

Clerk: To protect the store from people who bring in books they found or stole or bought more cheaply elsewhere. A rule's a rule.

Student: But a rule should be applied in a way that's consistent with the rule's purpose. I can prove that I didn't find or steal them or buy them more cheaply elsewhere. I bought them half an hour ago from that clerk over there.

Second Clerk: *[looks up]* I did ring up a sale to you. I don't remember what books you bought. I just scan the bar codes. Bring them over here and let's see if my register recorded the book titles.

[The two clerks compare the books to the register's record and explain to a supervisor who has wandered over.]

Supervisor: *[to the student]* We'll take all these books back and give you credit toward the books you need to buy now. The only reason we can do this is because we're confident that in these circumstances you actually did buy these books from us. Don't assume in the future that you can return things without a receipt.

§ 7.1   What Is Policy?

Notice the method through which the student won this argument. The student showed store employees that the purpose of the rule could be accomplished without enforcing the rule in the most obvious way. Instead, the store enforced the rule in a novel way—by treating the second clerk's memory and the store's internal records together as the equivalent of a receipt. If the student had not been able to persuade store employees to interpret their rule in light of its purpose, the student would have lost the argument.

Every rule of law, whether found in a statute or a case, has a purpose—a reason for being. That purpose is called the rule's *policy* or the *policy behind the rule*. Some policies are obvious. Why is it illegal to drive while intoxicated? You probably already know the answer.

Other policies are more complicated, and understanding them requires some special knowledge. Why is your internet service provider (ISP) not liable for defamation if you send email messages to a million people falsely and unjustly accusing Lizzo of stealing another singer's songs? Congress enacted a statute[1] exempting ISPs from liability for publishing defamatory material.

What problem was Congress trying to solve or prevent? If every ISP had to read and screen every email message that a website transmitted or made accessible

---

1. Part of the Communications Decency Act of 1996, 47 U.S.C. § 230(c) (Westlaw 2018).

through its equipment, the internet would suddenly become very slow and very expensive to use. And ISPs often would not be able to tell what is defamatory and what is not. Exempting ISPs from defamation for content transmitted through its service serves the public policy of ensuring efficient internet service.

Policy also exists in a wider sense—not tied to one specific rule. A broad policy might lead the law to adopt many separate rules. For example, courts everywhere like solutions that are easily enforceable, promote clarity in the law, aren't needlessly complex, and don't allow true wrongdoers to profit from illegal acts.

Other policy considerations may differ from state to state. In many states, for example, public policy favors development of land by building homes and businesses, while in states like Vermont policy prefers preservation of the environment and agriculture. Some states favor providing tort remedies even if additional lawsuits slow down courts, although in others the reverse is true.

§ 7.2   Why Courts Care About Policy

It is revolting to have no better reason for a rule of law than that so it was laid down in the time of Henry IV. It is still more revolting if the grounds upon which it was laid down have vanished long since, and the rule simply persists from blind imitation of the past.

—*Justice Oliver Wendell Holmes*

Law isn't just rules. It's rules *plus* their policies. To understand a rule, it's not enough to know its elements, results, and exceptions. You also need to know what the law is trying to accomplish through the rule. Every rule makes more sense when we understand why it exists.

Whenever courts doubt what a rule means or how it should be applied, the rule's purpose provides one solution to the problem. If you're not sure what a rule *means*, choose the meaning that's most consistent with the rule's purpose. If you're not sure *how to apply* the rule, apply it in whatever way is most consistent with its purpose. If you know the rule but not its purpose, you don't really know what to do with the rule. And if rules didn't have policies, they could be arbitrary and might cause more harm than good.

Policy is also important in a different context. When the law doesn't yet have a rule on a given subject and courts or legislators need to decide what rule to adopt, they consider the policies the law already has for other rules, and they try to choose a rule that achieves those policies. Policy thus is valuable not only in interpreting and enforcing existing rules, but also in adopting new rules.

§ 7.3   How to Recognize Policy in a Judicial Opinion

A rule itself doesn't tell you its policy. You need to look in the judicial decisions and statutes that are the sources of most law, or in commentaries on the law, such as law review articles. Sometimes, courts openly say something like "The policy behind this rule is . . . ." But more often a court will discuss policy without calling it policy—for example, by explaining what would happen if the rule did not exist. The rule's purpose is to prevent that from happening. With some practice, you will be able to spot a policy discussion in a judicial decision—and write about it in this course.

In the case below, a court used policy to decide whether to adopt a new rule.

Ash v. New York University Dental Center
564 N.Y.S.2d 308 (App. Div. 1st Dep't 1990)

ELLERIN, J.

The issue before us in this dental malpractice action is the validity of an agreement that plaintiff Arthur Ash was required to sign as a precondition to obtaining treatment at defendant New York University Dental Center which prospectively exculpated the various defendants from any liability for negligence in treating plaintiff.

Plaintiff seeks to recover for injuries suffered as a result of his aspiration, during dental treatment, of two dental crowns, which became lodged in his right lung and required surgical removal. Plaintiff [needed] substantial dental work which would cost over $6,000[, and he therefore sought treatment at the clinic associated with the defendant's dentistry school], where the work could be done [by dentistry students under supervision] for $3,000. . . .

When plaintiff arrived at the clinic . . . , he was required to sign a form containing the following provision: "In consideration of the reduced rates given to me by New York University, and in recognition of the risks inherent in a clinical program involving treatment by students, I hereby release and agree to save harmless New York University, its trustees, doctors, employees and students from any and all liability, including liability for its and their negligence, arising out of or in connection with any personal injuries (including death) or other damages of any kind which I may sustain while on its premises or as a result of any treatment at its Dental Center or infirmaries."

[P]laintiff testified that he believed the signing of this form was an insignificant registration procedure and he was never told, nor did he imagine, that he was relinquishing any of his legal rights. . . .

. . . There is no decision of the Court of Appeals [the state's highest court] that expressly deals with this precise issue. . . .

It is clear that the State's substantial interest in protecting the welfare of all of its citizens, irrespective of economic status, extends to ensuring that they be provided with health care in a safe and professional manner. Toward that end, the State carefully regulates the licensing of physicians and other health care professionals and monitors such activities to prevent untoward consequences to the public from "the ministrations of incompetent, incapable, ignorant persons." A similar concern for the enforcement of established minimum standards of professional care provides the underlying rationale for a cause of action for malpractice in favor of those who have been subjected to substandard care. Unquestionably public clinics such as defendant, which are used primarily by those who are unable to pay the rapidly escalating fees for private medical and dental care, play an important role in delivery of such care to those who may not otherwise be able to obtain it. However, important as this role is, it cannot serve as a basis for excusing such providers from complying with those minimum professional standards of care which the State has seen fit to establish. It is the very importance of such clinics to the people who use them that would create an invidious result if the exculpatory clause in issue were upheld—i.e., a de facto system in which the medical services received by the less affluent are permitted to be governed by lesser minimal standards of care and skill than that received by other segments of society.

There is, of course, no public policy against allowing patients of such clinics to agree to fewer amenities, longer waits or greater inconvenience in exchange for lower prices than they would pay elsewhere. Nor is there any public policy against such a clinic limiting itself to certain types of care or refusing to perform certain procedures. There cannot, however, be any justification for a policy which sanctions an agreement which negates the minimal standards of professional care which have been carefully forged by State regulations and imposed by law. . . .

The fact that defendant New York University Dental Center is a clinical program associated with an educational institution does not alter this conclusion. Defendant, of course, has a substantial interest in providing its students with clinical experience as part of their education. However, this interest cannot negate the State's overriding concern in seeing that defendants fulfill their equally important obligation to their patients. That obligation includes ensuring that students are sufficiently prepared and supervised so that the treatment which is provided to human patients is at least at the minimally acceptable reasonable level of skill and care. If defendants cannot fulfill this obligation, they must not hold themselves out as being providers of dental care. . . .

Other jurisdictions which have addressed attempts by health care professionals to relieve themselves of liability, particularly to those who stand in a disadvantageous bargaining position, have arrived at a conclusion similar to the one we have reached.

[For example, i]n *Emory Univ. v. Porubiansky* . . . the Supreme Court of Georgia refused to enforce a very similar contract in a setting identical to the one herein, stating: "A contract between a medical practitioner and patient must be examined in light of the strong policy of the state to protect the health of its citizens and to regulate those professionals that it licenses. . . ."

_____

This court was able to create new law only because existing law had a gap in it. How do we know there is a gap? The fifth paragraph tells us: "There is no decision of the Court of Appeals [the state's highest court] that expressly deals with this precise issue." The court used policy as a guide in filling that gap.

Exercise 7-A. A Cell Phone in Class

This rule appears in a course syllabus:

A student who uses any form of electronic communication during class will be counted as absent for the entire class.

Before class, a student set his cell phone to vibrate. During class, a friend in the parking lot sent him a text message saying the student's car was being stolen. The professor spotted the student reading the message and marked him as absent. The student protested.

Under this rule as written, who was right? Who *should* be right? How would policy considerations affect your answers?

8 Selecting the Right Authority

This chapter explains how to select the right legal authorities for your legal issues. The next two chapters explain how to use the two most important kinds of authority: statutes (Chapter 9) and cases (Chapter 10).

In reading this chapter, remember that the federal government and each state have separate bodies of law, which in most respects are independent of each other.

§ 8.1 The Hierarchy of Authority

Primary authority is the law itself. Its words have legal significance. Cases and statutes are the primary authorities most often used in legal reasoning. Others are constitutions, court rules, and administrative regulations. Primary authority is the product of a legislature, a court, or some other government entity empowered to make or determine law.

Secondary authority is commentary that explains the law but is not the law itself. Examples are law review articles, treatises, and other reference materials written by legal scholars. Secondary authority only summarizes, describes, or analyzes what a private person or group believes the law is (or should be). The author of secondary authority might know a lot about the law but lacks the power to create law itself.

From its name, you might think primary authority is always the best authority. While that is often true, identifying the best legal authority for resolving a particular dispute depends on the source of the primary authority and its relationship to the nature of the legal issue and the jurisdiction of the court that will decide it. Consequently, before selecting legal authorities to use in your case, you should answer the following questions:

- What *law* applies: federal or state?
- Which *kind of court* will decide your issue: federal or state?
- What *level of court* will decide the issue: trial court, intermediate appellate court, or the highest appellate court?

Courts use a complicated set of preferences—called the *hierarchy of authority*—to determine which authority they will follow. That hierarchy of authority can be visualized in this way:

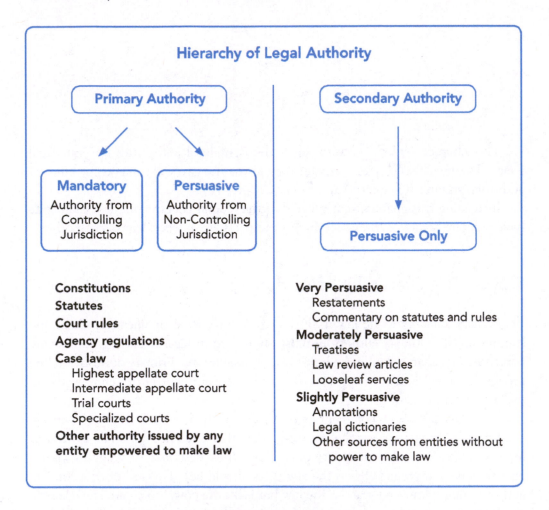

§ 8.1.1   Primary Authority

Primary authority (on the left side of the diagram) is the law itself—constitutions, statutes, cases, rules, and regulations. But not all primary authority is *mandatory authority* that your court *must* follow. Primary authority is *mandatory* only if issued by the federal or state government whose law controls the legal question.

Mandatory primary authority includes statutes and statute-like materials of the government with jurisdiction over the legal issue to be resolved. It also includes case precedents issued by those courts that have jurisdiction over the court that will decide the question. Those courts might be an intermediate appellate court or the jurisdiction's highest court of review (often, but not always, referred to as a supreme court). A lower-level court must follow those precedents because those higher courts have power to affirm or reverse the decision if the losing party challenges it on appeal.[1]

Regardless of jurisdiction, some mandatory authority outranks other mandatory authority. At the top of the ranking is the jurisdiction's constitution. Because a constitution is the fundamental law that creates the government, a jurisdiction's constitution prevails over all other forms of primary authority from the same jurisdiction that conflict with that constitution. This means that a legislature can only enact—and the executive may only enforce—statutes allowed by its constitution. When the statute and the constitution conflict, a court is empowered—by the constitution—to strike down the statute in whole or in part. The courts are similarly constrained by their constitutional authority. This means that the courts' power to create and reinterpret common law is subservient to the constitution that created the government of which the courts are a part.

Next in the hierarchy are statutes. Statutes generally control over case law because a legislature's power to enact new law or amend existing law prevails over the courts' power to interpret or reinterpret statutes and common law. Further, because statutes can give courts and administrative agencies the power to adopt court rules and regulations, statutes prevail over conflicting court rules or administrative regulations.

At the bottom of the hierarchy is the case law promulgated by the jurisdiction's courts. Within this ranking, case law from higher courts prevails over inconsistent case law from lower courts. For instance, a state's intermediate appellate court prevails over decisions by trial courts, and the state's highest court prevails over its appellate courts.

What happens when two mandatory authorities of the same rank are inconsistent with each other—for example, what if one state statute preserves a cause of action for alienation of affection, while another statute from the same state abolishes it? The court will first try to *reconcile* the two inconsistent authorities by applying interpretive

---

1. Because federal courts are divided into circuits, you must pay attention to which circuit has jurisdiction over the legal issue. For example, the U.S. Court of Appeals for the Third Circuit decides appeals from federal district courts in Delaware, New Jersey, and Pennsylvania. The U.S. Court of Appeals for the Sixth Circuit hears appeals from federal district courts in Kentucky, Michigan, Ohio, and Tennessee. A Sixth Circuit opinion is mandatory authority in a U.S. district court in Ohio because the Sixth Circuit can reverse that trial court's decision on appeal. The same Sixth Circuit opinion is mandatory primary authority for issues decided by other panels of the Sixth Circuit, which is bound by its own prior decisions. However, that same Sixth Circuit opinion is merely persuasive primary authority to a U.S. district court in Pennsylvania. That is because the Third Circuit—not the Sixth—hears appeals from federal trial courts in Pennsylvania. And that opinion is only persuasive primary authority in the Third Circuit and in the U.S. Supreme Court, which is superior to all federal circuit courts.

canons. (See Chapter 9.) If they cannot be reconciled, dates matter in deciding which one controls. A more recently enacted statute generally prevails over an older one. Similarly, a more recent case prevails over an earlier one issued by the same court.

§ 8.1.2   Applying the Hierarchy of Primary Authority

Mandatory primary authority. To apply some of these principles, let's try an example. Assume you represent a client who lives in Madison, Wisconsin. While she was attending a Bad Bunny performance in Chicago, Illinois, someone stole her car from the parking lot. Your client has since learned from her Facebook friends that a student from Knox College in Galesburg, Illinois, was spotted driving her car. She has asked you to sue to recover the car or its fair market value. How do you find the best authority for predicting the outcome?

Remember the questions listed earlier in this chapter:

- What *law* applies: federal or state? If state law applies, which one?

In a civil case for return of a stolen car, or for compensatory damages for the value of the stolen car, *state tort law* will govern the issues. But the tort law of which state? Because the car was stolen in Chicago, the claim arose there, and therefore Illinois tort law will most likely control the issue.

- Which *kind of court* will decide your issue: federal or state? If state, which one?

We know that the client lives in Wisconsin, and the theft occurred in Illinois. Civil procedure rules give her a choice where she files suit. Assuming the defendant who stole the car lives in Illinois, a federal court there would have diversity jurisdiction, but only if the amount at issue exceeds the jurisdictional threshold, currently $75,000.[2] Unless the car's fair market value exceeds the jurisdictional threshold for diversity jurisdiction in federal court, your client most likely will sue in state court in Illinois, where the car was stolen.

- What *level of court* will decide the issue: trial court, intermediate appellate court, or the highest appellate court?

No matter where the plaintiff files her lawsuit, we know it will be in a trial court. Which primary authorities are best in that trial court? Unless Illinois has a statute imposing civil liability for car theft, common law (found in case law) generally

---

2. 28 U.S.C. § 1332(a)(1) (2012).

controls for issues of Illinois tort law. Whether the plaintiff sues in a Wisconsin or an Illinois trial court, the court will be required to follow appellate court decisions interpreting the tort law of Illinois, where the car was stolen. If Illinois has enacted any statutes governing civil remedies for car theft, the trial court would be required to follow that mandatory primary authority as well.

What if the car is a brand new Porsche Taycan worth $90,000, which exceeds the $75,000 threshold for federal diversity jurisdiction? Then the plaintiff might decide to file suit in a federal district court. Would that change the best primary authority? No, it would not. Whether your client sues in federal or state court, the car theft involves the same issue of Illinois tort law. A federal court deciding a state law issue must follow state law, just the same as if a state court were to decide the issue. Here, that includes relevant Illinois cases and statutes—the same mandatory authority that would govern a state trial court. If a federal trial court rules against your client, the U.S. Court of Appeals for the Seventh Circuit would decide the appeal.

Nonmandatory primary authority. *Persuasive primary authority* may or may not be followed, at the court's election. For that reason, it's *nonmandatory*. Persuasive primary authority usually comes from a court that lacks the power to make law for the jurisdiction whose law controls the issue.

In the example above, the Illinois trial court might cite a Michigan appellate court case involving a car theft from a concert parking lot in Ohio. That case is *primary* authority because a Michigan appellate court can create Michigan common law. But it would not be *mandatory* because an issue of Illinois tort law is not controlled by either Michigan or Ohio law. The Michigan appellate case qualifies only as *persuasive primary authority* in this example because it was issued by a court that has no power to make Illinois law.

Just how persuasive is nonmandatory primary authority? If a court opinion isn't mandatory authority, its persuasive value depends on several factors. One of the most important is how *factually analogous* the persuasive authority is compared to your case. The more factually similar the Michigan appellate court case is to the facts of your case, the more persuasive it will be for the trial court resolving your client's issue. Other important factors are when the nonmandatory primary authority was decided, and whether it reflects a prevailing trend in the law. A trial court will be more persuaded by another jurisdiction's case if it has been issued recently or if it reflects a modern trend in developing the law.

Section 8.3 explains more about how you can use nonmandatory primary authority. But first, we need to show how primary authority differs from secondary authority. Before reading the next subsection, look back at the diagram at the beginning of this chapter to review what you have already learned about primary authority.

§ 8.1.3   Secondary Authority

As we explain in § 8.1, secondary authority explains the law but is not the law itself. For that reason, mandatory authority always outranks secondary authority. But in the hierarchy of authority, persuasive (nonmandatory) primary authority and secondary authority start out approximately equal in value. A court can either follow them or ignore them.

The most significant categories of secondary authority are restatements, which are formulations of the common law issued by the American Law Institute; treatises written by scholars; and articles and similar material published in law reviews and other periodicals.

Restatements are the most influential and persuasive form of secondary authority. Since 1923, the American Law Institute has commissioned scholars to draft restatements of the common law of contracts, property, torts, and several other fields. The purpose of a restatement is to express scholarly consensus about the common law.[3] A restatement consists of a series of black-letter rules organized into sections, followed by commentary and illustrations. Courts often cite restatements when deciding novel issues of state common law.

The persuasive value of a *scholarly treatise* depends on the author's reputation and whether the treatise has been kept up to date. Some outstanding treatises have been written by Wigmore (on evidence), Corbin (on contracts), Williston (on contracts), Prosser and Keeton (on torts), and Sutherland (on statutory interpretation). Some treatises are multivolume works, and some double as student hornbooks. In your law library, you will find subject-matter specific treatises that comprehensively address many legal issues in detail. If your research shows a gap in your jurisdiction's law, a treatise can reveal how other courts have handled the issue, and it can lead you to persuasive primary authority from other states.

Law reviews publish two kinds of material: articles (written by scholars, judges, and practitioners), and comments and notes (written by students). If an article is especially thorough and insightful, or is authored by a respected scholar, it might influence a court and might therefore be worth citing. Most articles, however, do not fit that description. The fact that an article has been published doesn't necessarily mean that it's influential. For example, a student comment or note influences a court in only the most unusual circumstances. But even when law review material would not influence a court, it might stimulate your thinking about the legal issue, and its footnotes can help you find cases, statutes, and other primary authority.

---

3. When a restatement is no longer up to date, a second or third version supersedes it.

Legal dictionaries, encyclopedias, digests, and annotations are also secondary authorities, but generally they are not very persuasive.[4] Their true function is to provide researchers with background information and to help them find primary authority. Dictionaries are often helpful in defining statutory terms, and courts regularly cite *Black's Law Dictionary* in particular to reveal the legal meaning of undefined statutory terms.[5] The other kinds of less persuasive secondary authority collect, analyze, and summarize case law on specific topics or issues. Use them to find primary authority relevant to your issue, and carefully analyze those authorities to find the ones that are most persuasive for your legal issue.

§ 8.2 Dicta and How Courts Use It

When citing to a court's opinion as primary authority, only the holding and the legal reasoning necessary to support it (including rules of law) are mandatory authority in future cases. Comments in an opinion that go beyond what is needed to state and support the court's holding are *obiter dicta*—a Latin term that means "words said in passing."[6] Because *dicta* is not a holding or support for a holding, it cannot be mandatory authority.

Why do courts bother to write dicta in the first place? Often dicta adds clarity to an opinion. Here are some examples:

- A court might want to make clear what the case is *not*: "If the plaintiff had presented evidence of injury to his reputation, he might be entitled to damages." But because that evidence was not before the court, whatever the court says about it is dicta, not a holding.

- The court might want to illustrate possible ways to generalize its decision to analogous situations: "When a minor is at the controls of a power boat—or for that matter a car or an airplane—she is subject to the standard of care expected of a reasonable adult." If the quote comes from a case dealing with injuries caused by a power boat when operated by a minor, it's part of the holding because it defines the legal standard for liability in that case. But the

---

4. Years ago, lawyers and judges cited legal encyclopedias and dictionaries more often because genuine legal authority was more difficult to find, especially in newer or smaller states. You will still see that done occasionally in older opinions printed in your casebooks and in some recent opinions from states lacking centuries of precedent. But generally legal encyclopedias and annotations are no longer considered acceptable or persuasive sources to cite as secondary authority.

5. Typically courts do not rely on nonlegal dictionaries as courts are preoccupied with the legal meanings of words rather than lay definitions. An exception to this might be a court resorting to a nonlegal dictionary when construing a term that has not yet been legally defined.

6. Although in Latin *dictum* is the singular and *dicta* is the plural, *dictum* is falling into disuse among lawyers and judges. More often, *dicta* is used for both the singular and the plural forms.

statement is merely dicta for similar cases involving cars and airplanes operated by minors.

- The court might make a suggestion to a lower court for proceedings on
  remand: "Although the parties have not appealed the issue of punitive damages, that issue will inevitably arise on retrial. We believe it necessary to point
  out that punitive damages are available only if the plaintiff proves that the
  defendant acted with malice." Because the issue of punitive damages was not
  disputed in this appeal, whatever the court says about the elements of proof
  on remand is merely dicta (although the trial court is highly likely to follow
  that dicta on remand).

Sometimes dicta is unintended. A judge might get carried away with extravagant
wording in an opinion, or might formulate the issue, the rule, or the determinative
facts in a way that makes it unclear whether a particular comment is within the scope
of the holding. Sometimes the holding is difficult to distinguish from dicta. Even
when a judge carefully defines the issue, rule, and determinative facts, readers—and
even judges—can reasonably disagree whether a particular statement in an opinion
is necessary to the resolution of the issue and therefore part of the holding.

Sometimes a court decision gives two separate and independent grounds for a
holding, either of which is sufficient by itself to support the result. When that happens, neither alternative ground is dicta. Both were the legal basis of the decision,
even if only one was necessary to support it. If the decision is challenged on appeal,
the appellate court will affirm if either ground supports the trial court's result.

It isn't wrong to refer to dicta in your legal analysis, but it is wrong to use it inap-
propriately. Dicta can never take the place of a holding, and it is inappropriate to
treat it as though it could. In short, dicta is only talk by the court. A holding is the
court's decision about the facts in the case. When you refer to dicta, identify it that
way either in the text or in the appropriate citation. For example: "The court said
in dicta that the same standard of care would apply to minors who operate cars and
airplanes." A holding is introduced differently: "The court held that a minor who
takes the controls of a power boat is subject to the same standard of care expected of
a reasonable adult." Or: "The court decided that the minor was liable to the injured
passenger."

§ 8.3 When Courts Use Primary Authority from Other Jurisdictions

There are two common situations when case law from another jurisdiction might
be cited as persuasive primary authority. The first is when citing to an opinion from

another state (if your case will be decided by a state court); the second is when citing to another federal circuit (if your case will be decided by a federal court).

In either situation, courts rely on cases from other jurisdictions only for guidance, and only when a gap appears in mandatory authority governing that issue. A gap exists when a jurisdiction's law does not fully settle an issue.

Courts can fill a gap in mandatory authority in two types of cases. One occurs when the unresolved issue is the kind normally resolved by common law. Because courts developed the common law, they continue to fill its gaps, and they are often guided by precedent from other jurisdictions when they do. The second involves a mandatory statute that, although it governs the issue, is so unclear that the court must decide what it means. In effect, the court fills the gap by interpreting how the statute applies in that situation. Courts might use another jurisdiction's precedent to fill that gap, but only some of those precedents will be relevant. For example, opinions interpreting another state's statute might persuade your court, but only if the other statute is very similar to the statute in your case. If the two statutes are *identical or nearly-identical*, precedent from the other state might be especially persuasive. If the two statutes take radically different approaches to solving the same problem, the other state's precedent is usually irrelevant.

If your state has no statute on the issue, precedent interpreting another jurisdiction's statute has no value at all. If your jurisdiction treats the issue as a matter of common law, the court will consider only precedent from other jurisdictions that also address the issue in common law.

In considering case law from other jurisdictions, a court will have several concerns. First, a court that must fill a gap will want to know the *majority rule*. A majority rule is a rule adopted by the majority of states (or circuits) that have considered the issue (not the number of specific courts or cases). A rule can be a majority rule even if most other jurisdictions have not yet addressed it. For purposes of determining the majority rule, each state or circuit is counted only once. When a jurisdiction has not addressed an issue before, the court will want to know how most other courts have resolved the issue, even if the issue is a novel one and most jurisdictions have not addressed it at all. The majority rule is often very persuasive, although some courts will decide to follow the *minority rule*, for instance, if a substantial number of other courts have taken a different but well-reasoned position on the issue or because it best fits within the jurisdiction's own policy considerations.

Second, if a majority of states or circuits follows one rule but a modern trend favors adopting a minority rule (in other words, the number of jurisdictions following the majority rule is falling), a gap-filling court would want to know that too. A modern-trend minority rule might be more appropriate for current conditions than an older majority rule that is declining in favor.

Third, a precedent case will be more persuasive to a gap-filling court if sound reasoning supports its solution to the issue. Careful and thoughtful legal reasoning impresses a court looking for precedent to follow.

With these considerations in mind, let's think through an example. Suppose Wyoming law controls. And suppose the issue involves Wyoming common law, and no Wyoming statute has changed it. Wyoming Supreme Court decisions would be mandatory primary authority for this issue. But suppose those cases, for one reason or another, do not clearly settle the issue, which creates a gap in Wyoming law.

To fill the gap in Wyoming law, the state trial court might consider persuasive authority from other state supreme courts that have decided the same common law issue. Those cases are primary authority because courts have the power to make law in their own states. But in Wyoming, they are only persuasive (nonmandatory) because Wyoming courts are not required to obey decisions from other state courts. A Wyoming court might follow the reasoning of a South Carolina court on a similar common law issue, but only if the Wyoming court is *persuaded* that the South Carolina court's reasoning does a good job of filling a gap in Wyoming law. If the Wyoming court concludes that the other state court's opinion is not very helpful for some reason, it might disregard that case. While it is still persuasive primary authority, it's nonmandatory because the Wyoming court has a choice whether to follow it.

§ 8.4　How to Use Persuasive Authority to Fill a Gap in Mandatory Law

To fill a gap in the law of the jurisdiction that will decide your case, you first need to establish a foundation by showing the court that a gap exists because no mandatory authority fully resolves the issue. Once you have provided that foundation, use persuasive authority to fill the gap.

§ 8.4.1　*Step 1:* Establish the Foundation

Because persuasive precedent is used most often to help fill gaps in a jurisdiction's mandatory law, you must first convince the court that an existing gap must be filled to resolve the issue.

To establish the foundation, define the gap and specify how the mandatory law fails to resolve the controversy. A particularly deep gap occurs when an issue is one of "first impression" in the state or circuit that will decide the case. *First impression* means that the courts in that jurisdiction has not yet addressed the issue.

Another type of gap occurs when cases from the jurisdiction's highest court are questionable due to age or poor reasoning. But be careful: A precedent is not infirm just because it's old or just because you dislike its reasoning. Age weakens precedent when society or culture has so changed that the precedent no longer represents contemporary public policy on the issue. And sometimes a more recent precedent case is questionable because it has been criticized in other courts' opinions or in treatises or law review articles.

If other states have enacted statutes addressing the issue and your state has not, that doesn't necessarily mean a gap exists in the law. Your state's courts might reason that when the state legislature has not enacted a statute to resolve the issue, the legislature in effect has deferred the issue to the courts for resolution by common law.

The following example concisely establishes a foundation in the first sentence:

> No court in this state has decided whether the sale of a newly built home implies a warranty of habitability. However, a common law warranty of habitability has been recognized in a growing number of states.

Here, the gap is clear: The state has no case law addressing whether the sale of a newly built home implies a warranty of habitability.

But things are not usually this clear-cut. For example, the state courts might have decided cases that have nibbled around the edges of the issue, or cases to which analogies could be made, or cases setting out public policy, or even cases that give the false impression of having resolved the question but in dicta. If so, the foundation is not complete until you have explained—in as much detail as the reader would need to agree with you—why the issue is still unresolved by the jurisdiction's law. For example:

> No reported decision in this state has determined whether a violation of § 432 is negligence per se. But the neighboring states of Colorado and Arizona have enacted similar statutes. [Explain why they are similar.] Courts in those states have interpreted those statutes to mean . . . .

Here, the state legislature has enacted a statute, but the courts have not yet decided a certain aspect of its meaning (whether a violation of the statute amounts to negligence per se). The foundation is established by the first sentence, which explains that no case in that state has decided the issue.

In laying the foundation, avoid lecturing the reader on basic principles in evaluating legal authority (e.g., "because no reported decisions in this state address this issue, it is necessary to look to the law of other jurisdictions"). A lawyer or judge already understands that when mandatory law doesn't exist on the issue, persuasive precedents are the next best alternative for filling the gap. Just show that the gap exists, and then move to fill it.

§ 8.4.2 *Step 2:* Fill the Gap

Once you establish the foundation, summarize the persuasive authority. For example, "Sixteen states have adopted this cause of action, and four have rejected it." Then explain the persuasive authority in detail. Include not only precedent from other jurisdictions but also highly persuasive secondary authority. A court convinced that a gap in law exists will often consult relevant restatement provisions, scholarly treatises, and law review articles. But keep your focus on the case law. The views of commentators generally play a secondary role in gap-filling.

§ 8.4.3   The Two Steps Summarized

Here are the two steps (explained above) in using nonmandatory authority to fill a gap in local law.

Step 1   Establish the foundation by doing all of the following (§ 8.4.1):
  • State the legal issue precisely.
  • Explain what related issues the jurisdiction's law *has* decided.
  • Identify the gap by demonstrating what the law *has* not yet decided.

Step 2   Fill the gap (§ 8.4.2).

§ 8.5   How to Select Persuasive Precedent to Fill a Gap

When selecting precedent to fill a gap in a jurisdiction's law, how do you decide which precedents are most persuasive? Once you have found a precedent case you plan to use, answer the following questions in approximately this order:

1. Is the precedent case factually on point with your case? If not, can you make a sound analogy to the facts of your case? If the precedent opinion is easily distinguished on its facts, it will not persuade your court to follow it.

2. How strong is the precedent's reasoning? Is the logic of the holding sound? Is it careful, thoughtful, and complete? Does it reach a just result? Well-reasoned precedents that reach just results persuade.

3. Which court decided the case? Was the precedent issued by the highest court in its jurisdiction? If so, it will be more persuasive. Or is it from a court that your jurisdiction's courts have treated as unusually influential in past decisions? Is the precedent from a state where relevant conditions are similar to those prevailing in your state? For example, a state whose economy is heavily based on manufacturing might be more persuaded by precedents from a state with a similar economic base, especially if the legal issue involves a labor dispute or an issue about job safety.

4. Is the policy reasoning of the precedent case consistent with public policy in your jurisdiction? For example, some state supreme courts have historically been leaders in creating new tort causes of action. If your state only reluctantly recognizes new torts, your court is unlikely to find precedents from those states persuasive.

5. How have other reported opinions treated the precedent? Have later courts discussed the precedent case or its legal rule with approval or with skepticism? Is it part of a general trend or a widely accepted body of law? Or is it a lonely straggler that other courts seem to be leaving behind?

6. How recent is the precedent case? Judges often treat recent opinions as more authoritative than older ones, simply because changing social conditions sometimes mean that a traditional legal rule is no longer suitable. On the other hand, a court might be wary of following a very recent precedent that other courts have not yet considered or that has not yet been tested through experience. That is especially true if the precedent addresses a novel issue or an issue of first impression in your jurisdiction.

Exercise 8-A. Distinguishing between Primary and Secondary Authority

Decide whether each of the following research materials is primary or secondary authority.

1. An administrative regulation issued by the Arkansas Department of Wildlife and Fisheries governing how to obtain a hunting license
2. A definition of "burglary" in *Black's Law Dictionary*
3. Rule 56 of the Federal Rules of Civil Procedure
4. An *American Law Reports* annotation collecting cases about liability for texting while driving
5. A trial court decision granting summary judgment to the defendant in a fraud case
6. A federal statute known as the Affordable Care Act
7. A provision of the Restatement (Second) of Torts defining the "concert of action" theory of liability
8. An opinion of the U.S. Court of Appeals for the Eighth Circuit deciding an issue of Missouri law
9. A regulation issued by the U.S. Fish and Wildlife Service defining the word "take" as used in the federal Migratory Bird Treaty Act, which makes it unlawful to take any migratory bird except as permitted by the agency's regulations
10. A paragraph from Prosser and Keeton's treatise explaining proximate cause

Exercise 8-B. Distinguishing between Mandatory and Persuasive Authority

You represent a client who has been prosecuted in federal court for possessing marijuana with intent to distribute, in violation of federal criminal statutes. Law enforcement officers found marijuana growing in the corner of an uncultivated field on her small family farm in Grinnell, Iowa, which she inherited from her grandparents. Your client lives with her wife in the old farmhouse, which is surrounded by a fence enclosing a large yard and a garden. The fenced yard covers about an acre of land. Your defense theory is that your client was never in "possession" of marijuana as defined by the statute because she did not know it was growing in the corner of an uncultivated field, located a half mile from the farmhouse.

First, determine whether each of the following is mandatory or persuasive primary authority. Second, for those you decide are persuasive authority, determine whether each one is highly persuasive, moderately persuasive, or slightly persuasive.

Before answering, review the questions at the beginning of this chapter. If you need more information to answer the questions, consult the resources mentioned in this chapter to find what you need. Use your legal research materials to identify the federal circuit in which Iowa is located.

1. A decision of the U.S. Court of Appeals for the Sixth Circuit interpreting the term "possession" as used in federal criminal statutes prohibiting a felon from possessing a firearm

2. A regulation of the U.S. Fish and Wildlife Service defining "possession" for purposes of the Endangered Species Act

3. A federal court rule determining whether a prejudicial statement by a criminal defendant is admissible against her at trial

4. A decision of the Iowa Supreme Court defining "possession" as used in state criminal statutes prohibiting possession of marijuana with intent to sell

5. A published decision from a different federal trial judge in Iowa defining the term "possession" in a case involving similar facts

6. An Iowa criminal statute defining "possession" for purposes of prohibiting possession of burglary tools

7. A North Dakota Supreme Court decision holding that a criminal defendant could not be found guilty for possession of marijuana without knowledge that the prohibited substance was either on his person or within the curtilage of his dwelling

8. A decision by the U.S. Court of Appeals for the Tenth Circuit affirming a conviction of a Kansas farmer for possession of marijuana with intent to distribute, in violation of the same federal statute, after the local sheriff spotted a patch of marijuana growing in a corner of the farmer's garden

Exercise 8-C. Using the Hierarchy of Authority

You are working on a case now pending in the U.S. District Court for the District of Nevada, located in the Ninth Circuit. You have been asked to find out whether a defendant who unsuccessfully moved to dismiss the case for insufficient service of process can later file a motion to dismiss for failure to state a claim on which relief can be granted.

Your legal research has located the following authorities, each of which squarely addresses your legal issue. Based only on the information provided in this exercise, make a preliminary ranking of the authorities in order of their respective mandatory and persuasive value in resolving the issue.

Catdog v. Amundsen—U.S. Court of Appeals for the Fourth Circuit, 2008

Great Basin Realty Co. v. Rand—Nevada Supreme Court, 2002

Matthewson's treatise titled *Federal Courts* (published last year)

Wilkes v. Jae Sun Trading Corp.—U.S. Court of Appeals for the Ninth Circuit, 1977

Pincus v. McGrath—U.S. Supreme Court, 1953

Mader v. City of Las Vegas—U.S. District Court for the District of Nevada, 2013

Federal Rule of Civil Procedure 12(b) (revised last year)

Barking Pumpkins Records, Inc. v. Sepulveda—California Supreme Court, 2009

Garibaldi v. City of Boulder—U.S. Court of Appeals for the Tenth Circuit, 2007

Ali v. Frazier—U.S. Court of Appeals for the Seventh Circuit, 1935

9 Working with Statutes

[T]he statutes of this Commonwealth . . . do not always mean what they say.

—*Henry David Thoreau*

§ 9.1 How Courts Interpret Statutes

Chapter 4 explains how to outline a statute. This chapter explains how to determine what the words and phrases in a statute mean.

When a reviewing court interprets a statute, the statute means whatever the court holds that it means, at least for lower courts within that court's jurisdiction. Without such a definitive case, however, lawyers and judges use eleven tools to determine a statute's meaning:

1. the *words* of the statute (which create a mandatory rule, a prohibitory rule, a discretionary rule, or a declaratory rule—see Chapters 2 and 4)
2. statutorily provided *definitions* of terms used (usually found in a nearby section of the same statute)
3. any statement of *purpose* found in the statute
4. the *context* at the time of enactment: the events and conditions that might have *motivated* the legislature to act
5. announcements of *public policy* in other statutes and in case law

6. judicial interpretations of the statute or some part of it
7. judicial interpretations of similar statutes
8. the statute's *legislative history*, which consists of the documents, like committee reports, created by various parts of the legislature during the course of enactment
9. a collection of maxims known as the *canons of statutory construction*
10. interpretations of the statute by administrative agencies charged with enforcing it
11. interpretations of the statute in treatises and law review articles by scholars who are widely recognized as experts in the field

§ 9.1.1 Judicial Approaches to Statutory Interpretation

In the absence of an authoritative court decision interpreting a statute, most judges begin by considering the *plain language* of a statute. Unless the statute itself defines terms differently, a court will interpret the words of the statute to carry the meaning most readers would give it. Courts generally assume that legislatures use words as nonlawyers would use them except where legal or other specialized terminology is needed. They reason that a statute's plain language best represents what the legislature intended when it enacted the statute.

Most statutory language is not as plainly written as lawyers and judges would like. Legislatures often draft statutes that apply to a wide range of situations and varying circumstances. When a legislature enacts a statute, it is nearly impossible to predict all the factual situations that will be within the statute's scope. Moreover, the legislative process is inherently characterized by compromise. When introduced in the legislature, a bill might be written in plain language. But throughout the political process of negotiation and compromise, the final language of the bill could be amended several times to appease various constituencies. One consequence of this process are the ambiguities that can creep in because more general language was used to garner votes for the bill. As a result, statutory language is often difficult to understand and apply to a specific set of facts.

When a court cannot determine the meaning of a statute from the language itself, or when a court decides that applying the plain language would reach an absurd result, the court will turn to other interpretive tools to sort out what a statute means. But judges vary in what interpretive tools they find persuasive. Each judge tends to adopt one or more of the following policy preferences when interpreting statutes:

- Intentionalism
- Purposivism
- Textualism

Intentionalism. The traditional approach that judges use in interpreting unclear statutes is to ascertain the *legislative intent*. Intentionalists consider a wide range of informational sources to figure out what the legislators who enacted the statute had in mind. Indeed, legislative history would seem to be the most direct evidence of the legislature's purpose. However, because of the chaotic nature of legislative work, legislative history can be incomplete and internally contradictory. Nevertheless, courts view some portions of the typical legislative history as particularly reliable, especially the reports of the committees that considered the bill.

Purposivism. Other judges are skeptical about the traditional approach to statutory interpretation because they question any judicial effort to search for the enacting legislature's subjective intent. Instead, a purposivist judge considers a variety of information to identify the *statutory purpose*. Occasionally, the legislature includes a statement of legislative purpose or a list of legislative findings in the statute itself. When it does, a purposivist judge gives particular consideration to that statement. More often, however, a judge tries to identify the legislative purpose by reviewing evidence that is extrinsic to the statute's wording, such as legislative history.

At first, it might seem that the *purpose* of a statute is not much different from the legislative *intent*. But the two reflect different perspectives. A purposivist judge wants to understand what public problem a statute was enacted to address or, more generally, the goal the legislature sought to achieve—a purpose external to the words of the statute itself. On the other hand, an intentionalist judge is more interested in interpreting the statute's words consistently with what the legislature must have thought the words meant.

Textualism. In contrast to the other two perspectives, a textualist judge primarily focuses on textual cues intrinsic to the words and literal context of the statute itself. Textualist judges consider not just the specific words whose meaning is disputed but also the statute as a whole. The judge might also consider how the same terms are used elsewhere in the same overall statutory scheme, reasoning that the legislature would not use the same terminology in different statutes to mean different things.

A textualist judge generally disregards evidence of subjective legislative intent and is less influenced by the public purpose the legislation was designed to accomplish. She focuses on the words themselves, read in context. However, a textualist judge often refers to extrinsic evidence in the form of dictionaries (both legal and general) to interpret ambiguous terms not otherwise defined in the statute.

As you gain more experience reading judicial opinions that interpret statutes, try to figure out which of these interpretive perspectives the author used to sort out the meaning of a black-letter statute or rule.

§ 9.1.2   Canons of Statutory Interpretation

If a court cannot determine the meaning of a statute based on its plain language, the court generally relies on one or more *canons of statutory interpretation*. A canon is a general guideline the courts have developed over time to help them figure out what unclear statutes mean. Although scholars have criticized the use of canons as arbitrary, courts continue to use them regularly to interpret unclear statutes. Depending on the judge's interpretive perspective (§ 9.1.1), they may be more likely to rely on some canons than others.

Canons are almost always judge-made rules of law, and you must prove them with legal authority, usually mandatory case law. However, sometimes they also appear in the statutes. For example, a few appear in 1 U.S.C. §§ 1-8. State statutes also include an assortment of canons, and states vary as to how many and which canons are codified in their statutes. Some state legislatures have even enacted statutes that overrule one or more of the traditional common law canons of statutory interpretation.[1] Be sure to check the statutes of your jurisdiction before researching the case law.

Courts employ a large number of canons of statutory interpretation, but these are some of the most common ones:

- A remedial statute should be liberally construed to address the harm the legislature intended to remedy.
- Criminal statutes should be narrowly interpreted in favor of the accused (*rule of lenity*).
- The expression of one thing implies the exclusion of alternatives (*expressio unius est exclusio alterius*).
- A general term following a list of specific terms will be construed in a manner consistent with the common features of the specific terms (*ejusdem generis*).
- Statutory words and phrases should be construed in the context of the entire enactment of which they are a part.
- Different statutes on the same subject (*in pari materia*) should be construed together.
- Statutes in derogation of the common law are strictly construed.
- A statute is presumed to operate prospectively only, unless the legislature has clearly expressed an intent to apply it retroactively.
- A strong presumption exists in favor of the constitutionality of a statute.
- A state statute patterned on another state's statute carries the interpretation the other state's courts have given it (*borrowed statute rule*).
- When a statute has been interpreted by the courts and the legislature has not later amended it, the legislature is presumed to have acquiesced in the judicial interpretation.

---

1. *E.g.*, KAN. STAT. ANN. § 77-109 (1997); 1 PA. CONS. STAT. ANN. § 1928(a) (West 2008).

§ 9.2   How to Discuss Statutes in Writing

Writing about a statutory question focuses on the *words of the statute* because most courts agree that a legislature signals its intent primarily through the words it enacts. For that reason, you should directly quote the crucial statutory term or phrase (inside quotation marks) in the relevant sections of your office memorandum or brief. Those words should be the most important focus of your brief answer, legal analysis, and conclusion.

In Exercise 9-A below, two courts repeatedly discuss variations of a single word in the controlling statutes: "carry," "carries," and "carrying" a firearm.

Because statutes are drafted to govern a wide range of circumstances, you might need to reformulate a rule expressed entirely in statutory language before you can easily apply it. (Chapters 2, 3, and 4 explain how.) But be careful when reformulating the statutory language into a more useful expression of the rule. If you oversimplify or distort the rule, trouble awaits. Quoting the key phrases of the statute helps.

From there, use the canons to the extent they reveal what the statute means for your issue. Only rarely will all of the canons do that. If one fails to help, skip it and use others.

Exercise 9-A. The Statutory Canons in Action

Title 18 U.S.C. § 924(c)(1) provides that "any person who, during and in relation to any crime of violence or drug trafficking crime . . . for which the person may be prosecuted in a court of the United States, uses or *carries a firearm* . . . shall, in addition to the punishment provided for such crime of violence or drug trafficking crime . . . be sentenced to a term of imprisonment of not less than 5 years." *Id.* (emphasis added).

Many of the canons of statutory interpretation are illustrated in the two cases that follow, which interpret the statutory words "carries a firearm." As you read the opinions, identify each canon in the margin where the author considers it in interpreting the statute. Explain the interpretive perspective used by the author of each opinion.

United States v. Foster
133 F.3d 704 (9th Cir. 1998)

KOZINSKI, CIRCUIT JUDGE.

What does it mean to "carry a gun"? . . .

Leon Foster and Sandra Ward manufactured methamphetamine. In 1989 the police got wise to them, pulled Foster over while he was driving his pickup truck and arrested him. In his truck bed, in a zipped up bag under a snap-down tarp, they found a loaded 9 mm semiautomatic and a bucket. Inside the bucket were a scale, plastic baggies, and some hand-written notes with prices.

Foster and Ward were convicted of conspiracy to manufacture and distribute methamphetamine in violation of 21 U.S.C. §§ 841(a)(1) and 846. Foster was also convicted of possessing methamphetamine, in violation of 21 U.S.C. § 844, and of carrying a firearm during and in relation to a drug trafficking crime, in violation of 18 U.S.C. § 924(c)(1). . . .

. . . Was Leon Foster carrying a gun when he drove with it in his truck bed?

. . . "Carry" has two differing relevant uses. It may mean to transport or even to arrange for something to be transported: "I had to carry my piano all the way across the country." But it may also mean to hold an object while moving from one place to another: "I carried that ball and chain wherever I went." This narrower sense applies particularly to weapons. If I were to say "Don Corleone is carrying a gun"— or even just "Don Corleone is carrying"—you would understand that the Don has a sidearm somewhere on his person. A synonym for carry in this sense is to "pack heat." Criminals who pack heat are obviously much more dangerous than those who do not.

In our caselaw, we first adopted the broad definition of "carry" as transporting in *United States v. Barber*, 594 F.2d 1242 (9th Cir. 1979). Interpreting section 924(c)(1)'s predecessor, we said "[i]n ordinary usage, the verb 'carry' includes transportation or causing to be transported. Nothing in the legislative history indicates that Congress intended any hypertechnical or narrow reading of the word 'carries.'" *Id.* at 1244. After [the Supreme Court's decision in *Bailey v. United States*, 516 U.S. 137 (1995)], we switched to the narrower (packing heat) sense in *United States v. Hernandez*, 80 F.3d 1253 (9th Cir. 1996). We held that "in order for a defendant to be convicted of 'carrying' a gun in violation of section 924(c)(1), the defendant must have transported the firearm on or about his or her person. . . . This means the firearm must have been immediately available for use by the defendant." *Id.* at 1258 (citations omitted). A number of recent cases follow the *Hernandez* definition. . . .

We can also speculate* as to what purpose a prohibition on carrying a gun during and in relation to a violent or drug trafficking crime might serve. Using or carrying guns makes those crimes more dangerous. A drug dealer who packs heat is more

---

* [*Court's footnote*] There is mercifully little legislative history on "carry" to burden our discussion. The original version of the section was added as a floor amendment by Representative Poff. *See United States v. Anderson*, 59 F.3d 1323, 1327 (D.C. Cir. 1995) (en banc). The general aim of the section seems to have been to ensure that violent criminals receive longer sentences, and to deter the use of guns. *See* 114 Cong. Rec. 22,231 (1968) (remarks of Representative Poff); *see also id.* at 22,230 (remarks of Representative Casey) and at 22,234 (remarks of Representative Harsha). The only references to "carry" concerned a proposed amendment to delete the word, apparently because it might affect people such as policemen who were authorized to carry a gun, then committed an assault without using the gun. "Carry" was deleted from Representative Casey's version of section 924(c)(1), but eventually Representative Poff's version, "carry" included, passed. *See United States v. Ramirez*, 482 F.2d 807, 814 (2d Cir. 1973).

likely to hurt someone or provoke someone else to violence. A gun in a bag under a tarp in a truck bed poses substantially less risk. . . .

On balance, the arguments point to the narrower definition: It fits the more specific dictionary definition, follows *Bailey* more closely, harmonizes better with the full statute, and flows from the likely purpose of section 924(c)(1). . . . A final argument for the narrower definition is the rule of lenity. Where a criminal law is ambiguous, we are wary of imposing criminal liability for conduct that the law does not clearly prohibit. *See Bifulco v. United States*, 447 U.S. 381, 387 (1980). . . .

The rule of lenity applies only where a statute has resisted the ordinary tools of statutory interpretation. *See Hanlester Network v. Shalala*, 51 F.3d 1390, 1397 (9th Cir. 1995) ("Canons of statutory construction, such as the Rule of Lenity, are employed only where 'reasonable doubt persists about a statute's intended scope even *after* resort to the language, and structure, legislative history and motivating policies of the statute.'") (citations omitted) (emphasis in original). We think these ordinary tools of interpretation point to the narrow definition; at worst (for Mr. Foster) they leave the scope of section 924(c)(1) in doubt. If Congress wants us to put people like Leon Foster in prison for a longer time, it can re-write the law to give us clearer instructions, perhaps by using the word "transport" in section 924(c)(1) as it does in various other sections of the firearm statutes.

We reaffirm our holding in *Hernandez* and its progeny that "in order for a defendant to be convicted of 'carrying' a gun in violation of section 924(c)(1), the defendant must have transported the firearm on or about his or her person. . . . This means the firearm must have been immediately available for use by the defendant." *Hernandez*, 80 F.3d at 1258. . . .

Shortly after the Ninth Circuit decided *Foster*, the United States Supreme Court came to the opposite conclusion in the following case.

Muscarello v. United States
524 U.S. 125 (1998)

JUSTICE BREYER delivered the opinion of the Court.

A provision in the firearms chapter of the federal criminal code imposes a 5-year mandatory prison term upon a person who "uses or carries a firearm" "during and in relation to" a "drug trafficking crime." 18 U.S.C. § 924(c)(1). The question before us is whether the phrase "carries a firearm" is limited to the carrying of firearms on the person. We hold that it is not so limited. Rather, it also applies to a person who knowingly possesses and conveys firearms in a vehicle, including in the locked glove compartment or trunk of a car, which the person accompanies. . . .

We begin with the statute's language. . . . Although the word "carry" has many different meanings, only two are relevant here. When one uses the word in the first, or primary, meaning, one can, as a matter of ordinary English, "carry firearms" in a wagon, car, truck, or other vehicle that one accompanies. When one uses the word in a different, rather special, way, to mean, for example, "bearing" or (in slang) "packing" (as in "packing a gun"), the matter is less clear. But, for reasons we shall set out below, we believe Congress intended to use the word in its primary sense and not in this latter, special way. . . .

This Court has described the statute's basic purpose broadly, as an effort to combat the "dangerous combination" of "drugs and guns." *Smith v. United States*, 508 U.S. 223, 240 (1993). And the provision's chief legislative sponsor has said that the provision seeks "to persuade the man who is tempted to commit a Federal felony to leave his gun at home." 114 Cong. Rec. 22231 (1968). . . .

From the perspective of any such purpose (persuading a criminal "to leave his gun at home") what sense would it make for this statute to penalize one who walks with a gun in a bag to the site of a drug sale, but to ignore a similar individual who, like defendant Gray-Santana, travels to a similar site with a similar gun in a similar bag, but instead of walking, drives there with the gun in his car? How persuasive is a punishment that is without effect until a drug dealer who has brought his gun to a sale (indeed has it available for use) actually takes it from the trunk (or unlocks the glove compartment) of his car? It is difficult to say that, considered as a class, those who prepare, say, to sell drugs by placing guns in their cars are less dangerous, or less deserving of punishment, than those who carry handguns on their person.

We have found no significant indication elsewhere in the legislative history of any more narrowly focused relevant purpose. . . .

We are not convinced by petitioners' remaining arguments to the contrary. First, they say that our definition of "carry" makes it the equivalent of "transport." Yet, Congress elsewhere in related statutes used the word "transport" deliberately to signify a different, and broader, statutory coverage. The immediately preceding statutory subsection, for example, imposes a different set of penalties on one who, with an intent to commit a crime, "ships, transports, or receives a firearm" in interstate commerce. 18 U.S.C. § 924(b). Moreover, § 926A specifically "entitles" a person "not otherwise prohibited . . . from transporting, shipping, or receiving a firearm" to "transport a firearm . . . from any place where he may lawfully possess and carry" it to "any other place" where he may do so. . . .

[P]etitioners say that our reading of the statute would extend its coverage to passengers on buses, trains, or ships, who have placed a firearm, say, in checked luggage. To extend this statute so far, they argue, is unfair, going well beyond what Congress likely would have thought possible. They add that some lower courts, thinking approximately the same, have limited the scope of "carries" to instances where a gun in a car is immediately accessible, thereby most likely excluding from coverage a gun carried in a car's trunk or locked glove compartment. See, e.g., [*United States v. Foster*, 133 F.3d 704, 708 (9th Cir. 1998)] (concluding that person "carries" a firearm in a car only if the firearm is immediately accessible). . . .

In our view, this argument does not take adequate account of other limiting words in the statute—words that make the statute applicable only where a defendant "carries" a gun both "during *and* in relation to" a drug crime. § 924(c)(1) (emphasis added). Congress added these words in part to prevent prosecution where guns "played" no part in the crime. See S. Rep. No. 98-225, at 314, n. 10. . . .

[P]etitioners argue that we should construe the word "carry" to mean "immediately accessible." And, as we have said, they point out that several Courts of Appeals have limited the statute's scope in this way. See, e.g., *Foster*, [133 F.3d] at 708. . . . That interpretation, however, is difficult to square with the statute's language, for one "carries" a gun in the glove compartment whether or not that glove compartment is locked. Nothing in the statute's history suggests that Congress intended that limitation. And, for reasons pointed out above, . . . we believe that the words "during" and "in relation to" will limit the statute's application to the harms that Congress foresaw.

Finally, petitioners and the dissent invoke the "rule of lenity." The simple existence of some statutory ambiguity, however, is not sufficient to warrant application of that rule, for most statutes are ambiguous to some degree. Cf. *Smith*, 508 U.S. at 239 ("The mere possibility of articulating a narrower construction . . . does not by itself make the rule of lenity applicable"). "The rule of lenity applies only if, 'after seizing everything from which aid can be derived,' . . . we can make 'no more than a guess as to what Congress intended.'" *United States v. Wells*, 519 U.S. 482 (1997). . . . To invoke the rule, we must conclude that there is a "'grievous ambiguity or uncertainty' in the statute." *Staples v. United States*, 511 U.S. 600, 619, n.17 (1994). . . . Certainly, our decision today is based on much more than a "guess as to what Congress intended," and there is no "grievous ambiguity" here. The problem of statutory interpretation in this case is indeed no different from that in many of the criminal cases that confront us. Yet, this Court has never held that the rule of lenity automatically permits a defendant to win. . . .

For these reasons, we conclude that the petitioners' conduct falls within the scope of the phrase "carries a firearm." The decisions of the Courts of Appeals are affirmed. . . .

Justice GINSBURG, with whom the CHIEF JUSTICE, Justice SCALIA, and Justice SOUTER join, dissenting.

. . . I would read the words to indicate not merely keeping arms on one's premises or in one's vehicle, but bearing them in such manner as to be ready for use as a weapon. . . .

For indicators from Congress itself, it is appropriate to consider word usage in other provisions of Title 18's chapter on "Firearms." . . .

Section 925(a)(2)(B), for example, provides that no criminal sanction shall attend "the transportation of [a] firearm or ammunition carried out to enable a person, who lawfully received such firearm or ammunition from the Secretary of the Army, to engage in military training or in competitions." . . .

. . . "Courts normally try to read language in different, but related, statutes, so as best to reconcile those statutes, in light of their purposes and of common sense." [*United States v.*] *McFadden*, [13 F.3d 463, 467 (1st Cir. 1994)] (Breyer, C. J., dissenting). So reading the "Firearms" statutes, I would not extend the word "carries" in § 924(c)(1) to mean transports out of hand's reach in a vehicle.

Section 924(c)(1), as the foregoing discussion details, is not decisively clear one way or another. The sharp division in the Court on the proper reading of the measure confirms, "[a]t the very least, . . . that the issue is subject to some doubt. Under these circumstances, we adhere to the familiar rule that, 'where there is ambiguity in a criminal statute, doubts are resolved in favor of the defendant.'" *Adamo Wrecking Co. v. United States*, 434 U.S. 275, 284-285 (1978) . . . ; see *United States v. Granderson*, 511 U.S. 39, 54 (1994) ("[W]here text, structure, and history fail to establish that the Government's position is unambiguously correct—we apply the rule of lenity and resolve the ambiguity in [the defendant's] favor."). "Carry" bears many meanings, as the Court and the "Firearms" statutes demonstrate. The narrower "on or about [one's] person" interpretation is hardly implausible nor at odds with an accepted meaning of "carries a firearm." . . .

The narrower "on or about [one's] person" construction of "carries a firearm" . . . fits plausibly with other provisions of the "Firearms" chapter, and it adheres to the principle that, given two readings of a penal provision, both consistent with the statutory text, we do not choose the harsher construction. . . .

Exercise 9-B. Plagiarism and the Board of Bar Examiners

This exercise is on the book's website.

10 Working with Cases

§ 10.1   Eight Skills for Working with Cases

If you find mandatory precedent on point—a case from the highest court in your jurisdiction deciding your issue on facts that exactly mirror yours—the legal issue is probably so straightforward that it requires little or no hard thinking. But that is rare. More often, you'll need to predict what a court would do using at least some of the following skills:

1. Evaluating a precedent case according to the hierarchy of authority and its mandatory or persuasive value (Chapter 8)
2. Isolating a precedent opinion's determinative facts and framing its holding either broadly or narrowly (Chapter 6)
3. Analogizing precedent cases on their facts (§ 10.2)
4. Distinguishing cases on their facts (the opposite of analogizing) (§ 10.2)
5. Identifying policy reasoning (§ 10.3)
6. Synthesizing fragmented authorities into a unifying rule that reconciles them (§ 10.4)
7. Reconciling conflicting or adverse authority (§ 10.5)
8. Testing the results for realism (§ 10.6)

The first two skills are explained earlier in this book. The others are explained in this chapter.

§ 10.2   Analogizing and Distinguishing Precedent Cases

If two cases are so factually parallel that the reasoning a court used to decide the first case should also govern the second, the cases are analogous. Distinguishing is showing that the facts of two cases are so fundamentally different that they should be decided differently.

For example, assume that your older brother graduated from high school and went to a large public university, and your parents bought him a used car. Four years later, you graduate from high school and plan to attend a small liberal arts college. You might argue that the situations are *analogous*, and if your brother got a car, you should get one, too.

But your parents might reason differently. They might say that your older brother needed a car to get around a huge university campus. But in your case, you can easily navigate your small college campus on foot without a car. Besides, your private college tuition is much more costly than your brother's tuition at a public university. Your parents might reason that the situations are so different that it would be unfair for you to expect to be treated the same as your older brother. In that case, your parents would be pointing out that the two situations are *distinguishable*.

Lawyers and judges are skilled at both analogizing and distinguishing cases. That is because the common law was developed entirely through case precedent and the principle of *stare decisis*, which both rely heavily on analogous reasoning to resolve legal issues.

A court is most likely to apply the same legal rule and reasoning to a new set of facts if it is persuaded that a previous case involving the same or similar facts was decided that way. Consistency in decision making helps make the law predictable. If judges decided cases based on what they thought was the fair result in each case without considering precedent, lawyers would have a much harder job predicting the outcome of a client's legal problem. Both analogizing and distinguishing cases support the policy of ensuring that the common law is predictable and fair.

Analogize and distinguish cases using these three steps.

Analogizing and Distinguishing Cases

Step 1   Make sure the legal issue in the precedent case is the same as the issue you're trying to resolve.

Step 2   Identify the precedent's determinative facts (§ 6.1). Don't look for mere coincidences between the precedent's facts and yours. Look instead for facts on which the precedent court's decision relied and that were crucial to the outcome.

Step 3   Compare the precedent's determinative facts to the facts of your case. If they match, you have an analogy, and you can use the precedent to predict the same outcome in your case. If not, the precedent is distinguishable from your case because the crucial facts differ.

Let's consider an example to show how these steps work.

The precedent. A landlord failed to repair a residential tenant's toilet for one week, in violation of the local housing code. A court held that the tenant could withhold her next monthly rent payment and use the money to repair the toilet herself.

Our facts. The owner of a refrigerated warehouse failed to maintain the refrigeration device, causing the commercial tenant's fruits and vegetables to spoil. The lease obligates the landlord to provide refrigeration. The tenant wants to withhold the next rent payment and use the money to repair the refrigeration device.

Step 1   Is the legal issue the same? Yes. In both, the issue is whether the tenant may deduct the cost of repairs from the rent payment.

Step 2   What were the determinative facts in the precedent?
- Landlord/tenant relationship
- Toilet problem
- Landlord violated housing code obligation to repair

Step 3   Compare the precedent's determinative facts to the facts in the current problem.

Precedent Facts
- Landlord/tenant relationship
- Toilet problem
- Landlord violated housing code

Our Facts
- Same
- No toilet issue
- No code governs commercial leases

But wait. Does the analogy fail because a residential toilet isn't the same as a commercial refrigeration device? Should it fail because commercial leases are not governed by a statute like the housing code? It's helpful when considering determinative facts to step back a bit from the concrete facts and consider why the facts mattered to the court's decision. In both cases, the equipment that failed was essential to the tenant's purpose for leasing the property. And in both cases, the landlord had an obligation (whether by law or under the lease agreement) to maintain the equipment that failed. Once we think about the two situations that way, Steps 2 and 3 might look analogous after all. Notice how they change below from those above.

Step 2   What were the determinative facts in the precedent?
- Landlord/tenant relationship
- Essential equipment failed (toilet)
- Landlord violated obligation to repair (housing code)

Step 3   Compare the precedent's determinative facts to the facts in the current problem.

Precedent Facts	Our Facts
• Landlord/tenant relationship	• Same, but a commercial lease
• Essential equipment failed	• Same—refrigeration essential
• Landlord violated obligation to repair	• Same—violated lease obligation to repair

In both cases, the landlord had an obligation to maintain something essential to the tenant's reason for occupying the rented space. The obligation arose from different sources, but an obligation is an obligation, whether imposed by statute (the housing code) or by contract (the lease). Although we cannot be certain that the outcome would be the same in both cases, drawing the analogy greatly increases the chances that if one tenant could deduct the cost of repairs from the rent payment, then the other tenant can, too.

If you were representing the landlord in the second case, how might you distinguish the facts of your case from the precedent? You might emphasize the difference between a residential tenant and a commercial tenant, and the difference between a repair obligation as a matter of statute (the housing code) and a repair obligation by contract (the lease). Or perhaps the commercial lease has another provision requiring the commercial tenant to immediately make the necessary repairs to mitigate damages, and then to bill the landlord for the out-of-pocket expense rather than deducting it from the next rent payment.

Even when two cases seem factually similar, experienced lawyers can find ways to distinguish them to persuade a court that the outcome in the second case should not be the same as the outcome in the precedent. The court will ultimately decide which party's arguments are most persuasive. The lawyer's job is to predict whether the judge will analogize or distinguish the precedent case.

§ 10.3   Identifying Policy Reasoning

In deciding cases, a court might seek to satisfy not just the elements of a rule but also the reason why the rule exists in the first place—its policy (Chapter 7). Policy considerations can minimize the importance of factual similarities or differences that do not matter to the underlying policy goal.

In our hypothetical landlord dispute, policy helps us understand why the precedent case was governed by a housing code and the second case was not. Parties to a commercial lease are often sophisticated actors that the law assumes are on equal footing, able to bargain with each other to protect themselves. If a commercial tenant needs refrigeration, the tenant can insist that the lease be written to require the landlord to provide it. But residential tenants often lack knowledge and market power to negotiate the terms of an apartment lease. If you have ever signed a lease, did it occur to you to negotiate for a provision requiring the landlord to fix the toilet or the stove or the heating system? Most likely not. The legislature has therefore enacted a housing code to protect residential tenants from landlords who might otherwise refuse to make repairs reasonably necessary for day-to-day living. Thus, a landlord who doesn't expressly contract to provide necessary repairs is nonetheless bound by the housing code to do so. Understanding the policy rationales can help us understand why, despite the different source of the obligation, the cases can be analogized on the basis of the landlord's obligations.

How do you find out what the law's policies are? Sometimes they will be expressly stated in the statutes themselves. (See § 9.1.1.) More often, policy discussions can be found in precedent cases, either expressly stated or implied. Courts don't often say, "We adopt this rule to achieve the following policies." More typically, a case will discuss the types of policy concerns the court is trying to address, the useful things the legal rule would accomplish, or the dangerous things that would happen without the rule. When a court talks about any of these concerns, the court is discussing policy, even if it never uses that word to describe it.

§ 10.4   Synthesis

Case synthesis is the process of unifying the reasoning of several opinions into a whole that stands for an overall legal rule or an expression of policy. Synthesis is necessary when you find many cases that are on point or when a statute or single case have not fully articulated the relevant legal rules.

By focusing on the common reasoning and generalized facts of a group of cases, synthesis finds and explains collective meaning that is not apparent from any single case read in isolation. Synthesis is plausible if it is logical, reasonable, and consistent with public policy. To test a synthesized rule, be sure it explains the court's reasoning and result in each of the synthesized precedents.

A synthesis does more than describe several cases, one by one. Don't synthesize by "mini-briefing" Case A, Case B, Case C, and finally Case D, and then stop. That is nothing more than a description of your raw materials.

To turn a description of several cases into a unified synthesis, step back and ask what the cases really have in common under the surface. Identify the common threads of reasoning or policy that appear in all four cases, tie the threads together, and organize the analysis around the threads—rather than around the individual cases. The reader cares more about the common threads than about the individual cases. In a synthesis, each individual case is important only to the extent it illustrates something about one of the common threads in legal reasoning.

It might turn out that Case B sets out the most convincing explanation to prove whatever element is in dispute. Cases A and D agree, and perhaps they are the only cases from other jurisdictions that have decided the issue. Case C might be a much older decision from the same state as the deciding court. It might support the same rule, but its reasoning might be less complete than in Case B. An effective synthesis would explain Case B in detail, using Cases A and D to show that other states agree. Case C might be mentioned with a brief citation and a concise explanatory parenthetical.

When working out a synthesis, make that clear to the reader. First, summarize the synthesis in an opening sentence:

> Although the Supreme Court has not ruled on the question, the trend in the appellate courts is to hold that a trial court may dismiss a criminal complaint if any of three kinds of government misconduct occurs.

A synthesis like this could take many pages to prove because you would later need to show that

- the Supreme Court really has not ruled on the issue (*You might discuss Supreme Court cases that come close and show how those cases don't resolve the issue, or you might note that the Court has declined to review a prior case raising that exact issue.*)
- appellate courts have held that each kind of government misconduct is grounds for dismissal (*You would write a separate synthesis for each kind of misconduct.*)

When you develop or discover a rule synthesis, you'll usually do it from the bottom up. First, work with the details of each case until you see their analogous features that suggest a synthesis. (See § 10.2.) However, when you explain your synthesis in writing to your reader, do the reverse. Begin by summarizing the synthesis, and then explain how the details of each case support it. Your first draft might not do that very well because your thinking develops as you write. (Writing is thinking.) But later drafts should reflect the top-down explanation that will make the most sense to your reader.

§ 10.5   Reconciling Authority

Reconciling authority is a hybrid of some of the other skills discussed in this chapter. If two cases on the surface seem to conflict with each other, you might be able to demonstrate that the conflict doesn't exist because the two decisions, on closer examination, actually stand for the same rule, espouse the same policy, or harmonize in some other way. Done that way, reconciliation has much in common with synthesis. Sometimes you can reconcile precedents by showing that one opinion is really analogous to another, even if the similarity isn't apparent at first glance. If you can reconcile cases in a plausible way, they are not distinguishable.

§ 10.6   Testing for Realism

The last skill in working with cases is *testing the result of your reasoning to see whether it would seem realistic to the judicial mind*. For example, would your reasoning seem reasonable to the typical judge? Does it reach a just result? Or would it produce impractical consequences?

Karl Llewellyn wrote that "rules *guide*, but they do not *control* decision. There is no precedent that the judge may not at his need either file down to razor thinness or expand into a bludgeon."[1] Indeed, experience at judging creates what Roscoe Pound once called "the trained intuition of the judge,"[2] an instinct for how the law ought to treat each set of facts. If the result of your reasoning would strike the judicial mind as impractical, many judges will reject it, even if you have effectively used all the other skills. If you don't test your result for realism, your analysis will be *formalistic* because it will do nothing more than comply with the letter of the law. Because the law is hardly ever certain, a skeptical judge can always fold back your reasoning and make analogies you did not make, build other syntheses, and so forth. Even worse, the judge might adopt the analogies, syntheses, and other constructs proposed by your adversary.

To test for realism, you need to understand how the judicial mind operates. That understanding might take a long time for you to develop fully, but you're learning it now through the decisions you read in casebooks, classroom discussions, and the writing you do in this course. Once you begin practicing law, you will also benefit from legal colleagues' reaction to the realism of your reasoning.

Although lawyers often write arguments based on equity, justice, and reasonableness, they *never put in writing* the kind of testing described in this section. How could you possibly reduce to writing a test for realism? If a lawyer concludes that the result of her reasoning would be inconsistent with the judge's trained intuition, the lawyer simply starts over again and builds a different analysis that a judge would accept.

Exercise 10-A. To Google or Not to Google?

You are sitting in your Contracts class, listening intently, while the professor introduces a hypothetical. One of the factors that would influence the result is the relative distance to deliver a product from Cincinnati, Ohio, to either Columbus, Ohio, or Lexington, Kentucky. You think you know which way is faster, but you'll get more accurate information if you use your laptop to check Google Maps.

---

1. Karl N. Llewellyn, The Bramble Bush 180 (1930).
2. Roscoe Pound, *The Theory of Judicial Decision*, 36 Harv. L. Rev. 940, 951 (1923).

Before you consult Google Maps while sitting in Contracts class, you recall the following:

- The syllabus allows computers in class, if used "only for purposes associated with the class."
- Last year the same Contracts professor noticed a student bidding on eBay during class. After that, the professor prohibited students from using laptops in class for the rest of the year, and everyone else in class resented the person who was caught.
- This semester, your Civil Procedure professor posted a message from a student about the Seventh Circuit's website providing information on standards of review. The professor's posting thanked the student for locating and sharing such useful information.

Use the skills of working with precedent to predict what the Contracts professor will do if you use Google Maps, following these steps:

1. Fill in the table printed below to see whether it helps you make a prediction. In the second and third columns, write a narrow and a broad interpretation of the rule applied in each precedent.
2. Synthesize by weighing the information together to determine whether the precedents combine to support one rule, a rule with an exception, or more than one rule.
3. Tentatively predict the result if you use Google Maps in Contracts class, based on the rule or rules you just synthesized.
4. Assess your tentative prediction by imagining arguments that can be made for each side. Would a narrow or broad interpretation of the rule lead to different results? Does your case include facts that seem significantly different from the precedent cases?
5. Weigh the arguments for the competing results, as a judge would. Which side is more likely to win, and why? This answer will be your final prediction.

It might help your legal analysis to draw a table like this one on a separate page, filling in the spaces for each precedent. After considering your entries in the table, does this visual diagram help synthesize a rule you can use to predict the result?

Case Synthesis Table

Precedent	Mandatory or persuasive?	Narrow reading	Broad reading	Policy
Syllabus rule				
Last year's eBay incident				
Internet value in Civ. Pro. class				

Part 2

The Process of Writing

11 Getting to Know Yourself as a Writer

§11.1 Product and Process

A writing course focuses on improving both the written *product* and the *process* of creating it. An office memo is an example of product. The process of writing is what you do at the keyboard while creating the memo, including what you're thinking while you type.

Process is harder to learn than product. Product is tangible. You can see it and hold it in your hand, and you can discuss in class what makes a document like the sample office memo in Appendix A effective or ineffective. Process is harder to observe because at least some of it happens in your mind.

There are many different effective processes of writing. If you put the 50 best-selling U.S. book authors into one room and asked them how they write, they may give you 50 different answers. But most effective writing processes share a few basic traits, which we discuss in this and later chapters of this book.

Beyond that, finding the process that works best for you can happen through self-examination while experimenting. This is called reflecting in action[1]—doing a professional task and simultaneously analyzing how you're doing it and whether you're doing it in the most effective way. You're essentially observing and assessing yourself while you're doing the work.

---

1. *See* DONALD A. SCHÖN, THE REFLECTIVE PRACTITIONER: HOW PROFESSIONALS THINK IN ACTION (1983), and DONALD A. SCHÖN, EDUCATING THE REFLECTIVE PRACTITIONER (1987).

§11.2   What Do You Do When You Write?

How do you go about writing? How did you write in the past, and how are you doing it in law school? Be honest with yourself. If you're open and self-critical about your process, you can improve it more quickly.

What do you *like* about the way you write? What *frustrates* you? What seems to cause the frustration? What would you like your process to be? What might it take for you to accomplish that? What methods have you tried to get there?

You don't need to wait until your next conversation with your professor to work on your writing process. You can brainstorm with another thoughtful student. Or, while writing, you can have an internal dialogue about what is working in your process and why.

§11.3   Voice

Voice is a personal quality in a person's writing, something that speaks from the page in that writer's own way. Some students enter law school with distinctive written voices of their own. In legal writing courses, they learn that their writing must conform to a number of professional standards. Does that mean that you can no longer write in a voice that's yours? No, but you might need to adapt it to a professional situation. Your voice in professional documents will grow into something different from what it was before law school, but it will still be distinctively yours—although recognizably professional. Most people who enter law school with distinctive written voices say later, after they have developed a professional voice, that they like the professional version.

§11.4   Confidence

You are already a writer, but writing in a new field at a higher level of proficiency, with new requirements, might make you feel as though you have lost the competency you thought you had before. Most students feel at least some of that uncertainty while learning to write at a professional level. The feeling of doubt is sharpest near the beginning. But gradually—very gradually—it's replaced with a feeling of *strength*. By the end of the legal writing course, many students feel much stronger as writers because they have *become* stronger. For now, please remember this: If in the weeks ahead you fall into doubt about your writing abilities, it will be because you're quickly learning a lot. It does not necessarily mean you're a bad writer. You might be a good one. Once you absorb what you're learning and start producing professional writing your prior confidence can return and might be stronger than before because you would now be reaching for mastery.

Many young lawyers report that while learning legal writing they felt discouraged, but that later they experienced a first moment of validation. That moment might have come late in a semester, when a legal writing professor told them that they had done something really well. Or it might have come in a summer or part-time job, when a supervising lawyer complimented them on a well-written memo. Or it might have come in court when a judge leaned over the bench and said, "It was a pleasure to read your brief, counselor." That first moment of validation was the beginning of the recognition of *mastery*. Mastery was not yet complete; it would take much longer for that to happen. But it had begun.

It takes a tremendous amount of work to get to that point. As Chapter 1 explains, getting there—and doing the work now—is essential to building a career in law.

§11.5   Learning Styles and Writing

This section explains three frequently discussed learning styles. Most people have some of the characteristics of two or all three styles.

Rather than classify your learning style one way or another, you might figure out which style or styles reflect your strengths and whether other styles illustrate strengths you want to develop. To become effective at learning writing or any other skill, it helps to identify your strengths so you can capitalize on them. But it also helps to identify areas where you need to grow so you can consciously work on improving those areas.

Auditory/sequential learners, or ASLs, absorb information most efficiently by listening. They would rather hear driving directions than look at a map. They tend to think in words rather than pictures. "Sequential" in "auditory/sequential" refers to thinking in a series of ideas that add up to a progression to larger conclusions, like this:

Traffic Stop Arrest
(If the police violate the Constitution during a search or interrogation, any resulting evidence or confession will be inadmissible at trial.)

if	then
police seize stolen property and get a confession	→ both need justification
probable cause for police to stop the car in traffic	→ police had legal authority to stop the car
no probable cause to search trunk	→ evidence found there will be inadmissible
driver consented to search	→ evidence admissible based on consent
driver in custody after stolen property found in trunk	→ *Miranda* warnings required
driver knowingly & voluntarily waived *Miranda* rights	→ confession admissible
evidence and confession admissible	→ ***driver will be convicted of possessing stolen property***

Visual/spatial learners, or VSLs, absorb information most efficiently by seeing— either reading words or looking at pictures, diagrams, or demonstrations. They would rather look at a map than listen to someone give driving directions. More than other people, they think in images, although they also think in words. When reading a story, they often "see" the action in their minds, as though watching a movie, or they create a mental diagram of the relationships among the people involved. "Spatial" in "visual/spatial" refers to several aspects of thinking, among them a tendency to start from an idea and branch out in several directions, sometimes simultaneously, like this:

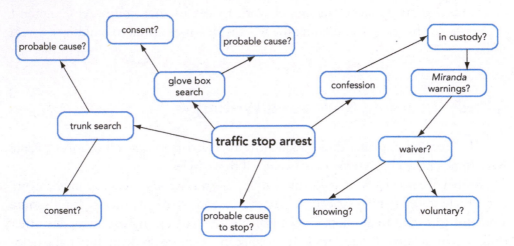

Tactile/kinesthetic learners, or TKLs, absorb information most efficiently through action. They learn best by doing something rather than by reading or hearing about it or looking at it, especially when action involves use of the sense of touch. They also learn well from experience. They would rather explore than look at a map or hear directions. They often think through doing because activity creates insights. While studying, TKLs often feel a desire to move about or do something with their hands because motion is thought.

Imagine that you buy something complicated, perhaps a PC with monitor, keyboard, printer, and speakers. Connecting everything and learning how to use it will be difficult. Inside the boxes are owner's manuals. If you have auditory/sequential strengths, your first instinct might be to read carefully the text in the manuals. If you have visual/spatial strengths, you might look first at the diagrams in a manual and consult the text only if the diagrams don't tell you clearly what you need to know. If you have tactile/kinesthetic strengths, you might toss the manuals aside and start fiddling with the equipment until you have figured out how to install it and how to use it.

This example is somewhat of an oversimplification, but researchers sometimes use it to illustrate differences among the three learning styles. Manufacturers know about learning styles. They put lots of diagrams in manuals for VSLs, and for TKLs they sometimes include a separate one- or two-page insert with essential information, titled something like "If You Hate Manuals, Use This."

When it comes to writing, people with auditory/sequential strengths tend to focus on the details, and in legal writing, they might intuitively understand how to show the steps of their reasoning in a logical sequence. Regardless of learning style, most students need to improve at explaining their reasoning steps *in depth*.

People with visual/spatial strengths might more quickly understand an entire situation. They might see the big picture at once. They can seem to sculpt a document rather than writing it from beginning to end. A leading researcher in this field says the following:

> For visual-spatials, writing is a lot like painting a picture. They may paint with broad strokes at first, filling in the details as they refine their pictures. In a painting, there's no particular order. You can start in the middle and work toward either end, or you can start at the end and work toward the beginning. I know a VSL who's a superb writer. . . . She cannot show anyone her rough drafts because they are full of holes. These are real gaps in the flow of writing where the picture hasn't formed yet. Being nonsequential in her thinking, she skips around the text, filling in the parts that are clear in her mind, and leaving large, gaping holes. Sometimes these holes are filled in her dreams, as her unconscious supplies the missing words or missing pieces of the picture.[2]

Less is known about TKLs and writing, except that some people with tactile/kinesthetic strengths say that writing helps them think because of the physical activity involved, especially when typing. Some describe this as thinking through their fingers.

In legal writing, *all* of these strengths can be valuable. You can continue to build your skills around the ones you already have. It isn't necessary to build up the others equally. No one is perfect or equally rounded, and all of us have uneven strengths. Many of the most famous writers can describe in abundant detail where they are weak in the writing process. And everyone can become more effective by identifying areas where they aren't strong and by trying to improve there.

Much of education is based on the erroneous assumption that all learners are auditory/sequential. A teacher stands at the front of the room and talks. Students are supposed to sit still for long periods of time. Most textbooks are masses of words with few or no diagrams. In law school, an exception to all this is in skills courses, where students learn to do things, like write memos or cross-examine witnesses.

Some researchers include learning style categories other than those discussed here, for example *verbal* (learning through reading and writing) and *oral* (learning through talking). These overlap with some of the categories explained earlier in this

---

2. Linda Kreger Silverman, Upside-Down Brilliance: The Visual-Spatial Learner 300 (2002).

section. Researchers are still discovering new aspects about learning styles, and much remains to be discovered.

If you want to know more about your learning style or styles, you might look at the books and articles listed in the footnote,[3] and do an internet search for the phrase "learning style." The books, articles, and websites explain how people with various learning styles can study more effectively and create more productive learning environments for themselves.

---

3. Ann L. Iijima, The Law Student's Pocket Mentor: From Surviving to Thriving 59-76, 103-106 (2007); Michael Hunter Schwartz, Expert Learning for Law Students (2d ed. 2008); Robin A. Boyle & Rita Dunn, *Teaching Law Students Through Individual Learning Styles*, 62 Alb. L. Rev. 213 (1998); M.H. Sam Jacobson, *Learning Styles and Lawyering: Using Learning Theory to Organize Thinking and Writing*, 2 J. ALWD 27 (2004); M.H. Sam Jacobson, *How Law Students Absorb Information*, 8 Legal Writing 175 (2002); M.H. Sam Jacobson, *A Primer on Learning Styles: Reaching Every Student*, 25 Seattle U. L. Rev. 139 (2001).

12 Inside the Process of Writing

Learning how to write like a lawyer is the beginning of learning how to make *professional decisions*. Some of those decisions are analytical, such as determining how a statute affects the client. And some decisions are practical, such as how to communicate most effectively to the reader.

§12.1 Five Phases of Writing

Writing happens in five phases:

1. researching authorities and analyzing what you find (see §12.3)
2. organizing your raw materials into an outline (§12.4)
3. producing a first draft (§§12.5-12.6)
4. rewriting through several more drafts (§12.7)
5. polishing (§12.9)

Writers rarely, if ever, start at the beginning, write until they get to the end, and then stop. And they rarely go through the five phases of writing in strict order, finishing one phase before starting the next one. Working in a rigid sequence could inhibit rather than enhance the writing process.

Instead, writers often circle back to reopen something already done and redo some aspect of it. For example, although much of the analytical work comes at the beginning, you'll continue to analyze while organizing, writing the first draft, and rewriting. While writing the first draft, you might decide to go back and rewrite something you wrote a few pages ago. While rewriting, you might reorganize.

Still, it helps to think about writing in the five phases listed above. Each phase is a different *kind* of work, requiring somewhat different skills.

§12.2   Managing Time

Suppose you receive an assignment with a deadline in three weeks. On the day you receive the assignment, you have two options.

The first is to toss the assignment aside when you get home and not think about it for two weeks, leaving only the last few days before the deadline to do the entire job. Many students did this in college and turned in their first draft as their final product. When they try it again in law school, the result is usually disappointing because law school writing requires much more preparation and many more drafts. When you're learning professional skills, each new task will usually take longer to accomplish than you might think because the complexities of the task aren't immediately apparent. (Later, with experience, you'll get much better at predicting how long it will take to get things done.)

The other option is to start working right away so you have the full three weeks to get the job done. Some students have very good internal clocks that pace them through the work without having to set a schedule for themselves. But for many students, time will get out of control unless they schedule. In this sense, planning the work includes

- *estimating* how long it will take to research, analyze the results, organize your raw materials, produce a first draft, rewrite it through several more drafts, and polish it,
- *budgeting* your time so that you can do each one of these tasks well, and
- *calendaring* each task.

When you first get the assignment, it can seem huge and intimidating. But once you break it down into a group of smaller tasks, it isn't as big any more, and it seems much more doable. Here is what Professor Amy Stein tells her students:[1]

> When I ask students if they have made a schedule for completing their work, they often look at me as if I have asked them to split the atom. Taking a series of complicated tasks and breaking them into manageable pieces is the best way that I know of to deal with the panic that comes from feeling that I have too much to do in too little time. Preparing a calendar will provide a master plan for all tasks, both work and play. . . .
>
> Building a schedule requires a certain amount of honesty. Students must know their own strengths and weaknesses and be able to answer several questions. . . . Do you work best in short, intense bursts or longer sessions? Where do you work the best? Are you a procrastinator? Are you a morning person or a night person?

---

1. Amy R. Stein, *Helping Students Understand That Effective Organization Is a Prerequisite to Effective Legal Writing*, 15 Persps. 36, 37 (2006).

A morning person should schedule research in the morning and thirty minutes on the elliptical bike at night. . . .

. . . It is marvelously satisfying to cross off what you have accomplished.

§12.3 Researching and Analyzing

Researching is finding relevant authority, such as statutes and cases.

Analysis is figuring out which authorities to rely on (Chapter 8), what they mean (Chapters 9 and 10), and how they govern the client's facts (Chapter 16). Students and lawyers often print out the authorities that research suggests might be relevant and mark them up while reading and rereading them, identifying the most significant passages. For statutes, it helps to outline them as you read (Chapter 4).

§12.4 Organizing Your Raw Materials into an Outline

For two reasons, good organization is crucial in legal writing. First, legal writing is a highly structured form of expression because rules of law are structured ideas. The structure of a rule controls the organization of its application to facts—and thus the organization of a written discussion of the rule and its application.

Second, your writing is measured by how well you educate a reader and convince the reader that you're right. Well-organized writing helps a reader understand you and your thinking. Organize so that you lead the reader through the steps in your reasoning.

Many students find that organizing in legal writing is challenging. That's why it takes several chapters in this book to explain how to plan and organize (see Chapter 13 and Chapters 16 through 20).

§12.5 Producing a First Draft

The purpose of a first draft is to get something written so you can start rewriting. A first draft accomplishes its entire purpose merely by existing.

Don't let the first draft scare you. Think of it as brainstorming, an opportunity write free from the worries of perfection that can interrupt your thoughts. Rewriting, which can take place a few minutes or a few days after you've done part of the first draft, is where you will turn a collection of ideas into a coherent document.

Your first draft doesn't even need to be good. You can write what Anne Lamott calls "shitty first drafts":

All good writers write them. This is how they end up with good second drafts and terrific third drafts. . . . I know some very great writers, . . . who write beautifully. . . . Not one of them writes elegant first drafts. All right, one of them does, but we don't like her very much. . . .

Almost all good writing starts with terrible first efforts. Start by getting something—anything—down on paper. A friend of mine says that the first draft is the down draft—you just get it down. The second draft is the up draft—you fix it up. . . . And the third draft is the dental draft, where you check every tooth. . . .[2]

Do your first draft as early as you possibly can. You can't start rewriting (§12.7) until you have a first draft to rewrite.

You don't need to write the first draft from beginning to end. You can start with any part of the document that you feel ready to write, no matter where in the document it will be. You can write the middle before you write the beginning, for example. If your mind is mulling over a certain part of the document, start writing that part. You can write the rest later.

§12.6   Overcoming Writer's Block

Suppose you sit down to write your first draft, but nothing happens. You stare at the computer screen, and it seems to stare right back at you. This doesn't mean you're an inadequate writer. Writer's block happens to everybody from time to time, even to the very best writers. What can you do to overcome it? Here are some strategies.

1. Do something unrelated for a while.   Prepare for class, do the dishes, or jog. While you're doing something else, your unconscious mind will continue to work on the first draft. After a while, ideas will pop into your conscious mind unexpectedly, and you'll need to sit down and start writing again. But be careful: In law, you're usually writing against a deadline, and doing something else can't go on for too long.

2. If the first paragraphs of a document are blocking you, start somewhere else.   The reader starts at the beginning, but you don't need to. A common cause of writer's block is starting to write at the beginning. The beginning of a document is often the hardest part to write. And in each part of the document, the first paragraph is often the hardest to write. One of the reasons is that if you're not sure exactly what you'll say, you won't know how to introduce it at the beginning.

---

2. Anne Lamott, Bird By Bird 21-22, 25-26 (1994).

3. Use writing to reduce your fear.   The most effective way to reduce anxiety is to start writing early—long before your deadline—and to keep on working steadily until you have finished. If you start early, you'll lose less sleep and be a happier writer. Many students procrastinate because they worry about writing. But procrastination *increases* anxiety and puts you further and further behind. The only way to break this cycle is to get started so you can bring the task under control.

4. Don't expect perfection in first drafts.   If you're chronically blocked when you try to do first drafts, it might be because you expect yourself to produce, in your first draft, a polished final version. That's expecting too much. Even well-known novelists cannot do it. Really bad first drafts are just fine. Keep reminding yourself that the first draft is the *least* important phase of writing. You can afford to write horribly in the first draft because you can fix everything during rewriting.

5. Start writing while researching and analyzing.   While you're reading a case, words you would like to say might flash through your mind. Type them or write them down. As you do, sentences might start coming to you. You sat down to research and analyze, but now you're writing. When you run out of steam while writing, go back to researching and analyzing.

Experienced writers keep their computer on or a notepad handy while reading statutes, cases, and other authority because researching, thinking, and writing are *one* process. To read is to trigger thinking, which can trigger writing. It doesn't matter that you're writing without consulting your outline. You can figure out later where to put what you're writing into the document.

6. Separate yourself from distractions.   If you're distracted by roommates or your phone, leave the distractions in one location while you work in another.

§12.7   Rewriting

There is no such thing as good writing. There is only good rewriting.

—*Justice Louis Brandeis*

A first draft is for the writer. You write to put your thoughts on the page. But in subsequent drafts, your focus should shift to the reader. How much will *this* reader need to be told? Will this reader understand what you say without having to read twice?

To answer these questions while you read your first draft, think about your audience. Pretend to be the reader for whom you're writing. Keep in mind the needs and sensibilities of the professional reader described in §1.2 at the beginning of this book.

Does your writing help this pragmatic person solve a problem? Will this skeptical person see issues that you have not addressed? Will this busy person become impatient wading through material of marginal value? Will this careful person be satisfied that you have written accurately and precisely?

You'll do a better job of impersonating the reader if, between drafts, you stop writing for some time, clear your mind by working on something else, and come back to do the next draft both "cold" and "fresh." Obviously, that can't happen if you put off starting the project and later need to do the whole thing frantically at the last minute. To make sure that you have time to rewrite, start on an assignment as soon as you get it, and then pace yourself, working at regular intervals within the time allotted.

There might not be a clear dividing line between writing a first draft and rewriting it. A writer working on the sixth page of a first draft can interrupt that to rewrite part of page three; return to page six to continue first-draft writing; interrupt that again to make changes in the introduction on page one; then return to page six for more first-drafting; and so on. The writer keeps moving back and forth because while one part of the brain is working on page six, another part is thinking about other pages. This is *recursive* rather than *linear* writing. You have finished a draft when you feel it's more or less complete, even if you know you'll need to return to it for more rewriting.

Most of the writing you'll do in the practice of law can be made effective in three to five drafts. The paragraphs you're reading now are our fifth draft. (Some parts of this book, however, required ten or twelve drafts.)

To experience what the reader will experience, some writers read their drafts out loud, which can alert you to wording problems. Bad phrasing often sounds terrible when you say it. Other writers can get the same effect without speaking because they have developed the ability to "hear" in their minds a voice saying the words they read.

While rewriting, you can test your draft for effectiveness by using the checklists in this book. Look for section titles that include the words "How to Test For. . . ."

Don't be afraid to cut material from your first draft. The fact that you have written something doesn't mean that you need to keep it.

Eventually, you'll notice, after putting the writing through several drafts, that the problems you find are mostly typographical errors and small matters of grammar, style, and citation. When that happens, you have moved from rewriting into polishing (§12.9), and the project is almost finished.

For many people, rewriting "is the hardest task of all."[3] Set aside a lot of time for it. Sometimes during rewriting, things will seem discouraging because you'll discover that problems you thought you had solved earlier are still there. At other times, when you piece things together well, you might experience relief, even exhilaration.

---

3. Peter Elbow, Writing With Power: Techniques For Mastering The Writing Process 121 (1981).

Rewriting may be the hardest phase of writing, but parts of it can be turned into a game. Read the preceding sentence again. While we were writing this book, the second part of that sentence—"parts of it can be turned into a game"—went through the following evolution:

1st draft: . . . there are ways of causing parts of rewriting to include the kinds of fun many people enjoy while playing games.

2d draft: . . . parts of rewriting can be turned into something that includes the fun of a game.

3d draft: . . . parts of it can be turned into a game.

How did this keep getting shorter and more clear?

Convoluted language was made simpler. Concepts that did not add understanding were taken out. If games are usually fun, what meaning does the word *fun* add to the word *games*? Rewriting tightened the draft by finding ways to say the same thing more vividly in fewer words.

Look again at the first-draft version above. During rewriting, you would notice its weakness in either of two ways. You might reread it and ask, "What's that supposed to mean? What was I trying to say?"

Verbs are a good target for places to improve your draft. Question 7 in §21.5 lists variations of the verb *to be*, which usually weakens writing. Your writing will become stronger and livelier if you replace *is, are, was,* and other forms of *to be* with action verbs. That doesn't always work, but if you look for opportunities to do it, you'll find some ways to make your writing stronger. The weakness in the first draft example above begins with "there are," which is a variant of the verb *to be.*

How can you find all the places where you have used variations of the verb *to be*? Use the "find" feature in your word processor to search for *is, are,* and *was.* Every time you find one, think about replacing the word with an action verb. Sometimes that will strengthen your writing, and sometimes it won't. Decide one way or the other. You can treat this as a game of search-and-destroy in which you get to say, "Hah! Zapped another one!"—at the end of which your writing will have more energy because you replaced so many *to be* verbs. You can make a list of other words that cause you trouble and do this for each of them.

Although rewriting focuses on the sentence level, it should also consider the big picture. Is your organization natural and effective? As you reread and rewrite, do you have doubts about your analysis? Don't limit yourself to "surface-level changes," but instead use rewriting as "an opportunity to re-see [your] work" as a whole.[4]

---

4. Patricia Grande Montana, *Better Revision: Encouraging Students to See Through the Eyes of the Legal Reader,* 14 Legal Writing 291, 292 (2008).

Don't confuse rewriting with polishing (§12.9). If all you do is fix typographical errors, awkward wording, grammatical errors, and errors in citation form, you're only polishing, and you have skipped rewriting completely. Rewriting is hard because much of it involves reimagining your first draft and reexamining the decisions you made there. Experienced writers report that they can really enjoy rewriting because of what they can achieve there. "The pleasure of revision"—another name for rewriting—"often arises when you refine what you intend to say and even discover that you have more to say, a new solution, a different path, a better presentation."[5] Research on the writing process has shown that experienced writers use rewriting for deep rethinking, and usually they reorganize the earlier draft.[6]

§12.8   Using Writing to Help You Think

Writing is thinking.

—*Deirdre McCloskey*

[T]here is no better way to master an idea than to write about it.

—*Robert H. Frank*

[L]earning to write as a lawyer is another way to learn to think as a lawyer.

—*Terrill Pollman*

Writing and rewriting will help you expand and refine your analysis. The writing process and the thinking process are inseparable. You can't rewrite without rethinking what you're trying to say.

While you're writing—in the first draft, in rewriting, or even in polishing—don't be afraid to change your mind about your analysis. Most writers have abandoned ideas that seemed valuable at first but nevertheless proved faulty when—in the end—they "wouldn't write."

Most writers have experienced the reverse as well: sitting down to write with a single idea and finding that the act of writing draws the idea out, fertilizes it, causes it to sprout limbs and roots, and to spread into a forest of ideas. The amount of

---

5. Christopher M. Anzidei, *The Revision Process in Legal Writing: Seeing Better to Write Better*, 8 LEGAL WRITING 23, 44 (2002).

6. *Id.* at 40.

thought reflected in a good final draft is many times more than the amount in the first draft because the writing process and the thinking process are inseparable, each stimulating and advancing the other.

§12.9 Polishing

This is the last phase. Allow more time to pass before coming back to the writing to polish it. If you're away from it for at least a day, you'll come back fresh and be able to see things you would otherwise miss.

Print the document so you can see it exactly the way the reader will see it. Readers often see problems on the printed page that aren't so obvious on a computer screen. Before returning to the computer to fix problems, mark up the printed copy.

Take one last look for wording that doesn't say clearly and unambiguously what you mean. This is the biggest reason for waiting at least a day. When you wrote the words, they seemed clear because at that moment you knew what you were trying to say. But after some time has passed, you're no longer in that frame of mind. If you're not sure what the words mean or what you intended them to mean, fix them.

And take one last look for wording that can be tightened up. Can you say it equally well in fewer words? If you can, do so.

Look for awkward wording, typographical and grammatical errors, and errors in citation form. Use your word processor's spellcheck function. Consider reading the document one sentence at a time, but from the back to the front. This can separate each sentence from the big picture and make it easier to spot errors. Make sure the pages are numbered.

Now you're done.

§12.10 Plagiarism

Plagiarism is using other people's words or ideas as though they were your own. You commit plagiarism if you lift words or ideas from *anywhere* else and put them into your own work without quotation marks (for words) and citations (for words or ideas).

You already know the ethical and moral reasons not to plagiarize. You heard them before law school. Here are three more reasons:

First, your writing actually gains value from appropriate citation to the sources of words and ideas. Much of what you write will have credibility *only* if you show exactly where words and ideas come from. Proper attribution of ideas will allow your reader to rely on your work and to give you credit for ideas that are truly yours.

Second, you'll feel better about yourself if you don't take words or ideas from someone else without giving them credit. You can have professional self-respect and pride in your own work only if you do it yourself. If you plagiarize, you won't have the satisfaction of knowing that you accomplished something important on your own merits—which, together with professional self-respect, is one of life's most important pleasures. Don't deprive yourself of it.

Third, it's so easy for a teacher to catch plagiarism that you should assume you'll be caught. A professor can take some of your words and search for them in any of the legal research databases to find the case or article from which they were taken. Many professors routinely do that. Professors can also electronically search other students' papers for words like yours. A professor who designed your assignment and grades the other students' papers knows where *all* the ideas came from. Even if you copy the structure of your paper from another student, that can be plagiarism, and a professor who grades both papers will notice it.

13 How Professional Writers Plan Their Writing

In college, students are sometimes told that they should do all the organizational work in an outline before starting the first draft. Professional writers rarely do that. Before starting the first draft, you need an organization to work from, but it can be flexible. During the first draft and during rewriting, experienced writers typically *reorganize* as they write. Chapter 20 explains a fluid outlining method that helps you write.

§13.1 Myths about Outlines

If you dislike outlining, it might be that you were taught an unnecessarily rigid outlining method. In college, you might have been told that before you can start writing, you must make an outline with roman numerals, capital letters, and Arabic numerals, like this (from a paper on the effectiveness of professional schools):

  I. Legal Education
    A. The First Year
       1. Large Classes
       2. The Casebook Method of Teaching
         [and so on]
    B. The Second and Third Years
      [and so on]
 II. Medical Education

This linear outline starts in one place and goes straight from I to II and later from III to IV to the end, with lower-level layers for detail along the way. It outlines the kind of paper you might have written in college and might write for a second- or third-year seminar in law school. Here, the student has chosen and researched an important topic. The end product—the paper the student eventually submits—might be very effective organized this way.

But differentiate between an *end product's* organization and the method through which a writer organizes the *first* draft. If the student starts with a linear outline on the first day of writing, that outline might make writing more difficult. Many professional writers don't plan their work by doing a detailed linear outline in advance.

Suppose you're sitting at the keyboard thinking about the project you're working on. Valuable thoughts are running through your mind. At that moment, you're in the groove. Ideas are popping into your mind. This mental state—which some social scientists call "flow"—doesn't happen every day, but you're lucky enough to be in it at this moment. You look at your linear outline (like the one above) and try to find a place to put one of the ideas you have in mind. While you're trying to find a place for that idea, all the other ideas in your mind recede. They seem to fly away. And it's hard to find a place in the outline for the one idea that's left because when you made the outline, that idea hadn't yet occurred to you. Trying to deal with your outline has obstructed the flow of ideas.

Or the situation is different: You're not in flow. You have not written anything yet. But you have made a linear outline. You stare at it and ask yourself, "What should I write under roman numeral I and before letter A?" Five minutes later, you have not been able to answer that question. You're focused on writing what the outline tells you to write first, but your imagination is dry. The outline hurts you. If you weren't trying to satisfy it, your mind might start thinking about some other part of the project, and ideas would start coming. But as long as you're staring at the outline, your mind shuts down. In fact, "one of the only virtues of linear outlining is that it looks neat, and that very virtue is its downfall. By working to make sure the outline is neat, we effectively cut off any additions or inserts, and new ideas. After all, we do not want to mess up our neat outline."[1]

The principal myth about outlining is that a linear outline helps *everyone* write better. Linear outlining helps some writers, but it hurts others. It might help those who naturally think in a linear fashion. If you don't naturally think that way, a linear outline made before writing might inhibit you from starting to write and might obstruct the flow of ideas while you write. (If the idea of flow interests you, you might look at some of the books in the footnote.[2])

Linear outlining can also interfere with what writing professors call the recursive nature of writing. Writing as a process doesn't go neatly from one step to the next. It goes back and forth from one aspect of writing to another and in several directions

---

1. Henriette Anne Klauser, Writing on Both Sides of the Brain 48 (1987).

2. *See* Mihaly Csikszentmihalyi, Finding Flow (1998); Mihaly Csikszentmihalyi, Flow: The Psychology of Optimal Experience (1990); Mihaly Csikszentmihalyi, Beyond Boredom and Anxiety (1975); Susan A. Jackson & Mihaly Csikszentmihalyi, Flow in Sports (1999); Optimal Experience (Mihaly Csikszentmihalyi & Isabella Selega Csikszentmihalyi eds., 1988); Susan K. Perry, Writing in Flow (2001).

at once (see Chapter 12). The process through which writers create can be messy. A messy process is fine as long as it leads to a neat and orderly final product.

This is why many students resist outlining in college. Outlining can seem like an arbitrary and useless requirement. But you still need to organize what you'll say, and you'll need to create an outline—but maybe not the way you were taught to do it in college.

§13.2 A Method of Planning Your Writing

Organizing really means two things: For the writer, organizing is structuring the document. It's part of the writing process explained in Chapters 11 and 12. For the reader, organization presents the writer's thoughts in a logical way with visible guideposts that keep her from getting lost. Thus, you'll organize before the first draft, just to get the writing started coherently. You'll also reorganize during the first draft and later during rewriting—so the reader can understand where in your document she is and where she is going.

Sometimes the original organization works well and doesn't need much reworking. But often you'll need to do a lot of reorganizing while rewriting until you find a structure that works. When you reorganize a lot, that doesn't necessarily mean you have been making mistakes and are now fixing them. Most of the time, reorganizing happens because the act of writing teaches you the analysis you're trying to write. *Writing is thinking.* You can't rewrite without rethinking what you're trying to say. Reorganizing is a natural part of rewriting. This makes outlining easier because it doesn't need to be perfect the first time.

Before a first draft: Make a fluid outline, which is just a flexible collection of lists on scratch paper or on your computer. Your raw materials (cases, facts, hypotheses, and so on) flow through it and into your first draft. Then, in later drafts, you can reorganize, if necessary, to meet the reader's expectations.

Begin by identifying the issues. For each issue, identify the rule or rules of law that control the answer. Then make a list of everything you found through research that proves a rule is accurate, and another list of everything that supports your application of the rule to the facts.

As you write about an issue during your first draft, cross off things on your list. When you have crossed off everything on that issue's list, go on to the next issue and its list. When you have done all the issues, you have completed a first draft of the Discussion if you're writing an office memo, or the Argument if you're writing a motion memo or appellate brief. Chapter 20 explains how to do all this effectively.

Many professional writers organize this way: by making lists or piles, knowing that they will be finished when everything is crossed out or a pile is empty. This method is only a suggestion. If you develop a different procedure that works better for you, use yours instead.

In later drafts: Linear outlines aren't inherently bad. Although linear outlines might obstruct producing a first draft, they can help to improve later drafts during rewriting. To do that, you would create *a post-draft linear outline*—a linear outline of what you have *already* written. That might seem strange, but for many writers it works. *A finished product should be organized the way a linear outline is—even if you used a fluid outline to produce your first draft.*

To find out whether this method would work for you, print a copy of your draft and read it, asking yourself whether you have incorporated a linear outline into your writing without realizing it. If the answer is yes, that increases the odds that you have organized effectively.

At each point in your draft where you state an important conclusion or start a new topic, write a heading reflecting that. The headings will resemble the items that would be listed in a linear outline. For example, if you were writing a seminar paper on the topic partially outlined at the beginning of this chapter, you would write in the margin "The Casebook Method of Teaching" at the point where you finish talking about whether large classes work well and are about to start talking about casebooks.

After you have done this to your entire draft, step back and look at your headings. For the moment, look at the headings alone and ignore the rest of your draft. You're trying to see the big picture. Do the headings appear in a logical order? Do they cover everything? Do they lay out the analysis clearly for the reader? If you answer yes to these questions, you might have a good organization—and you have now produced good headings, which you can insert into your draft if they would help guide the reader.

But if any of the answers is no, cut-and-paste to rearrange portions of your draft. Then reread everything to make sure that individual sentences and paragraphs still work well in their new locations. You might need to reword some things.

§13.3   Other Methods of Planning Your Writing

Some writers outline by writing on sticky notes and putting them on a wall. They then reorganize their outline by shuffling the notes around.

Some outline by making flowcharts in which the things to be written about appear in boxes or ovals with arrows showing their relationship to each other and the order in which they will be discussed. For some very visual writers, this accurately reflects how they think about what they are writing.

A few outline with mind-mapping software like Inspiration.

And some outline the linear way, with roman numerals, as illustrated at the beginning of this chapter. It has worked well for them, and they are happy with it.

Experiment with outlining processes until you find a method that works well with the way you most effectively work and think. The end result—the organization the reader sees—should be the best one for the material you're explaining. But the process of creating that organization should be the one that works best for you. As with so much else in writing, the result is for the reader, but the *process* of creating the result is for you.

Part 3

Office Memoranda

14 Writing an Office Memorandum

§14.1 Structure of an Office Memorandum

Form follows function.

—*Louis Sullivan (architect)*

A lawyer writes an office memorandum to determine how the law will treat a client's situation. Typically a junior lawyer will write a memo to answer a supervisor's legal question. The supervising lawyer might know the law generally, but not necessarily how the law treats the specific facts and issues in the case that triggered the legal question. The supervisor might use the contents of the office memo to advise the client or to plan a lawsuit or other action undertaken on the client's behalf. The office memo presents the legal research and analysis in a format that allows the supervisor to use her time most efficiently.

Purpose. Imagine that you are writing to a typical supervising lawyer. Your supervisor will read your memo for the purpose of making a decision for a client and will probably be under some pressure, especially time pressure. This busy person will be both careful and skeptical by nature.

You could answer your supervisor's question by having a conversation. But that takes time, requires both of you to be available, and leaves no written record to refer to later. When your supervisor assigns a written memo, that means she wants to use her time efficiently and at her discretion.

Good writers *anticipate* the questions a reader silently asks about the client's legal situation *before the reader even becomes consciously aware of those questions*. To do that, you must understand the legal analysis so well that you can prepare for your reader's questions and answer them in the order your reader expects.

Format. Office memo format varies from law office to law office, and even from case to case (a sample office memo is in Appendix A). But a typical office memorandum includes some combination of the following components, though not always in this order:

1. Memorandum heading
2. Issue or Issues
3. Brief Answer
4. Facts
5. Discussion (or Legal Analysis)
6. Conclusion (which may include Recommendations)

Some components of an office memo might seem repetitive. But a busy supervising lawyer rarely reads your entire memo from front to back. Rather, a lawyer reads only the part of the office memo needed for the immediate task ahead. For example, just before meeting with a client to advise about alternatives, the supervising lawyer might scan the Issue and the Brief Answer, and if time allows perhaps the Conclusion. When preparing a motion memorandum based on your office memo, she will study the Facts and the Discussion more carefully. Each memo component serves a specific purpose for your reader, depending on the task immediately at hand and the time available to review your work product.

Heading. The memorandum heading usually includes the word MEMORAN-DUM centered at the top of the page. The entries that follow identify the recipient (usually your supervisor), the writer (you), the date, and a brief reference to the client and subject matter.

The date in the memorandum heading is essential because you might learn additional facts after that date that may change the outcome of your analysis. The information you include in the reference line is also important because your employer is likely to file your office memo away for possible use in a later case involving similar facts and legal issues. For that reason, your entry should concisely refer to the subject matter of the memo, not just the specific case number, client name, or caption of the case your memo addresses.

Issue. Just after the heading, the Issue states the legal question that the memorandum resolves, along with the relevant factual context. Integrating the legal question with the relevant facts helps the reader quickly grasp the unique aspects of the client's case.

You can write the Issue as a question that invites a "yes" or "no" answer. For example, a good Issue might ask whether the client has a viable cause of action under a specific legal theory, such as negligence, based on the most salient facts.

Brief Answer. Immediately following the Issue, the Brief Answer begins by concisely stating your conclusion in a way that directly responds to the Issue (e.g., Yes. No.). In most cases you should qualify your prediction to reflect how certain or uncertain you are about the outcome. Because every set of facts is unique and the law is subject to change, it's risky to predict any outcome with absolute certainty. On the other hand, some questions lend themselves to more confident predictions than others. It's perfectly acceptable to give a qualified Brief Answer such as "Probably not" or "Most likely yes."

The Brief Answer also includes a short summary of the analysis supporting your prediction. Give the essence of the legal reasoning, the essential facts on which your conclusion depends, and a brief explanation showing how the rule applies to those key facts. The Brief Answer should provide a snapshot of your reasoning—no longer than one concise paragraph, without citing any legal authorities. Your detailed legal analysis and citations to the supporting legal authorities will appear later in the Discussion.

The following illustrates the Issue and Brief Answer components of an office memo analyzing a legal question about trademark law:

Issue

Can Joan's Jewelry run its proposed ads for engagements rings featuring the slogan "The Rock" without interfering with any rights owned by Dwayne Johnson, the actor who is also known as "The Rock"?

Brief Answer

Yes. Joan's Jewelry should be able to run the ads without infringing on Mr. Johnson's rights. The legal standard concerns the "likelihood of confusion" on the part of consumers. Here it is unlikely that consumers would confuse engagement rings with the muscular Mr. Johnson.

Here the Issue isolates the core facts crucial to the answer: a phrase that is associated with an actor, and a desire to use the phrase in a jewelry ad. The Brief Answer directly responds to the question and provides a concise summary of the writer's legal reasoning, given the client's facts. Note that it doesn't include a lengthy explanation of the law.

Statement of Facts. The Facts include the events and circumstances that are relevant to the Issue. A *relevant fact* is one that influences the outcome of the legal issue. A *determinative fact* is a relevant fact that is so critical that it might alone dictate the outcome of the legal issue.

How should the Facts be organized? Organize to help your reader. Often the Facts are stated chronologically, but organizing them by topic or subject matter is sometimes more helpful. Emphasize dates and times only when they are determinative or necessary to avoid confusing the reader. For example, a date might be determinative if the issue is whether a complaint was filed within the statute of limitations.

If your supervisor is thoroughly familiar with the factual background, this part of the memo might be short. You want to remind the supervisor about the essential facts rather than enumerate every factual detail.

But be sure to include any fact you will mention in your Discussion section. State both what you know *and what you don't yet know* about the client's situation. Sometimes you will later learn additional facts that lead to a different legal outcome. If your legal analysis leads you to a fact question that you need to resolve before you can reach a reasoned conclusion, include a notation in your Facts so your supervising lawyer can ask for that information.

The Facts should never include legal analysis or even references to the applicable legal rule. But a good Statement of Facts includes every fact that is determinative or relevant to the legal issues.

Discussion or Analysis. The Discussion, sometimes called the Analysis, is the largest and most complex part of the office memo. It explains and justifies the prediction set out in the Brief Answer. Chapter 16 explains how to write predictively in the Discussion section of an office memo. Chapters 17 through 20 explain step by step how to organize the Discussion.

If the Discussion is especially complex or analyzes several issues, break it up with subheadings, preferably written as complete sentences. Subheadings help the reader locate relevant portions of the Discussion and provide an outline for your legal analysis.

Conclusion. Lawyers follow different practices concerning the Conclusion. Some include it only if the analysis is so complicated that a reader would find a summary of the reasoning helpful. Others always include it. If your teacher asks you to include a Conclusion, summarize the points in the same order you presented them in the Discussion or Analysis section without citing legal authority. Sometimes the Conclusion is a good place to explain what you believe the lawyer or client should do next.

§14.2   Which Part of the Memo to Write First

One lawyer might write the Discussion before writing anything else, on the theory that the other components of the memorandum will be shaped by the insights gained while putting the Discussion together. For example, writing the Discussion first could help you identify which information to include in the Facts. Another lawyer might start by writing the Facts because they seem easier to describe and summarize. A third lawyer might be flexible, starting with whatever component of the office memo first begins to take shape in his mind, sometimes drafting two or more components simultaneously and rewriting each one to dovetail with the other.

One way of overcoming writer's block is to just start writing whatever part of the memo you are thinking about at the time. It's not necessary to write the parts in order from beginning to end. In fact, it's often more effective to do just the opposite.

Writing is thinking. If your mind is already thinking about one part of the memo, you are beginning to write even if your fingers have not yet touched the keyboard. As you begin writing, your thinking deepens and becomes more focused on the issue and the relevant facts. Insights will come as you write because your subconscious mind is already working out the legal reasoning for you. *Just get started.*

§14.3   An Office Memo's Audience

You are primarily writing an office memo to your supervisor, although others might eventually read it, including your coworkers and your client.

If you were sitting at a conference table in your law office looking your supervisor in the eye while explaining your research and analysis, you would choose your words and tone to communicate with that one person. In an office memo, you are doing the same thing, but in writing. In a first-year writing course, how can you write to a hypothetical supervisor when you don't yet have one of your own?

Think of someone you know whose intelligence, wisdom, and judgment you deeply respect. In your mind, let this person play the role of your supervising lawyer. In your first draft, write as though you are explaining your research and analysis to her. Assume that she is educated in the law even if that isn't true. The point is to write to a real human being who would be engaged with the subject matter when reading your document.

In later drafts, you are really writing to two people: your imagined supervisor and your professor. While your reader is knowledgeable about the law, don't assume that the reader knows what you know about the case and how the law applies. Even the most capable and experienced supervising lawyers rely on junior associates to identify the determinative facts of a client's case, research and analyze the applicable law, and apply the law to the facts to predict the outcome.

15 Interviewing the Client

Client representation starts with an interview. A person who wants a lawyer's help calls to make an appointment to discuss a criminal charge, the sale of real estate, or other concern. At the time of the appointment, that person and the lawyer sit down and talk. If the visitor has confidence in the lawyer, the visitor could become a client.

During that conversation, the lawyer learns what problem the prospective client wants solved, the client's goals in getting it solved, and what the client knows factually about the problem. The lawyer also learns about the client as a person and gives the client a reciprocal opportunity to learn about the lawyer. Then or later, the lawyer and client negotiate the contract through which the client hires the lawyer. But in this chapter, we focus on the main goals of the first interview: building a relationship with the client and fact gathering.

§15.1 Clients and Lawyers

Most clients aren't really interested in hiring "a lawyer." They want to hire a genuine and caring human being who can do legal work well. This first interview is your opportunity to establish yourself as that person.

You probably dislike it when a doctor treats you in a detached way as a case of flu, rather than as a person who has the flu. A doctor who treats you as a human being remembers that, even though she might have seen twenty patients with the flu that day, this is your only flu and your symptoms are, at least to you, unique. A doctor who treats you as a human being with flu-like symptoms might spend enough time with you to learn that you also have other symptoms inconsistent with the flu, and that you have a different illness that should be treated differently. If you have never been represented by a lawyer, you can imagine what clients experience during lawyer interviews simply by remembering how you have experienced contact with professionals such as doctors.

Treating the client as a person is called "client-centered lawyering,"[1] which means focusing your efforts around what the client wants rather than what you assume the client should want. Your client has hired you to accomplish the *client's* goal. And many clients can collaborate actively with you along the way, brainstorming with you about how to solve problems.

You must keep secret whatever the client tells you in private, which is the lawyer's duty of confidentiality.[2] There are exceptions. For example, the client may give the lawyer permission to reveal the client's confidences to other people. And a lawyer may reveal the client's confidences if necessary to prevent the client from committing a serious crime. States differ in defining these and other exceptions to the duty of confidentiality.

§15.2 The Interview

After the sort of pleasantries that people exchange when meeting one another, the lawyer says something like "How can I help you?" or "Let's talk about what brings you here today," or "I understand the bank has threatened to foreclose on your mortgage. You're probably worried. Where shall we begin?"

§15.2.1 Learning What the Client Knows

The best way to learn what the client knows is to listen to the client. Don't label the problem in your own mind until you have heard most of the facts. A client who starts by telling you about a dispute with a landlord might have claims for defamation and assault rather than one for breach of a lease obligation.

Don't jump in with questions right after the client tells you the nature of the problem. Before you intervene, give the client a complete opportunity to tell you whatever the client wants to talk about. Many clients want to make sure from the beginning that you hear certain things about which the client feels deeply. If you obstruct this process, you'll seem remote, even bureaucratic, to the client. And if you listen to what the client wants to tell you, you might learn a lot about the client as a person and about how the client views the problem.

In the beginning, encourage the client to present the facts in the way the client thinks best. After a while (sometimes pretty quickly), the client will want you to take the lead by asking questions.

---

1. David A. Binder, Paul Bergman, Paul R. Tremblay & Ian S. Weinstein, Lawyers as Counselors: A Client-Centered Approach (3d ed. 2011).

2. Model Rules of Prof'l Conduct, R. 1.6(a) (2013).

Most clients won't mind if you take notes on a pad of paper, but first explain that you want to be sure to remember everything the client tells you. While you take notes keep listening as you write, and make eye contact often. You might feel more comfortable taking notes on your laptop rather than a pad, but consider whether your client would feel comfortable as well. The computer screen places a barrier between you and your client at a time when you want to encourage interaction. A pad of paper is smaller and less obtrusive.[3]

§15.2.2 The Art of the Question

Explore the various aspects of the problem in detail with the client. On each topic, start with broad questions ("Tell me what happened the night the nuclear reactor melted down") and gradually work your way toward narrow ones ("Just before you ran from the control panel, what number on that dial was the needle pointing to?"). But do this gradually. If you jump too quickly to the narrow questions, you'll miss a lot of information. Ask broad questions until you aren't getting useful information anymore. Then go back and ask narrow questions about the facts the client didn't cover. While the client is answering the broad questions, you can note on a pad the topics you'll need to explore later using narrow questions.

Word your questions carefully. How you ask questions has a lot to do with the quality and quantity of the information you get. One of the marks of an effective lawyer is the ability to ask the right questions in the most productive way.

What are the qualities of a good question? First, it seeks information that you really need to know. Second, it's phrased in a way most likely to produce valuable information. Some words help jog the client's memory and encourage answers, while other words confuse, cloud memory, or provoke resistance. Third, a good question is asked in a useful sequence with other questions. When you start exploring various aspects of the problem in detail, try to take up each topic in logical order. Sometimes other questions logically should be asked and answered first. And ask one question at a time. If you ask two at a time, only one of them will be answered. And too much skipping around confuses you and the client.

Keep asking questions until you have all the details: when, where, who, how, and why. Get precise answers. "Last week" isn't good enough. You need "Thursday, at about 11 a.m., in the truck stop parking lot." If the client tells you about a conversation, ask who else was present, what else was discussed, how long the conversation lasted, how it started, how it ended, what words each person used, and so on. You'll need these details to analyze the situation. In nonprofessional life, vagueness and approximation are usually enough in conversations. But experienced lawyers know that only precision works.

---

3. Typically a lawyer will not audio-record a client interview.

Remember that lawyers often deal with topics that are difficult for clients to talk about, like divorce, the death of a loved one, or a criminal charge. Try to be both professional and empathetic in your interaction, allowing the client to speak as openly as possible.

Before the interview ends, make sure you understand the time line of events from beginning to end: What happened first, what happened next, what happened just after that, and so on.

§15.2.3   Listening and Talking

The ability to listen well is as important in the practice of law as the ability to talk well. The popular image of a lawyer is a person talking—to juries, to judges, to adversaries, to reporters. But in the end, the lawyer who succeeds is the one who also knows how to listen. If you don't listen carefully to an answer, you might as well not have asked the question. Knowledge is strength, and in the practice of law one of the most important means of gaining knowledge is to listen carefully. A strong listener learns to be comfortable with silence. A client's silence might suggest the client is uncomfortable with the topic, fearful of admitting something embarrassing, or just trying to remember or articulate his thoughts. In either case, don't rush to fill the silence with words.

When communicating with clients, talk and write in plain English. If you must use a legal term of art, explain its meaning in an uncondescending way. Use concrete, precise language rather than vague generalities. Behave in ways that encourage clients to tell you things that you need to know and to ask you questions about things that make them anxious.

§15.2.4   How to Conclude

Clients often want the lawyer to predict immediately whether the client will win or lose. Don't even try to make that prediction. You must research the law and might need more facts. And you need to think about it. Hasty predictions are often inaccurate.

But clients want assurance. What can you give them? Usually, it's enough to explain the work you'll do next. A client might not realize that lawyers don't know all the answers right away. But lawyers do know how to find the answers. You can convey to your client that you take the problem very seriously and want to help.

As a client leaves your office, two questions are typically running through her mind: Will this lawyer be able to accomplish what I want? And did this lawyer truly *hear me* and *understand me*? The law and the facts might prevent you from accomplishing what the client wants. But nothing should prevent you from hearing everything the client says, acknowledging the client's concerns, and understanding the client as a person.

16 Predictive Writing in an Office Memorandum

§16.1 Predicting in Writing

When a client hires a lawyer, the client often asks the lawyer to start making predictions pretty quickly: "Will I win?" "Is it worth fighting for this?" "Can the other side get away with that?" This chapter explains how to predict. Remember that prediction is an objective look at how the case, or a part of it, may be decided. Here the lawyer is not trying to persuade anyone of anything.

A lawyer predicts for either of two reasons. One is to help *the client* make a decision knowing how the law will respond ("if the client constructs her estate in this way, it will not be taxed"). The other is to help *the lawyer* make a tactical or strategic decision ("we can plead this claim because the evidence supports it").

Predictive writing is sometimes called *objective writing*, but objectivity only partly describes it. Any writing that makes a disinterested report of the law can be called objective. Predictive writing does more than that. It foretells how the law will resolve a particular controversy. Sometimes an office memo predicts explicitly, and sometimes it predicts implicitly:

explicitly: Ms. Olmstead will probably be awarded damages for trademark infringement.

implicitly: Ms. Olmstead probably has a cause of action for trademark infringement.

These two statements mean essentially the same thing. You can say it either way, unless you work in an office that prefers one or the other.

The first step in predicting is to develop arguments for each side on every issue. Think of the reasons why your client should win. And think of the reasons why the opposing party should win. To predict which arguments will persuade a court, you need to know the arguments the court will hear from each side. Then evaluate each argument by asking yourself whether it will probably persuade a judge. With those evaluations in mind, how would a court rule on each issue? Then step back and consider the matter as a whole. In light of your predictions on each individual issue, how will the court decide the entire controversy?

In predictive writing, don't hide from the bad news, whether it is a fact that makes your case tough, or a law that will make it hard for your client to win. Also be ready to qualify your prediction if that is appropriate. Don't guarantee a result unless you are certain. And when you aren't certain, explain why.

§16.2   An Example of the Predictive Process: Taylor and Garrett

Assume that in our jurisdiction the crime of common law burglary has been codified in the following form and renamed burglary in the first degree:

> **Criminal Code § 102.** A person commits burglary in the first degree by breaking and entering the dwelling of another in the nighttime with intent to commit a felony there.

This part of the statute is preceded by a definitions section:

> **Criminal Code § 101.** Definitions:
> (a) A "breaking" is the making of an opening, or the enlarging of an opening, to permit entry into a building, or a closed off portion of one, if neither the owner nor the occupant has consented.
> (b) A "closed off portion" of a building is one divided from the remainder of the building by walls, partitions, or the like so that it can be secured against entry.
> (c) A "dwelling" is any building, or closed off portion of one, in which one or more persons habitually sleep.
> (d) An "entering" or an "entry" is the placing, by the defendant, of any part of his body or anything under his control within a building, or a closed off portion of one, if neither the owner nor the occupant has consented.
> (e) "Intent to commit a felony there" is the design or purpose of committing, within a building or closed off portion of one, a crime classified in this Code as a felony, if the defendant had that design or purpose both at the time of a breaking and at the time of an entering.
> (f) "Nighttime" is the period between sunset and sunrise.
> (g) A dwelling is "of another" if the defendant does not by right habitually sleep there.

The legislature has also enacted the following:

> **Criminal Code § 10.** A person is not to be convicted of a crime except on evidence proving guilt beyond a reasonable doubt.
> **Criminal Code § 403.** A battery causing substantial injury is a felony.

Assume—just to make things simpler—that none of these sections has yet been interpreted by the courts, and that you are therefore limited to the statute itself. That is a unusual situation. You'll typically be working with judicial decisions that have interpreted the statute.

Taylor and Garrett are students who have rented apartments on the same floor of the same building. At midnight, Taylor was studying, while Garrett was listening to a Harry Styles album with his new four-foot concert speakers. Taylor had put up with this for two or three hours, and finally she pounded on Garrett's door. Garrett opened the door about six inches, and when he realized that he couldn't hear what Taylor was saying, he stepped back into the room a few feet to turn the volume down, without opening the door further. Continuing to express outrage, Taylor pushed the door fully open and strode into the room. Garrett turned to Taylor and ordered her to leave. According to Taylor, she felt this to be "too much" and punched Garrett so hard that he suffered substantial injury.

The punch was a felonious battery under Criminal Code § 403. *Is Taylor also guilty of burglary in the first degree under Criminal Code § 102?* Your first reaction might be "no," and your reasoning might be something like this: "That's not burglary. Burglary happens when somebody gets into the house when you're not around and steals all the valuables. Maybe this will turn out to be some kind of trespass." But in law a satisfactory answer is never just "yes" or "no." An answer includes a sound *reason*, and regardless of whether Taylor is guilty of burglary, this answer is wrong because the reasoning is inadequate. A correct answer is determined only by applying all the relevant rules to the facts. Anything else is a guess.

A lawyer might start thinking predictively in the following way. These would be the lawyer's thoughts:

First-degree burglary (from § 102) has six elements and no exceptions. In § 101, the legislature defined each of the elements as well as some terms used in defining the elements. Taylor is guilty only if each element is proved beyond a reasonable doubt (§ 10). So I'll make a list of the elements and annotate each element with relevant facts:

1. *breaking*: When Taylor pushed the door back, she enlarged an opening into Garrett's apartment, which is a closed off portion of a building, and neither Garrett nor the landlord consented to that.

2. *and entering*: Taylor "entered" by walking into the apartment, which neither Garrett nor the landlord consented to.
3. *the dwelling*: Nothing suggests that Garrett doesn't habitually sleep in his own apartment. He was there at midnight, although he obviously wasn't sleeping at the time. It's a dwelling.
4. *of another*: And it isn't Taylor's dwelling. She lives down the hall.
5. *in the nighttime*: Midnight is in the nighttime.
6. *with intent to commit a felony there*: Taylor committed a felony under § 403 when she hit Garrett. The issue is *when* she formed the intent to do that. Because of the way § 101(e) defines this element, it isn't satisfied unless she had the intent to hit him both when she did the breaking *and* when she entered Garrett's apartment. If she formed the intent to hit him *after* she entered, the element isn't satisfied. Here are the arguments:

guilty: Taylor was already furious, and she walked right over and punched Garrett, without hesitation.

not guilty: After Taylor's breaking and entering and before the punch, Garrett turned on her and ordered her to leave, and she'll testify that she was reacting to what he did. She felt it to be "too much." She might have been angry when she pushed the door open and walked in, but anger doesn't necessarily include an intent to hit somebody. She isn't guilty unless the evidence proves beyond a reasonable doubt that she formed that intent before or during the breaking and entering—not afterward.

The not guilty argument looks better. It creates reasonable doubt that undermines the guilty argument (unless the jury decides she's not telling the truth).

So the prosecution can prove every element except the last one. And since they'll be missing an element, she'll be acquitted.

This is how a lawyer might *think*. But if you were asked to *write* that prediction in the Discussion portion of an office memorandum, you might write something like the following. (This Discussion is relatively simple because it doesn't evaluate any judicial opinions. If these statutes had been interpreted by courts, the Discussion would be more complex.)

Discussion

Taylor will probably be acquitted of first-degree burglary because the evidence does not show beyond a reasonable doubt that she had formed the intent to commit a felony when she broke and entered Garrett's apartment. The evidence will prove, however, that she committed the other five elements of first-degree burglary. Under § 102 of the Criminal Code, a person is guilty of burglary if he or she (1) breaks and (2) enters (3) the dwelling (4) of another (5) in the nighttime (6) "with intent to commit a felony there." Under § 10, she can be convicted only "on evidence proving guilt beyond a reasonable doubt."

The prosecution will easily prove the third, fourth, and fifth elements. Section 101(c) defines a dwelling as "any building, or closed off portion of one, in which one or more persons habitually sleep." Nothing suggests that Garrett does not habitually sleep in his own apartment. That apartment is, to Taylor, the dwelling of another. Section 101(g) would define it as her dwelling only if she habitually slept there and had a legal right ("by right") to do so. Neither is true. These events transpired between sunset and sunrise, which satisfies § 101(f)'s definition of nighttime.

Taylor's pushing open Garrett's door was a breaking. A breaking includes, among other things, "the enlarging of an opening, to permit entry into . . . a closed off portion" of a building "if neither the owner nor the occupant has consented." Crim. Code § 101(a). Garrett's apartment is a "closed off portion" of a building, which § 101(b) defines as "one divided from the remainder of the building by walls, partitions, or the like so that it can be secured against entry." It would be difficult to imagine an apartment that is not thus divided from the building in which it is located. During the incident in question, Garrett opened his front door about six inches after Taylor knocked on it to complain of noise. When she pushed open the door and walked into his apartment moments later, he immediately ordered her out. The initial opening of six inches would not have been enough to admit Taylor, and Garrett's prompt order to leave shows beyond a reasonable doubt that he had not consented to her opening the door farther. And nothing suggests that Taylor had consent from an owner of the apartment, who might have been someone other than Garrett.

Taylor's walking into Garrett's apartment was an entry, which § 101(d) defines as "the placing, by the defendant, of any part of his body or anything under his control within a building, or a closed off portion of one, if neither the owner nor the occupant has consented." Taylor walked into Garrett's apartment, and the circumstances do not show consent to an entry for the same reasons that they do not show consent to a breaking.

But the prosecution will not be able to prove beyond a reasonable doubt that Taylor had already formed the intent to assault Garrett at the time she broke and entered. Section 101(e) defines "intent to commit a felony there" as "the design or purpose of committing, within a building or closed off portion of one, a crime classified in this Code as a felony, if the defendant had that design or purpose both at the time of a breaking and at the time of an entering." Taylor will testify that when Garrett turned around and ordered her to leave while she was protesting his noise, she found this to be "too much" and punched him. A reasonable explanation is that her intent was formed after she was already in Garrett's apartment. No words or action on her part show that she had the intent to punch Garrett before she actually did so. Although, in her anger, she might have contemplated an assault before or when she broke and entered, there is a difference between considering an act and having the "design or purpose of committing" it. Her actions before she struck Garrett show no more than an intent to complain.

Thus, unless the jury decides that Taylor is not telling the truth, she will be acquitted of first-degree burglary because the evidence does not show beyond a reasonable doubt that she had the intent to commit a felony when she pushed open Garrett's door and walked into his apartment.

This material could be organized effectively in other ways, too. *Resist the temptation to copy uncritically the style of this example.* It might not be appropriate to your assignment or to your own approach to the analysis. The issues here are not difficult, and the facts given are few. The writing you do in law school will require both more extensive discussion and deeper analysis than in this example.

§16.3   How to Test Your Writing for Predictiveness

While rewriting, ask yourself the following questions.

1. Have you refused to hide from bad news?   If the client's case is weak, it's better to know that now. Predictive writing is frank diagnosis. Advocacy has another time and place.

2. Have you edited out waffling?   Your readers will expect you to take a position and prove it. Mushy waffling with words like "seems," "appears," and their synonyms makes your advice less useful to clients and supervising lawyers. Supervisors and judges are grateful for concreteness, whether or not they agree with you. If somebody disagrees with you, lightning won't strike you down on the spot. (It isn't waffling to say that "the plaintiff probably will win an appeal" or "is likely to win an appeal." No prediction can be a certainty.)

3. Have you told the reader whether your prediction is qualified in any way?   For precision, a prediction should at least imply how confident you are of it. Is the underlying rule a matter of "settled law," and are the facts clear-cut? If your prediction is qualified, state precisely the variables on which the prediction is based, such as "The defendant will probably prevail unless . . . ."

4. Have you concentrated on solving a problem, rather than on writing a college essay?   A college essay is a vehicle for academic analysis—analysis to satisfy curiosity—rather than practical problem solving for clients. Legal writing is practical. Solve the problem you were asked to solve. Solve it completely. But don't insert into your writing essays not essential to solving the problem. Here's an example of writing that *does not* solve a problem:

> Common law courts developed the crime of burglary because in the middle ages, with no police and no electric lights, life was much more dangerous at night. People bolted their doors and windows when the sun went down, but they still felt vulnerable because of the advantage darkness gave to criminals. The courts classified burglary as a felony with the same punishment as murder (execution by hanging) so that people could sleep at night with some sense of security. Modern statutes have reduced the punishment to imprisonment. They often retain something like the common law formulation of burglary as the most serious form of the crime. Lesser statutory forms might omit some of the elements of common law burglary and might be called second- or third-degree burglary or breaking and entering.

This is interesting. It even explains why Goldilocks wouldn't be charged with common law burglary. She got into the bears' house during the daytime, and she didn't have a felonious intent, even though she later ate their porridge and slept in their beds. But it doesn't help predict whether Taylor will be convicted and therefore doesn't belong in Taylor's predictive memo.

Part 4

Organizing Analysis

17 CREAC: A Formula for Structuring Proof of a Conclusion of Law

This and the following chapters explain how to structure the Discussion section of an office memo as well as the Argument section of a motion memo or appellate brief.

§17.1 The Need to Organize with Care (Kendrick and Jordan)

After a long day in the library studying for exams, Jordan and her friends walked to the student lounge, bought cans of apple juice from vending machines, poured the juice into clear plastic cups, sat down, and chatted. One of the group suggested that before going back to the library to study for a few more hours, they have a contest to see which of them could do the most convincing job of pretending to be drunk. Kendrick, who was eating pizza nearby, took out his cell phone and, without Jordan's knowledge, filmed her while she was clearly winning the contest.

Kendrick posted the video on YouTube under the title "Jordan Drunk in the Student Lounge." Nothing on the YouTube page suggested that she wasn't actually drunk.

The next day Jordan received a very attractive job offer from a law firm. Like many job offers, this one was conditioned on a background check. Among other things, the firm searched the internet for websites on which Jordan's name appeared. When the firm came across the YouTube video, it rescinded the offer. Jordan tried to persuade the firm that she hadn't actually been drunk and that she'd had nothing to do with putting the video on YouTube. But by then the firm had filled the position with another applicant. Other firms that had interviewed Jordan didn't return her phone calls, and she thinks that's because they have done background checks of their own.

Jordan has hired your law firm, which is not the one that rescinded the job offer. Your supervisor has decided that a lawsuit would make sense only if YouTube would be liable for posting the video. You and your supervisor have already determined that Jordan will win a lawsuit against Kendrick for defamation and invasion of privacy. But suing Kendrick alone wouldn't help because it will be years before he earns enough money to compensate Jordan.

A television station would be liable under your state's common law of defamation and invasion of privacy if it had broadcast the video with the title Kendrick posted on YouTube. And a newspaper or magazine would be similarly liable if it had published still frames from the video with the same caption. Your supervisor has asked you to research whether the federal Communications Decency Act of 1996 would prevent recovery against YouTube, which isn't a television station, newspaper, or magazine. After reading the statute and the case law interpreting it, you believe that Jordan can't recover against YouTube.

When you write the Discussion section of an office memo or the Argument in a motion memo or appellate brief, what will you say first? What will you say after that? How will you organize the many things you have to say? And in how much detail will you say them? Those questions are answered in this and the following chapters.

§17.2   A Formula for Organizing Analysis

A supervising lawyer reads an office memo to prepare for making a decision. So does a judge who reads a motion memo or appellate brief. They will make different kinds of decisions. The lawyer will decide how to advise the client or handle the client's case. The judge will decide how to rule on a motion or appeal. But both look for tightly structured analysis that makes your conclusion seem inevitable.

§17.2.1   CREAC

The reader who must make a decision understands your analysis most easily when you organize it using the following formula—or some variation of it.

CREAC Organization

To prove a conclusion of law:

C — State your **Conclusion**.

R — State the primary **Rule** that supports your conclusion.

E — **Explain** and prove the rule by analyzing legal authority.

A — **Apply** the rule's test (elements or factors) to your facts.

C — *(optional)* If explaining or applying the rule is complicated, sum up by restating your **Conclusion**.

What do the ingredients in the CREAC[1] formula mean?

C: The **Conclusion** of law is your determination of how the law treats certain facts. It is what you are trying to prove. In predictive writing, it can be expressed as a determination ("The Communications Decency Act prevents recovery against YouTube") or as a prediction ("Jordan probably will not be able to recover against YouTube for defamation or invasion of privacy").

R: The **Rule** is the primary one on which you rely in reaching your conclusion. Other rules might also be involved, but this is the main one on which your analysis rests.

E: Rule **Explanation** is proof—using authority such as statutes and cases—that the main rule on which you rely really is the law in the jurisdiction involved. The reader needs to know for certain that the rule exists in the jurisdiction and that you have expressed it accurately. Explain how the authority supports the rule, analyze the policy behind the rule, and counteranalyze reasonable arguments that might contradict your interpretation of the rule. A subsidiary rule might help explain the main rule. A subsidiary rule guides application of the main rule or works together with it in some way important to your analysis. For example, a conviction in a criminal case requires proof beyond a reasonable doubt. In the Discussion example in Chapter 16, notice how that rule of evidence interacts with the main rule that defines first-degree burglary.

A: Rule **Application** demonstrates that the rule + the facts = your conclusion. Explain *why* your result is what the law has in mind, using legal authority, policy considerations, counteranalyses, and any subsidiary rules needed.

---

1. The CREAC formula is identical to the paradigm for structuring proof of a conclusion of law—often called just *the paradigm*—which first appeared in Richard K. Neumann, Jr., Legal Reasoning and Legal Writing 111-125 (1990), and which has continued to be called *the paradigm* in subsequent editions of that book.

C: Depending on the complexity of your analysis, you might need to state your **Conclusion** again. If your treatment of a given issue is three pages long, the reader probably needs a sentence or two at the end wrapping up by restating the conclusion you have just proved. On the other hand, if your analysis is two paragraphs long, the reader might not need to be reminded; you can just go on to the next issue without restating something you said only a few sentences earlier.

Although the CREAC formula *helps* you organize, it will take some effort to learn how to use it effectively. But once you have learned that, writing will become easier because you won't need to struggle to figure out how to organize a mass of information. The CREAC formula will organize it for you.

§17.2.2   Why Readers Prefer CREAC Organization

Your readers are practical and busy people who read your memo or brief to help them make a decision. Because skepticism results in better decisions, readers will be skeptical about what you say. To present your thinking effectively, organize it to meet the ways that law-trained readers tend to process information. Here is what things look like from the typical reader's point of view:

State your **conclusion** first because a practical and busy reader needs to know what you are trying to support before you start supporting it. If you state your conclusion only after the analysis that supports it (or in the middle of that analysis), some or all of your reasoning will seem pointless to the reader, who doesn't yet know what you're trying to prove. Effective writers usually state their conclusions boldly at the beginning of a Discussion or Argument. This may take some getting used to because it differs from the way writing is done in college. And in conversation, aggressively stating a controversial conclusion before explaining its background data and reasons can seem opinionated or arrogant.

Far from being offended, however, the reader who has to make a decision is grateful not to be kept in suspense. That kind of reader becomes frustrated and annoyed while struggling through sentences without understanding their relevance because the writer hasn't yet stated the proposition the writer intends to prove.

Next, state the **rule** because, after reading a conclusion of law, a skeptical lawyer or judge instinctively wants to know what principle of law requires that conclusion. After all, a core idea of law is that things are to be done according to the rules.

Then **explain** and prove the rule because the reader will refuse to believe you until you establish that the rule really is controlling law and you educate the reader on how the rule works. The skeptical lawyer or judge won't accept a rule statement as genuine unless it's proved with authority. Do all this *before* you apply the rule to your facts. The reader won't accept the rule until you show that it's law and how it operates.

Then **apply** the rule. Once you have done that, you have proved a conclusion of law.

If what you have said is complicated, restate your **conclusion** to wrap things up.

§17.3 Rule Explanation and Rule Application

Your casebooks in other courses are full of examples of rule explanation and rule application. Judicial opinions usually start with a statement of the facts of the case. After that, a court typically begins discussing the law. In the legal discussion, you can often see exactly where the court stops explaining the law generally and starts applying the law to the facts of the dispute. If you were to draw a line across the page at that point, above the line would be rule explanation and below it would be rule application. If the opinion decides several issues, you might find a dividing point for each issue. If you want to get some practice in recognizing the difference between rule explanation and rule application, you might try looking for this dividing point when you read cases for other courses. The more recent the case, the more apparent the dividing point will be. Older cases tend to be somewhat less organized.

Authority, policy, and counteranalyses can appear both in rule explanation and in rule application. Sometimes authority used in rule explanation might reappear in rule application, but for a different purpose.

For example, suppose that *Alger v. Rittenhouse* held that a boat crew who caught a shark became its owner, to the exclusion of the fisherman who hooked but lost the shark an hour earlier. In your case, ranchers trapped a wild mustang in their corral. The mustang immediately jumped over the fence and galloped onto land owned by your client, who captured it. In rule explanation, you can use *Alger* to prove that your jurisdiction has adopted the rule that a wild animal becomes the property of the first person who reduces it to possession. And in rule application, you can use *Alger* again—this time to show that your client satisfies that rule because her facts are analogous to those of the boat crew, and that she thus owns the mustang.

A rule's *policy* is the rule's reason for being (Chapter 7). Each rule of law is designed to accomplish a purpose, such as preventing a particular type of harm. When courts are unsure what a rule means or how to apply it, they interpret the rule in the way most consistent with the policy behind it. Thus, policy can be used to show both what the rule is (in rule explanation) and how to apply it (in rule application).

A *counteranalysis* evaluates the arguments that could reasonably be made against your conclusion. Counteranalyses can appear in rule explanation or in rule application. In the comic strip below, Calvin refuses to consider a counteranalysis even after his tiger friend Hobbes prompts him. In predictive writing, the counteranalysis objectively evaluates each reasonable contrary argument, honestly assessing its strengths and weaknesses. You must say whether your conclusion can withstand attack. And you must consider the possibility that other analyses might be better than the one you have selected.

In persuasive writing in a motion memo or appellate brief, a counteranalysis is called a *counterargument*. It doesn't objectively consider contrary points of view. It argues against them, stressing their weaknesses and showing their strengths to be unconvincing. Calvin might be more comfortable writing persuasively rather than objectively.

§17.3.1   How to Explain a Rule

To explain a rule, do the following:

1. Prove that the rule is law in the jurisdiction where the dispute will be decided.   If the jurisdiction adopted the rule by statute, quote the key words of the statute, and show how the courts' interpretation of the statute is consistent with your understanding of it. If the rule is part of the jurisdiction's common law, prove that with cases. If the jurisdiction has a gap in its law on this subject, show how cases from other jurisdictions would persuade local courts to adopt the rule you are using.

2. Prove that you have stated the rule accurately.   Sometimes whatever you say to prove that the rule is law also shows that you have stated it accurately. Sometimes you'll need to add some extra discussion to give the reader confidence that you haven't misstated the rule.

3. Explain how the rule operates.   Some information about how courts have interpreted and applied the rule will give the reader an overview before you start rule application. But don't include information irrelevant to your issue.

4. Explain the policy behind the rule—if that would help the reader understand the rule.   What is the law trying to accomplish through the rule? You don't need to explain the policy behind the cause of action for negligence. Every lawyer learned in the first year of law school that the policies behind negligence are to deter people from behaving in ways that are unreasonably dangerous to others and to compensate those who are injured through others' unreasonably dangerous behavior. But the reader might not know the policy behind the rule that a judge is forbidden to ask jurors how they reached their verdict. That might need to be explained so that the reader can see how your analysis of the rule is consistent with its policy.

5. If any arguments could reasonably challenge your explanation of the rule, show why they are not persuasive in the counteranalysis. If you can't do that, consider changing your mind.

6. If any subsidiary rules are essential to the analysis, prove and explain them as well. A subsidiary rule is one that operates with the primary rule to resolve the issue. Usually, less explanation is needed for subsidiary rules because they are less important. Not all subsidiary rules need to be explained in rule explanation.

§17.3.2 How to Apply a Rule

To apply a rule to your facts, do the following:

1. State, in summary, what happens when you compare the facts to the rule. Here are some examples:

All of these elements are supported by the facts.

McGillicuddy did everything the law of adverse possession requires of her.

Cobb did not proximately cause Crawford's injury, although the facts support the other elements of negligence.

None of these elements are supported by the facts.

2. Show, in detail, why that result occurs. Go through the rule's elements—all of them. But concentrate on the elements that are difficult to analyze, and allocate less space to others. Use legal authority to support your analysis. Show how the facts are equivalent or analogous to those in precedent cases. Use the outline of your rule explanation as an outline or checklist of the legal conclusions you must state about your client's facts in rule application. For instance, if your issue is whether a joke can form the basis of a contract, your rule explanation might read:

[1] A joke can form the basis of a valid offer when the statement is deemed to manifest mutual assent to enter into a contractual obligation. *See Barnes v. Treece*, 549 P.2d 1152, 1155 (Wa. App. 1976). [2] Mutual assent requires that

both parties demonstrate an objective intent to enter into a contract. *Id.* [3] In assessing whether there is sufficient mutual intention to enter into a contract, the parties' subjective intent is irrelevant. *Id.* [4] Rather, sufficient manifestation of intent exists when a reasonable observer would believe that a sincere offer was being made. *Id.* [5] Indicators of this objective manifestation of intent include negotiation between the parties over terms, actions in reasonable reliance on the contract, as well as a signed writing that specifies the terms of the agreement such as price, delivery date, and an item description. *Id.* [6] Further, even if an offer was made in jest, later conduct can reaffirm the contract if a reasonable person would so conclude. *Id.*

Each of these numbered sentences would require a conclusion in rule application about your client's facts. Thus, your rule application would include conclusions on [1] whether the joke manifested mutual assent; [2] whether the parties demonstrated an objective intent to enter into a contract; and so on. In between each conclusion, you would provide supporting facts and analysis to explain to the reader why that is the appropriate conclusion given the law and the specific facts of your client's case.

3. Unless it's obvious, show how the result is consistent with the rule's policy. See paragraph 4 in §17.3.1.

4. If any arguments could reasonably challenge your application of the rule, show, in a counteranalysis, why those arguments aren't persuasive. If you can't do that, consider changing your mind.

Exercise 17-A. Changing Planes in Little Rock

Wong has sued Keating in an Arkansas state court. Wong has never lived in Arkansas, and none of the events that led to *Wong v. Keating* happened in that state. But Wong sued in Arkansas because his lawyer has confidence in the juries there. The only time Keating has ever set foot on the ground in Arkansas was for 45 minutes while changing planes at the Little Rock airport. The only way for Keating to get to Shreveport, Louisiana, where she had a job interview, was to fly into Little Rock on one flight and then fly from Little Rock to Shreveport on another. During those 45 minutes, while Keating was walking in the airport from her incoming gate to her outgoing gate, a process server, acting on Wong's behalf, served Keating with a summons and complaint in *Wong v. Keating*. Keating has moved to dismiss on the ground that Arkansas has no personal jurisdiction over her. Wong claims that service in Arkansas gives Arkansas personal jurisdiction over Keating.

Below is an analysis of this issue. Find the components of the CREAC formula, which are set out in the box in §17.2.1.

Arkansas has personal jurisdiction over Keating. Under the Due Process Clause of the Fourteenth Amendment, a state is authorized to exercise personal jurisdiction over a defendant who is served with a summons while the defendant is voluntarily inside the state. *Burnham v. Superior Court*, 495 U.S. 604 (1990). That is true even if service of the summons is the only connection between the state and the plaintiff, the defendant, or the plaintiff's claim. It is true when a defendant does not reside in the state, is only traveling through the state, and has no connection to the state except for the trip during which the defendant was served. *Id.* at 617-619, 635-639. And it is true even when none of the events or circumstances alleged in the plaintiff's complaint happened in the state. *Id.* at 620-621.

The defendant in *Burnham* was a New Jersey resident who had traveled on business to southern California and then to northern California to visit his children. The plaintiff was the defendant's wife, who had him served in a divorce action while he was in northern California. Four justices of the Supreme Court joined in an opinion by Justice Scalia and reasoned that, under precedent going back two centuries, a state has "the power to hale before its courts any individual who could be found within its borders." *Id.* at 610. Another four justices joined in an opinion by Justice Brennan and reasoned that the defendant's presence in the state at the time of service was a purposeful availment that satisfies the minimum contacts requirements of *International Shoe v. Washington*, 326 U.S. 310 (1945). The ninth justice (Stevens) concurred separately on the ground that both rationales were correct. Because there was no majority opinion, it is not settled which rationale supports the rule, although the rule had the unanimous support of all nine justices.

Regardless of the rationale, service on Keating in the Little Rock airport created personal jurisdiction in Arkansas. Keating was present in Arkansas at the moment of service. The process server's affidavit is evidence of that, and Keating concedes it. Moreover, she does not claim that she did not know she was in Arkansas or that she was in the state under duress. She bought her airline ticket knowing she would have to change planes in Little Rock, and her presence was therefore voluntary.

Keating argues, however, that she was not in Arkansas long enough to be subject to the state's jurisdiction, even if she was served in Arkansas. She points out that the *Burnham* defendant had traveled to California to conduct business there and visit his children, spending nights in hotels and purposely availing himself of the benefits of the state. Keating contends that this case is distinguishable from *Burnham* because her destination was Louisiana rather than Arkansas, and because she was on the ground in Arkansas for less than an hour and only for the purpose of getting to Louisiana.

This case cannot be distinguished from *Burnham*. The Scalia opinion stressed that the state's jurisdiction extends to any visitor, "no matter how fleeting his visit." *Id.* at 610. And the Brennan rationale would treat Keating's decision to use the Little Rock airport for a connecting flight as purposeful availment supporting minimum contacts because Keating gained a benefit from her presence in Arkansas. Any other result would be unsupportable policy in an era of modern travel. There is no practical way to craft a rule that would clearly distinguish between a presence in the state that is too short to support personal jurisdiction and a presence that is long enough, which is why the Supreme Court held in *Burnham* that any presence is long enough if the defendant is served while physically present.

Moreover, Keating's presence in Arkansas was not limited to her 45 minutes inside the airport. She might have been validly served while either of the airplanes on which she flew was on the tarmac or even in the air over Arkansas. Service of process on a passenger in an airplane that flew over Arkansas but never landed in the state has been sustained because at the moment of service, the passenger was inside Arkansas even though not on the ground. *Grace v. MacArthur*, 170 F. Supp. 442 (E.D. Ark. 1959). The *Grace* court reasoned that there is no real difference between a passenger on an airplane that passes through Arkansas airspace and a passenger who travels through the state by train or bus without disembarking. *Id.* at 447.

Thus Arkansas has personal jurisdiction over Keating, and her motion to dismiss should be denied.

18 Varying the Sequence and Depth of Rule Explanation and Rule Application

§18.1 Varying the CREAC Formula to Suit Your Needs

You can vary the CREAC formula set out in Chapter 17 in two ways. First, you can vary the *sequence* in which the components appear. The next section in this chapter explains how. Second, in rule explanation and in rule application, you can vary the *depth* to suit the amount of skepticism you expect from the reader. Later sections in this chapter explain how.

In addition, when you have more than one issue or sub-issue, you can *combine* separate CREAC analyses into a unified explanation of several issues and sub-issues. Chapter 19 explains how.

§18.2 Varying the Sequence

In some situations, you might vary the sequence of the CREAC formula's components—for example, by stating the rule first and the conclusion second—although the order should not be illogical or confusing. Think long and hard before deciding to vary the sequence in the box shown in §17.2.1. If you do vary it, you should be able to give a good reason for doing so. Because of the reader's needs, described in §17.2.2, *rule explanation should be completed before rule application begins.* In an office memo, variations in sequence usually don't work well. They're more useful in motion memos and appellate briefs, where varying the sequence might fit into a strategy of persuasion.

§18.3   Varying the Depth of Rule Explanation or Rule Application

Depending on the situation, rule explanation or rule application can be very short, very long, or somewhere in between. In one instance, rule explanation might need only a sentence, while rule application might require three pages. In another instance, the reverse might be true. Or each of them might be four or five pages long—or four or five sentences long. How can you tell how much depth is needed? Ask these three questions:

First, *how much depth will convince the reader that your conclusion is correct?* That depends on the reader's level of skepticism, which in turn depends on how complicated the issue is and how important it is to the decision the reader must make.

Second, *how much depth will convince your reader that she does not personally need to read the authorities on which you rely?* This second question poses a need-to-read test: If your reader would find it hard to agree with you without reading the authorities herself, you haven't gone into enough depth. A reader's need to consult the statutes and cases depends on the context. A reader is more likely to feel that need with a crucial and difficult issue than with a simple, peripheral, or routine one.

Third, *how much depth would help the reader make an informed decision?* If the reader were to go to the statutes and cases, would she be startled to find things you have left out? Part of your job is choosing what to leave out. The reader counts on you to cut out the things that don't matter. But don't leave out so much that you deprive the reader of some of the information needed to make the decision.

Don't explore an issue in more depth than a reader needs. Your writing should not include things that are merely true; it should include what is relevant to the reader's understanding of the issue or issues. Your reader is a busy person, almost as intolerant of too much explanation as too little. If you include a great deal of detail about peripheral issues or about routine propositions with which your reader will easily agree, she can feel stuck in quicksand.

Students often underestimate the skepticism of legal readers. If you're not sure how much analysis to include, err on the side of making a more complete analysis until you have gained a better sense of your reader's expectations.

Rule explanation and rule application can each be developed in a way that is *comprehensive* or *substantiating* or *conclusory*. The rest of this chapter explains how, using the facts from Jordan's possible claim against YouTube introduced in §17.1.

§18.4   Comprehensive Analysis

A comprehensive explanation includes whatever analyses are needed to satisfy a reader's aggressive skepticism. This is the full treatment. In the example below, notes in the margin show where each component of the CREAC formula begins. Can you locate policy discussions and counteranalyses?

Conclusion   YouTube has been immunized by federal law from liability for the video and words posted by Kendrick on YouTube's website.

Rule   Under the Communications Decency Act of 1996, a defendant is immune from liability if (1) the defendant is a "provider or user of an interactive computer service," which the statute defines to include a website; (2) the plaintiff has pleaded a state law claim; (3) the state claim requires the plaintiff to prove that the defendant is a "publisher or speaker of any information"; and (4) the information at issue in the plaintiff's claim was "provided by another information content provider," which the statute defines to include a person, other than the defendant, who puts information on the defendant's website. 47 U.S.C. § 230(c)(1), (e)(3), (f)(2), (f)(3) (2012). The immunity test is in § 230(c)(1), (e)(3). The other subsections are definitional.

Rule Explanation begins   In the leading case interpreting these subsections of § 230, a plaintiff sued America Online, alleging that AOL allowed users to post anonymous messages on its website that defamed him and put his life in jeopardy. *Zeran v. Am. Online, Inc.*, 129 F.3d 327 (4th Cir. 1997). According to the complaint, the messages purported to be advertisements for "Naughty Oklahoma T-Shirts" with what the court described as "offensive and tasteless slogans related to the April 19, 1995, bombing of the Alfred P. Murrah Federal Building in Oklahoma City." *Id.* at 329. The messages said that viewers could purchase the t-shirts by calling the plaintiff's home telephone number. Although the plaintiff knew nothing about this and was not selling t-shirts of any kind, so many outraged people called him at home that at times he "was receiving an abusive phone call approximately every two minutes." *Id.* Several calls included threats to his life, and he had to seek police protection. *Id.* The plaintiff alleged that AOL was slow to remove these messages from its site, and that every time one was removed, another was posted, which AOL failed to prevent. *Id.*

The Fourth Circuit held that the Communications Decency Act barred the plaintiff's claims against AOL. *Id.* at 339. Even though the messages defamed him, AOL was immunized because, in the words of § 230(c)(1), (1) AOL is a "provider . . . of an interactive computer service"; (2) the plaintiff's defamation and negligence claims were based on state law; (3) publication is an element of defamation, requiring the plaintiff to prove that AOL is a "publisher or speaker of . . . information"; and (4) the information at issue in the plaintiff's claim was "provided by another information content provider," the anonymous poster. *Zeran*, 129 F.3d at 332. Section 230 even immunized AOL from liability for delays in removing the messages after the plaintiff informed the company of their defamatory character and their effect on him. *Zeran*, 129 F.3d at 339.

The plaintiff in *Zeran* argued that a website is no different from the publisher or distributor of a newspaper, book, or magazine, which would be liable for defamatory words it publishes. But the court held that even though a website is easily analogous to a print publisher, Congress had immunized websites anyway. "By its plain language, § 230 creates a federal immunity to any cause of action that would make service providers liable for information originating with a third-party user of the service," such as the unknown person who posted the false messages about the plaintiff. *Zeran*, 129 F.2d at 330.

Other Circuits have interpreted § 230 in the same way. *Doe v. GTE Corp.*, 347 F.3d 655 (7th Cir. 2003) (holding internet service provider immune from liability for a user's invasion of plaintiff's privacy); *Batzel v. Smith*, 333 F.3d 1018 (9th Cir. 2003) (holding website operator immune for defamatory email message posted on its website); *Ben Ezra, Weinstein & Co. v. Am. Online, Inc.*, 206 F.3d 980 (10th Cir. 2000) (holding AOL immune for inaccurate information posted on bulletin boards about stocks).

According to § 230's legislative history, Congress added subsections (c)(1) and (e)(3) to overrule a case that held that Prodigy could be liable for defamatory statements posted on one of its bulletin boards. S. Rep. No. 104-230, at 194 (1996); H.R. Conf. Rep. No. 104-458, at 194 (1996); 141 Cong. Rec. H84691-70 (1996). The case was *Stratton Oakmont, Inc. v. Prodigy Services Co.*, 1995 WL 323710 (N.Y. Sup. Ct. May 24, 1995).

In the statute itself, Congress enunciated the reasons for this immunity: "to promote the continued development of the Internet" and "to preserve the vibrant and competitive free market that presently exists for the Internet and other interactive computer services, unfettered by Federal or State regulation." 47 U.S.C. § 230(b)(1) & (2). "Congress recognized the threat that tort-based lawsuits pose to freedom of speech in the new and burgeoning Internet medium. . . . Section 230 was enacted, in part, to maintain the robust nature of Internet communication and, accordingly, to keep government interference in the medium to a minimum." *Zeran*, 129 F.3d at 330. People like the plaintiff in *Zeran* would be left without a remedy, but Congress considered the vitality of the internet to be more important than insuring recovery by every plaintiff aggrieved by information distributed over the internet. *Id.*

Rule Application begins

Here, YouTube can satisfy the immunity test in subsections (c)(1) and (e)(3). First, YouTube operates a website. It is therefore, in the statute's words, "a provider or user of an interactive computer service."

Second, defamation and false light invasion of privacy are state law claims. The immunity provisions of § 230 were enacted to prevent defamation claims against websites when the defamatory words were not generated by the website operator. That is why defamation claims failed in *Zeran* and *Batzel*. *Doe* treated invasion of privacy claims the same way.

Third, publication by the defendant is an element of both defamation and false light invasion of privacy. Thus, both claims would require Jordan to prove that YouTube was, in the statute's words, the "publisher or speaker of [the] information" that defamed her and invaded her privacy.

Finally, that information was not provided by YouTube. Instead, it was, in the statute's words, "provided by another information content provider." That was Kendrick.

This result is consistent with Congress's purpose in enacting the immunity provisions in § 230. As a practical matter, YouTube cannot review every video posted on its website without incurring business expenses so great that they could easily make the website unprofitable and cause weeks or months of delay in posting video clips that are the very reason for YouTube's existence. If the law imposed liability on YouTube for failing to conduct these investigations, the site could be forced to shut down. Congress did not immunize interactive computer service providers like websites from all informational liability, but only liability for information provided by others, like Kendrick. They remain liable for information that they generate themselves.

Even though a television station, newspaper, or magazine would have been liable under state law for defamation and false light invasion of privacy for publishing Kendrick's video with the words that he posted on YouTube, § 230 immunizes YouTube from these state law claims. The courts have uniformly enforced the distinction between internet service providers and conventional media.

Conclusion (again)   Thus, Jordan will not be able to recover from YouTube.

§18.5 Substantiating Analysis

A substantiating analysis goes less deeply into the writer's reasoning. It supports the conclusion but without comprehensive detail. A substantiating analysis works when the reader is less skeptical because the issue is not central to the problem you are addressing. A substantiating analysis would be inadequate if the issue is crucial or difficult. A substantiating analysis might look like this:

Conclusion   YouTube is immune from liability for the video and words Kendrick posted on YouTube's website.

Rule   A defendant is immune if (1) the defendant is a "provider or user of an interactive computer service," including a website; (2) the plaintiff has pleaded a state law claim; (3) the state claim requires the plaintiff to prove that the defendant is a "publisher or speaker of any information"; and (4) the information was "provided by another information content provider," defined to include a third party who puts information on the defendant's website. 47 U.S.C. § 230(c)(1), (e)(3), (f)(2), (f)(3) (2012).

Rule Explanation begins   In the leading case interpreting these subsections of § 230, a plaintiff sued America Online for allowing anonymous postings on its website that defamed him and jeopardized his life. *Zeran v. Am. Online, Inc.*, 129 F.3d 327, 339 (4th Cir. 1997). The Fourth Circuit held that AOL was immune because (1) AOL was a "provider . . . of an interactive computer service"; (2) the plaintiff's defamation and negligence claims grew out of state law; (3) to prove defamation, the plaintiff had to prove that AOL was a "publisher or speaker of . . . information"; and (4) the information was "provided by another information content provider," the anonymous poster. *Id.* (quoting § 230(c)(1)). Section 230(f)(3) defines "another information content provider" to include a third party who puts information on the defendant's website.

Other circuits have interpreted § 230 in the same way. *Doe v. GTE Corp.*, 347 F.3d 655 (7th Cir. 2003); *Batzel v. Smith*, 333 F.3d 1018 (9th Cir. 2003); *Ben Ezra, Weinstein & Co. v. Am. Online, Inc.*, 206 F.3d 980 (10th Cir. 2000). In the statute itself, Congress enunciated the reasons for this immunity: "to promote the continued development of the Internet" and "to preserve the . . . free market that presently exists for . . . interactive computer services, unfettered by Federal or State regulation." 47 U.S.C. § 230(b)(1) & (2).

Rule Application begins   YouTube can satisfy the immunity test in § 230(c)(1) and (e)(3). First, YouTube operates a website and is therefore "a provider or user of an interactive computer service." Second, defamation and false light invasion of privacy are state law claims. Third, both claims require Jordan to prove that YouTube was the "publisher or speaker of [the offending] information." Finally, that information was "provided by another information content provider" (Kendrick). § 230(f)(3).

This result is consistent with the congressional purpose of the immunity provisions. YouTube cannot practically review every video posted on its website, and if the law imposed liability on YouTube for failing to do so, the site could be forced out of business.

What in the comprehensive explanation in §18.4 is missing here? If you and your supervisor were trying to figure out whether to sue YouTube, would the substantiating analysis be sufficient?

§18.6 Conclusory Analysis

A conclusory analysis does no more than allude to some of the more important reasons supporting your conclusion. The CREAC formula components are all included in the example below, but in abbreviated form except the rule itself. The only rule explanation is the statutory citation that proves the rule.

A conclusory analysis is appropriate *only* when the reader will easily agree with you, or when the point is not important to your analysis. In those situations, a reader would find a more detailed analysis tedious.

Conclusion	YouTube is immune from liability for the video and words Kendrick posted on YouTube's website.
Rule	A defendant is immune if (1) the defendant is a "provider or user of an interactive computer service," including a website; (2) the plaintiff has pleaded a state law claim; (3) the state claim requires the plaintiff to prove that the defendant is a "publisher or speaker of any information"; and (4) the information was "provided by another information content provider," including a third party who puts information on the defendant's website. 47 U.S.C. § 230(c)(1), (e)(3), (f)(2), (f)(3) (2012).
Rule Explanation	
Rule Application begins	YouTube can satisfy this test. First, YouTube operates a website and is therefore "a provider or user of an interactive computer service." Second, defamation and false light invasion of privacy are state law claims. Third, both claims require Jordan to prove that YouTube was the "publisher or speaker of [the] information" in question. Finally, that information was "provided by another information content provider," Kendrick.

§18.7 Cryptic Analysis

Beginning students sometimes write analyses so cryptic as to be less than conclusory.

> Jordan will not be able to recover from YouTube because it satisfies all four requirements under the Communications Decency Act of 1996 and is therefore immune from Jordan's claim. 47 U.S.C. § 230(c)(1), (e)(3), (f)(2), (f)(3) (2012).

This example omits the rule on which the conclusion is based, and it doesn't show in any way how the rule applies to the facts. It would *never* satisfy a skeptical reader.

19 Advanced CREAC: Organizing More Than One Issue

§19.1 Introduction

If you have more than one issue, the reader will need a separately structured CREAC proof for each one. That can happen when

- more than one element of a rule is at issue (see §19.2)
- more than one claim or defense is at issue (see §19.3)
- a dispute involves separate but related issues (see §19.4)

Each issue will have its own conclusion. Adding all those conclusions together produces an *ultimate conclusion*. When you organize your writing, you'll state the ultimate conclusion first, which will cover all the issues—like a big umbrella:

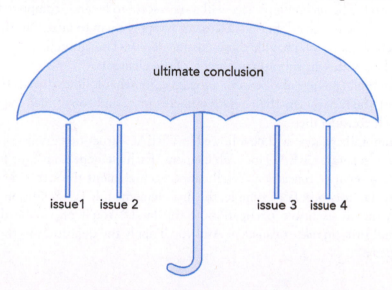

ultimate conclusion

issue1   issue 2   issue 3   issue 4

§19.2   How to Organize When More Than One Element or Factor Is at Issue

If you need to resolve more than one element of a test, you'll have an ultimate conclusion for the rule as a whole, together with a conclusion for each individual element—in this instance from the test for adverse possession:

Ultimate Conclusion		Melrose will probably be able to gain title through adverse possession to the land known as the Ironwood Tract.
Conclusions on Issues	*Element 1*	Melrose has been in actual possession of the Ironwood Tract.
	Element 2	Melrose possessed the land continuously for at least ten years.
	Element 3	Melrose possessed it openly and notoriously for the entire ten years.
	Element 4	Melrose's possession has been hostile to the owner's rights.
	Element 5	Melrose possessed the land under a claim of right or title.

When you write this analysis, your opening or umbrella passage will state the ultimate conclusion ("Melrose will probably be able to gain title to the client's Ironwood Tract") and the essence of the reason ("because she has satisfied all the elements of adverse possession"). Your umbrella passage will also recite the *rule* on which the ultimate conclusion is based (the test for adverse possession, which has five elements). The umbrella passage will at first seem to be an incomplete CREAC structure because it won't define the elements or apply them to facts. But the discussion of each element will provide those missing details. The umbrella passage simply covers and organizes the subordinate proofs of the elements.

The umbrella passage also sets out a roadmap for what follows. It tells the reader what issues you'll consider, their relative importance, and sometimes the order in which you'll consider them.

Your umbrella passage will be followed by CREAC-structured discussions for the elements—a separate CREAC for each element. Each element is an issue for which you'll have a separate *conclusion*. You'll define each element through a definitional or other declaratory *rule*. For example, the first elements rule is a definition: "Actual possession means exclusive occupation of the land." You'll prove the definition through authority in *rule explanation*. And you'll apply the definition to the facts in *rule application*.

§19.3   How to Organize When More Than One Claim or Defense Is at Issue

Suppose your supervisor wants to know whether the client will be awarded damages in a tort case. You need to figure out whether the client has a cause of action (one issue or a cluster of issues). And you anticipate that the defendant will raise the affirmative defense of sovereign immunity. Although this situation is more complex than when several elements of a single rule are in dispute, you'll handle it in the same way (see §19.2).

Build an umbrella CREAC structure, and underneath it prove each of the conclusions through separate CREAC-structured analyses. For example, the ultimate conclusion might be that the client will be awarded damages because she has a cause of action (first conclusion) and the defendant has waived sovereign immunity (second conclusion). Thus:

Ultimate Conclusion	The client will be awarded damages.
Conclusions on Issues	*The claim* The client can prove negligence.
	Element 1 The defendant owed the client a duty.
	Element 2 The defendant breached it.
	Element 3 The client suffered injury.
	Element 4 The breach proximately caused the injury.
	The defense The defendant has waived the affirmative defense of sovereign immunity.

Because negligence has four elements, the first issue is divided further into the four sub-issues shown above. At the beginning of your analysis of Issue 1, include an umbrella passage limited to whether the client has a cause of action for negligence.

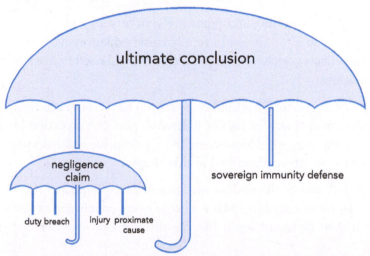

§19.4 How to Organize Other Types of Separate but Related Issues

Suppose someone sues your client, and your supervisor wants to know whether the lawsuit can be dismissed on forum selection grounds (because it was brought in the wrong court). You'll have to resolve some or all of the following issues: (1) Does this court have subject-matter jurisdiction over this kind of case? (2) Does this court have personal jurisdiction over your client? (3) Is this court the right venue for this lawsuit? To resolve these issues, you'll use the same umbrella CREAC structure explained in §19.2:

Ultimate Conclusion	The court will not dismiss this lawsuit on forum selection grounds.
Conclusions on Issues	*Issue 1* The court has subject-matter jurisdiction.
	Issue 2 The court has personal jurisdiction over our client.
	Issue 3 The court is the proper venue.

Here, too, if an issue involves a test with more than one element, you'll include an umbrella passage limited to that issue.

§19.5 How to Work with Multi-Issue Situations

Many students feel confused at first by how to organize multi-issue situations. But within a few weeks, you might begin to gain confidence in organizing this way. And within a year or two, most students instinctively think in structured proofs because it becomes second nature. This section provides some suggestions for getting to that point.

Step 1 While researching and planning your writing, ask yourself how many issues you have. If you have a hard time identifying issues, ask yourself how many conclusions of law a court would need to reach to resolve the dispute.

Step 2 Now, figure out what kind of issues you have. For each issue, is it part of the cause of action, part of a defense, part of a procedural requirement, or something else? Identifying the type of issue will help you choose one of the structures described in this chapter.

Step 3 Select one of the multi-issue structures explained in this chapter, and adapt it to your case. Make a list of every conclusion of law you'll prove in your memo or brief, like the lists of issues earlier in this chapter.

Organize the conclusions logically—for example, elements of a cause of action first, then defenses. Treat this list of conclusions as the beginning of an outline. Chapter 20 explains how to complete this outline and turn it into a memo or brief.

Step 4 At the beginning of an umbrella passage, use a roadmap paragraph to explain your umbrella CREAC to the reader. An introductory roadmap paragraph outlines your discussion so the reader knows what to expect as you explain the details. It states your ultimate conclusion ("The client should be awarded damages," for example) and then states the conclusions on sub-issues that support that ultimate conclusion. If some elements of a test are at issue and others aren't, the roadmap paragraph is the place to make that clear. Most judges say that a well-written roadmap paragraph is essential in helping them understand what a lawyer is trying to say.[1] Here's a typical roadmap paragraph, which you might use to introduce the discussion outlined in §19.3:

> The client will be awarded damages for destruction of its warehouse. The evidence supports all four of the elements of negligence. The defendant owed a duty to the plaintiff to keep the loading dock clear and breached that duty by leaving explosive materials on the loading dock overnight. The client's injury, destruction of its warehouse, is uncontested. The property damage was proximately caused by the defendant's breach when the materials it left on the loading dock exploded. In addition, sovereign immunity has been waived by § 419 of the Highways Code.

After reading this umbrella paragraph, the reader knows that you'll discuss each of these issues in detail later in your analysis.

---

1. Kristen K. Robbins, *The Inside Scoop: What Federal Judges Really Think About the Way Lawyers Write*, 8 Legal Writing 257, 273 (2002).

20 Working with CREAC in First Drafts and in Later Drafts

§20.1 Using CREAC to Outline and to Begin Your First Draft

The CREAC formula explained in the preceding chapters can help you organize your legal analysis. It will also help keep your material from getting out of control. Getting used to writing with the CREAC formula takes some effort, but once you're used to it, organizing your writing becomes much easier *because the formula shows you where to put things*.

This section describes one method of working with CREAC. It's only a suggestion for the first time you write. If you develop a different process that works better for you, use that instead.

In the method described here, you'll label everything so that you know where it goes and then plug it into whatever variant of the formula best fits your situation. The first time you try this method, it might seem a little awkward. But by the second or third time, it will begin to feel more natural because it fits the way people instinctively work and takes less effort than other methods of organizing.

Step 1 Figure out how many issues you have. You'll analyze each using a separate CREAC structure. Chapter 19 explains how.

Step 2 For each issue, identify the rule that is central to and governs the answer. You might also use other rules, but for the moment focus on the rule that—more than any other—compels your answer.

Step 3 Inventory your raw materials. For each issue or sub-issue, sort everything you have into two categories: rule explanation and rule application. Some methods of sorting may work better for you than others, and over several writing assignments you might experiment to find the method that best fits the way you write.

One method is to go through your notes and write "RE" in the margin next to everything that you might use in rule explanation, and "RA" next to everything you might use in rule application. Some ideas or authorities might be useful in both rule explanation and rule application. Write "RE/RA" next to them. If you have several issues, you can work out a shorthand for marking them separately, such as "#3 RE" for "rule explanation on issue 3" or "#1 RA" for "rule application on issue 1." If you have printed out cases, write these notations next to each part of the case that you'll use. Go through your facts, too, marking the ones that are important enough to talk about during rule application.

Step 4 Think about how all these things add up.   If you haven't yet drawn a conclusion, do it now. If you decided previously on a conclusion, check it against your raw materials to see whether it still seems like the best conclusion.

Step 5 Make a fluid outline.   Your notes are now complete enough to be organized into some variation of the CREAC formula. You can do that by making the fluid outline described in §13.2.

For each issue, take a piece of paper and write four headings on it, using abbreviations for the CREAC components (for example: "concl," "rule," "RE," and "RA"). You can do this on a computer instead if you feel more comfortable typing than writing.

Under "concl," write your conclusion for that issue in whatever shorthand will remind you later what your thinking was (for example: "no diversity—Wharton citizen of Maine"). Under "rule," do something similar. Under "RE," list your raw materials for rule explanation. For each item listed, don't write a lot—just enough to remind you at a glance of everything you have. Under "RA," do the same for rule application. Make sure that everything you have on that issue is listed on that page. *This is your outline page for the issue.*

Suppose that for rule explanation on a certain issue you've listed six resources (cases, facts, and so on). You haven't yet decided the order in which you'll discuss them when you explain the rule. In most situations, that decision will be easier and better if you don't make it while outlining. The best time to decide is just before you write that issue's rule explanation in your first draft. *You don't need to know exactly where everything will go before you start the first draft.* When you decide, just write a number next to each item ("1" next to the first one you'll discuss, "2" next to the second, and so on).

Step 6 Start writing. Choose the issue you feel most comfortable writing about. Put that issue's outline page (from Step 5) where you can see it while you work. Using what you have on the outline page, write a complete sentence stating your conclusion for that issue. Then write the other CREAC components.

As you cover each thing listed on the issue's outline page, cross it off. When everything has been crossed off, go on to another issue, and use the same process to write it.

Your first draft probably won't use everything that you listed on your outline pages. Some material won't seem as useful while you're writing as it did when you were sorting. But don't throw anything away yet. During rewriting, you might change your mind and decide to use it after all.

§20.2 How to Test Your Writing for Effective Organization

While reviewing your work, ask the following questions.

1. Have you organized around tests and elements, rather than around cases? Readers will be frustrated if you dump before them the cases you found in the library. A mere list of relevant cases, with a discussion of each, does not help a decision maker, who needs to understand how the *rules* affect the facts. The law is the rules themselves, and a case merely proves a rule's existence and accuracy. Professors sometimes call this problem *case-by-case-itis*. It is easy to spot in a student's paper: The reader sees a series of paragraphs, each devoted to a single case. Instead, organize around *ideas*, such as issues, arguments, or a test's elements or factors.

2. Have you collected closely related ideas in one place, rather than scattering them? If you have three reasons why the defendant won't be convicted, first list them all in one place, and then explain each separately. The reader looking for the big picture can't follow your analysis if you introduce the first reason on page one; mention the second for the first time on page four; and surprise the reader with the third on page six. If you have more than one item or idea, listing them in a roadmap paragraph at the beginning helps the reader keep things in perspective. It also forces you to organize and evaluate your thoughts. Roadmap paragraphs help tell the reader where you're going.

3. Have you accounted for all the issues and discussed them in logical order? If you have several issues, have you organized them so the reader understands how everything fits together?

4. For each issue or sub-issue, have you stated your conclusion? If so, where? State it precisely so the reader knows from the very beginning what you intend to demonstrate. In an office memo, your conclusions will be predictions, either expressed ("Kolchak will probably be acquitted of robbery") or implied ("The evidence does not establish beyond a reasonable doubt that Kolchak is guilty of robbery").

5. For each issue or sub-issue, have you stated the rule or rules supporting your conclusion? If so, where? Don't merely describe the cases and assume your reader will figure out what rule they stand for. Formulate a credible rule, and prove it by analyzing the authority.

6. For each issue or sub-issue, have you explained the rule? If so, where? See §17.3.1 for how to evaluate your rule explanation.

7. For each issue or sub-issue, have you applied the rule to the facts? If so, where? See §17.3.2 for how to evaluate your rule application.

8. Have you completed rule explanation before starting rule application? Before you start rule application, the reader needs to know that you have accurately stated the rule and that it really is law. If you don't do those things first during rule explanation, many readers will find it harder to agree with your rule application. You might use some authorities first in explaining the rule and again in applying the rule. But that doesn't mean rule application and rule explanation can be mixed.

9. In both rule explanation and rule application, have you explained your reasoning fully? Explain each step in your reasoning. Don't leave anything out. One way to discipline yourself to do this well is to ask "Why is that true?" about each conclusion you make. Then make sure your writing completely answers that question. Your conclusions must be supported by facts that are connected to the conclusion by their inferences. The inferences are what makes that fact matter given the rules you are applying. To ensure you do this well, ask "So what?" about each fact you refer to in your analysis.

10. Have you created a post-draft linear outline to test your organization? A post-draft linear outline is explained in §13.2.

Part 5

Working Effectively with Details

21 Writing Effective Paragraphs and Sentences

This chapter explains how to structure paragraphs and sentences to help the reader easily follow your reasoning. Paragraphs are the building blocks of your legal analysis. Sentences are the bricks. Your reader will struggle to understand unless you pay careful attention to structuring your analysis block by block and brick by brick.

§21.1 Paragraphs Reveal the Organizational Details

Most readers subconsciously use paragraph divisions to learn how a writer's thoughts fit together. They assume that each paragraph substantiates or explores a separate and distinct idea or subject. They also assume that the first or second sentence in each paragraph states or implies that idea or subject and shows how it relates to matters already discussed in previous paragraphs. To the extent that you frustrate these assumptions, your writing will be less helpful to the reader and therefore less influential.

An effective paragraph has the following five characteristics:

1. *Unity:* It proves one proposition or covers one subject. Material more relevant to other propositions or subjects is relocated to a more appropriate paragraph.
2. *Completeness:* It includes whatever is needed to prove the proposition or cover the subject of that paragraph.
3. *Internal coherence:* Ideas are expressed in a logical sequence that the reader can follow without having to mentally edit the paragraph while reading and without having to refer to other paragraphs.
4. *Readable length:* It is neither so long that the reader gets lost, nor so short that valuable material is underdeveloped or trivialized.
5. *Thesis or topic sentence:* An effective paragraph announces or implies its purpose at the outset. Its first or second sentence states or implies its thesis or topic and, if necessary, makes a transition from the preceding material.

§21.2   Descriptive and Probative Paragraphs

The way you write a paragraph depends on whether you are *describing* something or *proving* something. Compare these paragraphs:

Descriptive	Probative
In January in Death Valley, the average high temperature is about 65°, and the average low is about 37°. Spring and fall temperatures approximate summer temperatures elsewhere. In April and in October, for example, the average high is about 90°, and the average low about 60°. July is the hottest month, with an average high of about 116° and an average low of about 87°. The highest temperature ever recorded in Death Valley was 134° on July 10, 1913. Average annual rainfall is about 1.5 inches.	The climate in Death Valley is brutal. At Furnace Creek Ranch, the highest summer temperature each year reaches at least 120° and in many years at least 125°. The highest temperature recorded in Death Valley—134°—is also the highest recorded anywhere on earth. In the summer sun, a person can lose four gallons of perspiration a day and—in 3% humidity—die of dehydration.

A *topic* is a subject or category of information, such as "Death Valley weather." After reading the descriptive paragraph, you know some weather details about Death Valley. Descriptive paragraphs give factual information about things. If a descriptive paragraph confuses a reader, she might ask, "What is this paragraph about?"

A *thesis* or *proposition*, on the other hand, begins a probative paragraph with a statement that can be proved or disproved—such as "the climate in Death Valley is brutal." After reading the probative paragraph, you have a reaction to that proposition. You might agree or disagree. A probative paragraph should try to *prove* something about the subject matter or topic. If a probative paragraph confuses a reader, she might ask, "What is this paragraph supposed to prove?"

Probative and descriptive writing often appear in the same legal document. In an office memo, for example, the Facts are mostly descriptive, and the Discussion is mostly probative.

Even in probative writing, some paragraphs are more descriptive than others. If it takes three pages to prove a particular proposition, at least a few paragraphs in those three pages will describe the raw materials involved—facts, cases, or statutes, for example. Proving a proposition means explaining *how* the relevant legal authority and determinative facts support it. Most readers need a description of those raw materials before you can convincingly explain how they prove something when artfully woven together.

§21.3 Proposition Sentences, Topic Sentences, and Transition Sentences

The first or second sentence of a probative paragraph is the *proposition sentence* because it clearly states the proposition. The rest of the paragraph should prove the proposition.

In contrast, a descriptive paragraph provides details about a topic. The first or second sentence is the *topic sentence*, which identifies the topic by expressly stating it or implying it. If the context implies the topic, sometimes the topic sentence can be omitted from the paragraph. But in most cases, including a topic sentence helps the reader understand by revealing your internal organization step by step.

Although in descriptive writing a topic can sometimes be implied, in probative writing the proposition should be expressly stated. *A practical reader needs to know what you are trying to prove before you start proving it.* Law-trained readers are always practical because they must make decisions after reading a lot of material in a limited amount of time. Careful paragraph structure is an important part of helping your reader understand information as quickly and efficiently as possible.

Both descriptive and probative paragraphs are much more effective if they include *transition words or phrases* to show the reader how each paragraph is connected to the material before or after it. If paragraphs are the blocks that build your analysis, transitions are the mortar that hold the blocks in place. Transitions are the mark of a professional writer, who thoughtfully adds connections between each block of writing to help the reader follow what she is communicating. A transition most often appears at the beginning of a paragraph but may also appear at the end, serving as a bridge to the next paragraph or topic. Often the first sentence of a paragraph can both state a proposition or topic and make a transition.

§21.4 How to Test Your Paragraphs for Effectiveness

In first drafts, paragraphs are seldom structured well. To identify the paragraphs in need of improvement, ask the following questions.

1. Does each paragraph serve just one purpose? Prove one proposition or describe one topic. Remove and relocate material that is more relevant to other propositions or topics.

2. Have you told the reader each paragraph's proposition (if probative) or its topic (if descriptive) near the beginning? If your reader has to wait until later in the paragraph to learn its proposition or topic, the reader might need to read the paragraph two or three times to figure out its purpose. However, a topic sentence might not be necessary if the topic is clearly implied by the context.

3. Have you broken up long paragraphs so the reader does not get lost inside them? Your reader will be confused by paragraphs that wander on aimlessly or endlessly, addressing multiple topics. A busy reader relies on paragraph divisions to take a momentary mental breath before proceeding to the next thought. Think about a case you recently read in one of your casebooks that had unusually long paragraphs.[2] You probably felt tired and confused by trying to understand its internal organization and reasoning. That is how a lawyer or judge feels when navigating a document with paragraphs that are too long.

A paragraph that is too long probably lacks *unity* as well because it includes two or more topics or propositions. Writers of long paragraphs often shift topics without realizing it. If you tend to write paragraphs longer than a half-page, look for the natural topic shifts inside the paragraph. After identifying each individual topic or proposition, break up the material into digestible chunks, so they become separate paragraphs that address distinct topics. Lead your reader from one paragraph to the next by adding effective transitions.

4. Within each paragraph, have you expressed your ideas in a logical and effective sequence? When a paragraph confuses but nothing is wrong with its length or the wording of individual sentences, the paragraph usually lacks *internal coherence*. That happens when ideas within the paragraph are presented in a sequence that makes it hard for the reader to understand how they fit together to prove the proposition or illuminate the topic. Using transitions to show the connections between sentences can make it easier for the reader to follow the analysis. (See §§21.3 and 22.3.)

§21.5   How to Test Your Sentences for Effectiveness

Just as paragraphs build documents, sentences build paragraphs. All of the characteristics of an effective paragraph depend upon the internal structure and sequence of the sentence components. Sentences usually do not become fully effective until the polishing stage. But at the first draft and rewriting stage, ask the following questions.

1. Does the sentence deliver the subject and verb to the reader as soon as possible? The verb holds a sentence together by connecting its words to an idea. In fact, a sentence is usually incomprehensible until the reader finds both the subject and the verb. The longer it takes the reader to find both, the harder your reader must work.

---

2. An example in your Civil Procedure casebook is *Pennoyer v. Neff*, 95 U.S. 714 (1878).

For example, try reading this sentence:

> The defendant's use of email spam to solicit contributions to a fake charitable organization purportedly engaged in disaster relief and his use of the contributions to buy a vacation home for himself constitute fraud.

A sentence like this cannot be understood in a single reading because it is "front-loaded." A frustrated reader searches for the verb ("constitute") and finds it nearly at the end of the sentence, after plowing through a 32-word compound subject ("The defendant's use of email spam to solicit contributions to a fake charitable organization purportedly engaged in disaster relief *and* his use of the contributions to buy a vacation home for himself"). Once the reader locates the verb, she must read the sentence again to understand it—because everything that came before the verb made no sense the first time.

During first drafts, writers often ask themselves, "What shall I talk about next?" and then write down the answer. That answer becomes the subject of a sentence, no matter how unreadable the result. We all do this in first drafts, but in rewriting you should spot the problem and fix it. There are two ways to fix the front-loaded sentence above.

You can fix a front-loaded sentence by reshuffling it to deliver the verb to the reader quickly:

> <u>The defendant committed fraud</u> by using email spam to solicit contributions for a fake charitable organization purportedly engaged in disaster relief, and by using the contributions to buy a vacation home for himself.

Or you can break up the sentence into two or more shorter sentences:

> <u>The defendant committed fraud</u>. He used email spam to solicit contributions for a fake charitable organization purportedly engaged in disaster relief, and he used the contributions to buy a vacation home for himself.

2. Have you put the verb near the subject and the object near the verb? Many readers get lost in a sentence when something has been inserted between the subject and the verb.

> The Wabash Garage Orchestra, <u>even though it includes 32 musicians, some with cellos or other large instruments,</u> played the Philip Glass Violin Concerto while sitting in trees in Fabian Smedley's backyard.

In this sentence, 32 musicians and several large instruments have been inserted between the subject (Wabash Garage Orchestra) and the verb (played).

The same problem occurs when the verb and its object are interrupted by other words. To help your reader, move the interrupting clause or phrase to the end of the sentence (or to the beginning), leaving the subject and verb (or the verb and its object) relatively close together.

phrase or clause moved to end	The Wabash Garage Orchestra played the Philip Glass Violin Concerto while sitting in trees in Fabian Smedley's backyard, <u>even though the orchestra includes 32 musicians, some with cellos or other large instruments.</u>
phrase or clause moved to beginning	<u>Even though the Wabash Garage Orchestra includes 32 musicians, some with cellos or other large instruments,</u> they played the Philip Glass Violin Concerto while sitting in trees in Fabian Smedley's backyard.

3. Have you put the most complex and detailed part of the sentence at the end?   To understand a sentence, a reader must figure out its structure. Readers do this quickly and subconsciously. When they cannot figure out the structure easily, they have to read the sentence again—or they lose interest, ignore the sentence, and read on without ever learning what the offending sentence meant. Consequently, the reader might misunderstand what will appear to be an incomplete analysis.

Compare these examples:

complex part at beginning	<u>Because the defendant's website is interactive and allows a person in any state to order a catalog, send a message to the defendant, and purchase beer or wine by typing in credit card and other information,</u> the court held that it has jurisdiction over the defendant.
complex part in middle	The court held that <u>because the defendant's website is interactive and allows a person in any state to order a catalog, send a message to the defendant, and purchase beer or wine by typing in credit card and other information,</u> the court has jurisdiction over the defendant.
complex part at end	The court held that it has jurisdiction over the defendant <u>because the defendant's website is interactive and allows a person in any state to order a catalog, send a message to the defendant, and purchase beer or wine by typing in credit card and other information.</u>

Most readers find the third example the easiest to read because the first thing they see is a subject, verb, and object ("The court held that it has jurisdiction over the defendant"). Once they understand the basic sentence structure, the complex part at the end makes more sense.

4. Have you put what you want to emphasize at the beginning or at the end of the sentence? The beginning or end of a sentence is more obvious than the middle. Some writers call them *stress positions*. Sometimes, the end is more obvious just because that is the last thing the reader reads before going on to something else. And sometimes the beginning is more obvious—for example, if the sentence is the first one in a paragraph. If you want a theme or idea to resonate in the reader's mind, take advantage of the stress position in a sentence and put that information there.

5. When a sentence compares two ideas, have you used the most effective structure and wording? Some sentence structures show contrast better than others. For example:

> The Supreme Court has held that a defendant waives an objection by not making it at trial, <u>but</u> the Court has also held that, even without an objection, a conviction should be reversed when a prosecutor's conduct was as inflammatory as it was here.

The word *but* buried in the middle of a long sentence only weakly alerts the reader that one idea (waiver by failing to object) is knocked down by another (but not if the prosecutor's conduct is inflammatory). Everybody writes this kind of sentence in rough drafts, but you should recognize and cure it during rewriting.

> <u>Although</u> the Supreme Court has held that a defendant waives an objection by not making it at trial, the Court has also held that a conviction should be reversed, even without an objection, when a prosecutor's conduct was as inflammatory as it was here.

"Although" signals the reader from the beginning that the first clause will turn out not to matter. Contrast can also be effectively shown when *but* appears at the beginning of a sentence:

> The Supreme Court has held that a defendant waives an objection by not making it at trial. <u>But</u> the Court has also held that a conviction should be reversed, even without an objection, when a prosecutor's conduct was as inflammatory as it was here.

No rule of grammar forbids occasionally starting a sentence with *but* or *and*. But avoid overdoing it.

6. Is the subject of the sentence doing something concrete? Does the sentence use a verb in the active voice? If not, do you have a good reason for using passive voice? A sentence is easier to understand when it uses concrete words to paint a picture full of active imagery. First, figure out who is (or was, or will be) doing something. Make the one who acts the subject of the sentence. Then choose a verb in the active voice that expresses the subject's action or conduct.

When you choose a verb in the active voice, it describes what the subject is doing or has done ("Maguire *sued* Schultz"). But a verb in the passive voice makes the subject of the sentence the receiver or victim of the action ("Schultz *was sued by* Maguire").

Here are two more examples:

active   The student missed the deadline.

passive   The deadline was missed by the student.

In the active voice example, the *student* is the subject, who acted by missing the deadline. In the passive voice example, the deadline—an inanimate abstraction—is the subject of the sentence. And the reader must wait until the end of the sentence to find out who missed it.

The passive voice can be vague, weak, wordy—and just plain boring. For that reason, write most sentences in the active voice. But sometimes passive voice works better. For example, passive verbs might be more effective when you do not know who acted, when the identity of the actor is unimportant, or when you want to deemphasize the actor's identity. For example, compare these:

active   The Department of Public Welfare has wrongfully terminated Ms. Blitzstein's aid-to-dependent-family benefits fourteen times in the last six years.

passive   Ms. Blitzstein's aid-to-dependent-family benefits have been wrongfully terminated fourteen times in the last six years.

Depending on the context, the passive sentence might not be vague. Here, the reader might know that the Department is the only agency capable of terminating aid-to-dependent-family benefits. And to some readers, the passive sentence could be stronger and more interesting. To a judge who is asked to issue an order to stop this nonsense, the passive would be stronger because it emphasizes the outcome in a way the judge might find more appealing. Generally, a judge is more likely to sympathize with the victim of a faceless bureaucracy (the passive example) than condemn a named government agency for acting maliciously or incompetently (the active example).

7. Have you avoided using forms of the verb *to be*? *To be* verbs include *is, are, was, were,* and some other forms that occur less often. In law, people do things to other people and to ideas and objects, which are best described by concrete verbs that help the reader *see* the action. Variations on the verb *to be* fail to bring the story to life for the reader. Even worse, when a form of *to be* is used in combination with the word *there,* the resulting sentence is weak, wordy, and devoid of imagery.

None of this is to say that the verb *to be* and its variations are never useful. *To be* verbs can effectively describe a condition or status ("the defendant is guilty"), and they work well to signal a declaratory rule ("the sentence for first-degree murder is 40 years without parole"). But, the overuse of *to be* verbs creates problems such as when they obscure action. Writing creates temptations to use *there is* and its variations (*there are, there were*). Editing them out usually creates stronger and tighter wording. For example:

weak	There is a possibility of action in the near future by the EPA to remove these pesticides from the market.
much better	The EPA might soon prohibit the sale of these pesticides.
weak	There are four reasons why the plaintiff will not recover.
much better	The plaintiff will not recover for four reasons.

In the "weak" examples, the reader can barely tell who has done what to whom because the weak verb and lofty tone obscure action. The subjects and verbs do not stand out and take charge. In the "much better" examples, the reader immediately knows what is happening without reading the same words twice. The subjects and verbs stand out and the sentences are more direct.

Early drafts often include sentences like the weak examples above, but rewriting should produce final drafts that more closely resemble the much better ones. While rewriting, look for sentences like the weak ones. Figure out what is *really* going on (who is doing what?). Use your word processor's "find" function to locate each of the four most common forms of the verb *to be—is, are, was,* and *were.* Then search for each instance of *there* used in combination with one of these verbs. Each time you find one, ask yourself whether you can rewrite the sentence using an active verb to bring the action to life. We bet you can.

8. Have you used concrete verbs that communicate *exactly* what the reader needs to know? Help the reader by choosing concrete verbs that clearly communicate your meaning. Here are some examples of vague verbs that frequently fail to meet the reader's needs because they raise more questions than they answer:

Apply. "The Freedom of Information Act *applies* to this document." Does that mean the document must be published in the *Federal Register*? Or does it mean that the document must be given to anyone who asks for a copy? Or that the document must be made available to the public for photocopying, but not at government expense? Or does it give the government permission to refuse to do any of these things? Replace *applies* with a verb that communicates exactly what the Act does.

Deal with. "The court *dealt with* common law larceny." What exactly did the court do to larceny? Did the court define that term? Define only one of the elements? Clarify the difference between larceny and false pretenses? Decide that the legislature impliedly abolished the crime of larceny when it enacted a theft statute? Delete *dealt with* and insert a verb that tells exactly what the court actually did.

Indicate. "The defendant *indicated* that he was interested in buying hashish." How did he do that? By nodding affirmatively when asked if that was his desire? By asking, "Is hashish sold in this neighborhood?" By saying, "I want to buy some hash"? The law might treat each of these possibilities differently, and the reader needs to know exactly what happened.

Involve. "Section 452(a) *involves* the Rule Against Perpetuities." That sentence says only that § 452(a) has some connection with the Rule Against Perpetuities. Has § 452(a) codified the Rule? Modified it? Abolished it? Use a verb that specifies exactly what § 452(a) and the Rule Against Perpetuities have to do with each other.

Say or Said. "The court *said* that the defendant's conduct was unconscionable." Courts hold, conclude, or reason. The reader expects you to analyze the law and explain what it *means*. To do that, use a specific word that communicates exactly what the court *did*, not just what it said. Courts *say* things only in dicta. On the other hand, a judge writing a concurrence or dissent does not act for the court, and therefore can accurately be described as having *said* things. For clarity, when you use the word *say*, specify the context: "The court said in dicta," or "Justice McGillicuddy said in dissent."

Do not use the word *say* to refer to words found in a statute: "Section 243(a) says the plaintiff is not entitled to exemplary damages." Statutes are called Acts because the legislature does something by enacting them. Statutes *provide, create, abolish, prohibit, penalize, define,* and more. Whether you are analyzing case law, statutes, or some other legal authority, use specific and concrete verbs that explain what the law *means and does*, not just what it says.

9. Have you broken up sentences that are too long or too complicated for the reader to understand easily the first time? Express the sentence's ideas in fewer words, or split the sentence into two or more shorter sentences. Or do both.

Legal ideas and concepts are difficult for a writer to communicate clearly, and even more difficult for the reader to comprehend. Long, convoluted sentences that try to impress by doing too much in fact do just the opposite. They fail to persuade because the reader gives up in frustration. You have reached the benchmark for excellent writing when your reader understands each step of your analysis *effortlessly*.

10. Have you violated any of these guidelines *only* when you have a very good reason? Writing is creative work, and when you have a good reason, go ahead and break the rules. To test whether your reason is a good one, try to articulate for yourself *exactly* what it is. Your professor might ask you to explain it.

Exercise 21-A. Probative and Descriptive Paragraphs

Write two paragraphs—one descriptive and the other probative—about the first month or two of law school.

1. Descriptive paragraph. Summarize what happened during your first month or two of law school. Describe some of the things you saw, heard, read, and wrote. Do not try to prove any belief you might have about the first month or two of law school. Just describe your experiences without characterizing them.

2. Probative paragraph. State a proposition about the first month or two of law school that you might use to persuade a friend who is considering whether to apply for admission. After the proposition sentence that characterizes your experience, continue by explaining the reasons for your characterization to prove the proposition.

For example, the opening sentence of this paragraph might read, "The first month or two of law school is hard," or "puzzling," or "exciting," or "fun," or "challenging," or any other characterization you choose. Then add "because," and complete the proposition sentence by listing and explaining the most important facts that led to your characterization. Then finish the paragraph by proving the proposition.

Exercise 21-B. Editing for Effective Sentence Structure

Each of the following sentences was written by a first-year law student. First, identify the structural problem or problems with each sentence. Then rewrite each sentence to resolve the problems and to make its meaning clear to the reader.

1. New York Civil Rights Law § 51 says that the commercial use of any person's name or likeness, used for an advertisement or to profit by selling, without having first obtained written consent, may sue for damages.

2. Although Ms. Roland is a person who was injured by the nonconsensual use of her picture for advertising and trade purposes by Online Images, Inc. and the incidental use of her photograph by the New York State Division was unlawful.

3. The question presented in this case is whether or not a minor who has entered into a cell phone contract in the State of Ohio can disaffirm said contract, taking into consideration whether the cell phone could, given the exception for necessities, be considered "necessary" and, assuming a disaffirmance was allowed, if there were time restrictions to which a minor would be subject.

4. Exemplary damages are allowed when it is found that a company or person used an image knowing that they do not have consent.

5. There is no cause of action for a plaintiff for invasion of privacy just because they are cast in a "false light."

6. Online Images, Inc. knew it did not possess written consent of Ms. Roland for the use of her photograph, thus satisfying the requirement for the jury to consider an award for exemplary damages.

7. The element of knowing use is usually a question for the jury once it has been found that compensatory damages are warranted.

8. The enactment of § 51 was immediately preceded by a lawsuit in which a young woman could not recover damages when a company nonconsensually used her photograph in a national advertising campaign because New York did not have a common law or statutory right of privacy.

22 Effective Style: Be Clear, Vivid, and Concise

It took me seven years to write this show. This is no overnight success.

—*Lin-Manuel Miranda, writer, composer,*
and lyricist of the musical Hamilton

In first drafts, style is usually pretty awful. Most writers achieve effective style only through rewriting and polishing, as they look for opportunities to make the earlier draft more clear, vivid, and concise.

§22.1   Clarity and Vividness

If the reader thinks something you wrote is unclear, then it is, by definition.

—*Deirdre N. McCloskey*

Unclear writing can make it hard or impossible for your reader to agree with you. Even if a reader—with effort—could figure out what you mean, readers in the legal profession usually cannot give you that effort. They don't have the time. A judge's impartiality means they won't be invested in reaching the conclusion you advocate. If your writing lacks clarity, a disappointed senior lawyer might return your memo and ask you to rewrite it. A judge who can't understand your argument could rule against your client.

Your writing should be so clear that your reader can understand it *effortlessly* and without needing to ask you any follow-up questions.

In the comic strip, Calvin foresees being rewarded for writing papers using dense prose. His toy tiger Hobbes is already suffering the same frustration a legal reader feels when confronting unclear legal writing. Successful lawyers understand that *clear writing* is what gets the job done.

Vividness goes a step further than clarity. Clear writing communicates a *message*. Adding vividness—by creating an image in the reader's mind using descriptive, concrete words—can make the message memorable and convincing. Vividness is not always necessary in legal writing. But add vividness to your writing when you see an opportunity so your message stays in the reader's mind.

Flowery, important-sounding words almost always make your writing less clear and vivid than simple and straightforward ones. For example, do not write *utilized* instead of the simple, straightforward word *used*. You might have read *Pierson v. Post*, with sentences like, "Both parties have regarded him, as the law of nations does a pirate, '*hostem humani generis*,' and although '*de mortuis nil nisi bonum*,' be a maxim of our profession, the memory of the deceased has not been spared."[1] It is unlikely you understood that sentence's meaning on the first—or even third—reading without consulting a Latin dictionary. Thank goodness we don't have to write like that because, unlike law students, legal readers will not have the time or inclination to read your sentences two or three times.

Judges want clear, concise writing in legal briefs. In one experiment, some appellate judges and their law clerks were asked to assess the persuasiveness of contorted writing in "legalese." Others were asked to evaluate the same material rewritten in "plain English." They considered the original legalese version "substantively weaker and less persuasive than the plain English versions."[2] And the judges and law clerks assumed that the lawyers who wrote the plain English versions worked in higher-prestige jobs.[3] Being able to translate legalese into plain English demonstrates the writer understands the law well enough to explain it clearly.

---

1. 3 Caines 175, 180 (N.Y. Sup. Ct. 1805).

2. Robert Benson & Joan B. Kessler, *Legalese v. Plain English: An Empirical Study of Persuasion and Credibility in Appellate Brief Writing*, 20 Loy. L.A. L. Rev. 301, 301 (1987).

3. *Id.* at 301-02.

§22.2 Conciseness

> The present letter is a very long one simply because I had no time to make it shorter.
>
> —*Pascal*

First drafts are usually too wordy. That tendency serves one purpose of the first draft, which is often to brainstorm and think through the issue while writing. In later drafts, you can tighten up the writing by finding ways to say the same thing in fewer words so your reader can understand your message more quickly and easily. Later drafts might expand with new *ideas* because the process of rewriting and responding to feedback helps you see what was missing from earlier drafts. Rewriting for conciseness helps make room for these new ideas.

Compare the following two versions of the same sentence. The facts—though not the words—come from *Sherwood v. Walker*,[4] a mutual-mistake-of-fact case discussed in many Contracts casebooks.

verbose	It is important to note that, at the time when the parties entered into the agreement of purchase and sale, neither of them had knowledge of the cow's pregnant condition.
concise	When the parties agreed to the sale, neither knew the cow was pregnant.

How did the verbose first draft become the tight rewrite? Look at the following revisions:

Verbose Original		**Concise Rewrite**
It is important to note that	⟶	[deleted]
at the time when	⟶	when
entered into the agreement of purchase and sale	⟶	agreed to the sale
neither of them	⟶	neither
had knowledge of	⟶	knew
the cow's pregnant condition	⟶	the cow was pregnant

Do not edit out meaning. In the example above, it would be a mistake to eliminate so many words that a reader would not understand that the cow was pregnant when sold and that neither the buyer nor the seller then knew about the pregnancy.

---

4. 33 N.W. 919 (Mich. 1887).

§22.3   How to Test Your Writing for Effective Style

While rewriting, ask the following questions.

1. Is everything crystal clear for the reader?   Sometimes a phrase or a sentence will seem clear in a first draft. But when you read it again while rewriting, you are not so sure. You have an advantage the reader lacks: You know what you meant to say. Put yourself in the position of your reader. Pretend that you are leaving for a vacation as soon as the reader begins reading and that you will not be available for follow-up questions. Will the meaning be clear to that person? Try to read your draft like the supervisor who will read your office memo or the judge who will read your motion memo or brief.

It will be easier to read your writing from the perspective of your reader if you allow some time to pass before going back to your draft. A day or two doing something else will help you return to the draft refreshed. Try to read quickly like a busy person and skeptically like someone who must make a decision. Try reading it out loud; you may hear something different in your words than you intended in writing them. Is everything clear? If not, fix the problem.

2. Have you used transitions to show relationships between ideas? Transitional words can help lead the reader through ideas by specifying their relationships with one another, and by identifying ideas that are most important or compelling. Section 21.3 explained the use of transitions to connect one paragraph to the next. They can be used in a similar way to help the reader see connections between sentences. The Transitions table shows how transitions can be used.

You can use transition words or phrases at the beginning of a paragraph (§21.3), at the beginning of a sentence, or inside a sentence. Choose the spot that best makes the point without confusing the reader.

3. Have you replaced unnecessarily complicated verbs with simple ones?   When you have a choice, use shorter phrases and simpler words to replace unnecessarily complex verb forms. Use concrete action verbs rather than abstractions (better to "agree" than to "reach an agreement"). See the Simplifying Verbs table.

A similar problem that can obscure meaning is turning common nouns and adjectives into abstract verbs. For example, the word *impact* is a noun, but it is sometimes used as an abstract verb rather than the more concrete action words *change* or *alter*. For clarity, use nouns to refer to *things* and verbs to describe concrete *action*. Nominalizing verbs and "verbing" nouns both create unnecessary barriers between you and your reader.

Transitions		
Purpose	**Examples**	
to introduce new, related ideas	additionally and besides furthermore	in addition (to) in fact moreover

to explain how ideas relate to one another	after
	afterward
	at the same time
	before
	finally
	on these facts
	specifically
	in fact
		not only . . ., but also
		under these
		   circumstances
		first, . . . second, . . .
		   third, . . . *(when
		   listing reasons)*

to point out similarities	analogously similarly	like
to introduce a connection	accordingly as a result because consequently	for that reason therefore thus
to point out differences, inconsistency, or lack of causation	although but conversely despite even if even though unlike however	in contrast in spite of instead of nevertheless on the contrary on the other hand
when introducing examples	for example for instance such as	
to explain time relationships	later previously	then next

Simplifying Verbs	
Delete	**Replace with**
entered into an agreement	agreed
gave consideration to	considered
had knowledge of	knew
was aware of	knew
is able to	can
is binding on	binds
made a determination	determined
made allegations of	alleged
made a motion for	moved for
made the argument	argued
made the assumption	assumed
took into consideration	considered

4. Have you streamlined unnecessarily wordy phrases? For example:

<table>
<tr><td colspan="2" align="center">Streamlining Phrases</td></tr>
<tr><td align="center">Delete</td><td align="center">Replace with</td></tr>
<tr><td>due to the fact that</td><td>because</td></tr>
<tr><td>for the purpose of</td><td>to</td></tr>
<tr><td>for the reason that</td><td>because</td></tr>
<tr><td>in the case of</td><td>in</td></tr>
<tr><td>in the event that</td><td>if</td></tr>
<tr><td>in the situation where</td><td>where (or when)</td></tr>
<tr><td>subsequent to</td><td>after</td></tr>
<tr><td>with regard to</td><td>regarding</td></tr>
<tr><td>with the exception of</td><td>except</td></tr>
</table>

5. Have you deleted throat-clearing phrases (also known as "long wind-ups")? Phrases like the ones below waste words, divert the reader from your real message, and introduce a shade of doubt and an impression of insecurity. They might be acceptable in first drafts to help you get your thoughts onto the page. But in rewriting, delete them.

> It is significant that . . .
> The defendant submits that . . .
> It is important to note that . . .
> It could be argued that . . .
> It is clear that . . .

6. Have you used lists connected with transitions to express coordinated ideas? When you discuss several ideas together, lead the reader forcefully by making that clear, perhaps through some sort of textual list introduced by a roadmap sentence. For example: "The court rejected that position for four reasons . . .," followed by sentences or paragraphs that begin with transitions to show how they connect to the roadmap ("First, . . . Second, . . ." and so on).

7. In a series or list, have you used parallel construction, making sure that every item in the list uses consistent grammatical structure? Readers are instantly confused by sentence structures that lack internal consistency.

For example, when introducing a series of offenses or claims, use a gerund to introduce each one. The sentence below is grammatically incorrect. Compare the underlined words.

> Martha Stewart was convicted of <u>obstructing</u> justice, <u>making</u> false statements to government investigators, and <u>because she conspired</u> with her broker to commit various crimes.

You can see the structural problems more easily when the sentence is tabulated vertically:

Martha Stewart was convicted of
- <u>obstructing</u> justice,
- <u>making</u> false statements to government investigators, and
- <u>because she conspired</u> with her broker to commit various crimes.

Parallel construction requires you to structure each item in a list using the same grammatical form as the others to establish a predictable pattern for the reader. Failing to do that distracts the reader because she expects sentences and paragraphs to follow internally consistent structure. Martha Stewart's list of offenses is not internally parallel. While the first and second items begin with gerund phrases ("*obstructing* justice" and "*making* false statements"), the third item is a dependent clause (beginning with "because") followed by a subject ("she") and a verb ("conspired").

If you frustrate the reader's expectations by using inconsistent grammar forms, she might have to reread the sentence to be sure she understands its message. In the example above, correct the problem by revising the third item in the list to begin with a gerund form like the others:

> Martha Stewart was convicted of <u>obstructing</u> justice, <u>making</u> false statements to government investigators, and <u>conspiring</u> with her broker to commit various crimes.

8. Have you used legal terms of art only when appropriate? When a term of art communicates an idea peculiar to the law, use that term. It conveys the idea precisely, and often it makes long and convoluted explanations unnecessary. For example, do not write "The court issued an order *telling the defendants to stop* building the highway." Instead, use precise wording: "The court issued an order *enjoining the defendants* from building the highway."

But use a legal term of art *only* when necessary to convey its exact legal meaning. If you use a term of art unnecessarily, perhaps because it sounds lawyer-like, your reader might assume you have misunderstood either the legal term or the law itself.

9. Have you edited out legalese? Notwithstanding grievous misconceptions of what is ubiquitously known to be fit and proper, said lawyer noises, by instrumentalities undisclosed herein, have been entirely expurgated, expunged, and otherwise eliminated from this textbook, both heretofore and hereinafter. (*Translation:* That stuff has been banished from this book.)

The most influential memos and briefs are written in real English.

Ouch	It would be accurate to say that Elvis has left the building.
Still Bad	Elvis has departed from the premises.
Just Fine	Elvis has left the building.

Some lawyerly wording conveys genuine meaning, and some does not.

meaningless	Elvis has clearly and unequivocally left the building.
meaningful	Uncontroverted evidence shows that Elvis has left the building.

Why is the phrase "clearly and unequivocally" meaningless? Elvis has either left the building or he has not. Writing something like "clearly and unequivocally" pounds the table without adding meaning. But "uncontroverted evidence" says that some evidence shows that Elvis has left, and no other evidence shows that he has not—which makes it easy for a court to decide that he has gone. We would expect to read in the next sentence about the two dozen witnesses who can testify that they saw Elvis walk through the stage door, step into a stretch limo, and disappear into the night.

It can take some time to learn how to distinguish between legalese and true terms of art (see question 9 above). When you come across a word or phrase used exclusively by lawyers, ask the following questions.

- Is it part of a rule of law you have read in a case or a statute—for example, an element of a legal test?
- Is it the name of a concept that is part of the law, including the policies or the reasoning behind a legal rule?

If either answer is "yes," you probably have a legal term of art, although legalese does appear in some statutes and older cases. If both answers are "no," you probably have legalese (although it might be a term of art). These questions will not produce completely accurate answers every time, but they increase the odds of correctly categorizing a word or phrase.

Do not use legalese. But do use genuine terms of art when necessary to convey your meaning precisely.

10. Have you properly placed modifiers next to the specific words they modify to clarify your meaning? When people talk in conversation, their modifiers sometimes wander all over sentences, regardless of what those words are intended to modify. But in formal writing, more precision is required to avoid confusing the reader. For example, each of these sentences means something different:

- The police are authorized to arrest *only* the person named in the warrant.
  [*They are not authorized to arrest anyone else.*]
- The police are authorized *only* to arrest the person named in the warrant.
  [*They are not authorized to deport her or do anything else except arrest.*]
- *Only* the police are authorized to arrest the person named in the warrant.
  [*No one else, including a civilian, is authorized to arrest her.*]

To help your reader understand your meaning, place a modifier—in this example, the word *only*—as close as possible to the word or term it modifies.

11. Have you used gender-neutral wording whenever appropriate? The English language has traditionally used the masculine pronouns *he*, *his*, and *him* to refer generally to all people. English lacks a gender-neutral singular pronoun that means any person. However, it has become acceptable to use "they" as a gender-neutral singular pronoun or when referring to a nonbinary person. In formal legal writing, do not use masculine pronouns when you intend to refer to all persons. For example, the following sentence would be wrong because it uses the masculine pronoun "his" to refer to lawyers in general:

To calendar a motion, an attorney must file his motion papers with the clerk.

replace the pronoun	To calendar a motion, an attorney must file <u>the</u> motion papers with the clerk.
make the actor plural	To calendar motions, <u>attorneys</u> must file their moving papers with the clerk.
eliminate the actor	A motion is calendared by filing the motion papers with the clerk.

Here are some solutions:

Choose the solution that fits your goal. Here, the last solution is the most concise one. But if you want to warn lawyers who carelessly forget to file their moving papers, that point is lost if the sentence uses passive voice and does not mention lawyers at all.

12. Have you punctuated correctly?   Correct punctuation is not decoration. It is essential because proper punctuation makes writing clear and easy to understand. Many readers will question your analytical ability if you fail to observe accepted rules of punctuation.

Before law school, you might have been able to get by without learning the rules of punctuation. But in legal writing, poor punctuation can miscommunicate meaning. In one case, a client lost a million dollars over a misplaced comma.[5] You would not want it to be *your* misplaced or missing comma.

§22.4   Our Style and Yours

If you notice clarity, vividness, or conciseness in our writing, it might be worth emulating whatever we did to achieve that—*if* doing so would work well in the assignment you are working on. (That's a big *if*.)

But in memos and briefs, the informal style of this book is *not* appropriate. A textbook's audience is students, who often learn more easily when the material is explained in a friendly tone. But the writing you submit to senior lawyers and judges should be formal in tone and style. For example, our own memos and briefs never contain contractions (two words merged with an apostrophe). They might be appropriate to use in an informal letter to a client, but they have no place in formal documents. For similar reasons, in our memos and briefs you would see far fewer dashes and italics than you see in this book. In a formal document, an occasional dash or italicized word or phrase might help make a point, but they should be used sparingly.

Here are some guidelines for office memos, motion memos, appellate briefs, and other formal documents:

- *contractions:* Don't.
- *italics:* Rarely, and we mean *rarely.*
- *dashes:* Rarely—unless you have a good reason to set something off so obviously.

Exercise 22-A. Style, Sentences, and Rewriting

In each passage, identify the problems with sentence structure, clarity, and conciseness. Then rewrite the passage.

1. Facebook is being used more frequently by people in their twenties and thirties, which means that teenagers are being marketed to less.

---

5. *See* Ian Austen, *The Comma That Costs 1 Million Dollars (Canadian)*, N.Y. Times, Oct. 25, 2006.

2. Because the defendant made statements to the effect that the plaintiff was not able to have knowledge of the actual date of Beyonce's birth, the plaintiff brought suit against the defendant with allegations of defamation. The defendant made a motion for summary judgment and made the argument that the court should give consideration to the plaintiff's admission, in an earlier lawsuit, that he lacked knowledge of Beyonce's date of birth. After making a determination that the plaintiff had previously made an admission that he lacked knowledge of Beyonce's date of birth, the court made entry of judgment for the defendant and made provision for the defendant to obtain recovery of costs.

3. On the ground that the client's video is a violation of YouTube's user agreement, which makes prohibited material that is "unlawful, obscene, defamatory, libelous, threatening, pornographic, harassing, hateful, racially or ethnically offensive, or encourages conduct that would be considered a criminal offense, give rise to civil liability, violate any law, or is otherwise inappropriate," YouTube's management effectuated a removal of the video from the website, and the client would like to know whether she has a cause of action against YouTube.

4. Jackson was employed as a bouncer at Savannah's nightclub. His job was to screen the people who were in line outside, admitting only those whose coolness was obvious. ("Coolness" and "cool" are business terms with specific meanings that are understood throughout the nightclub industry.) There were three reasons why Jackson was fired by Savannah. First, the people he admitted to the nightclub were not cool. Second, the people he left on the sidewalk were cool. Third, he was not liked by Savannah.

23 Citing and Quoting Authority

Lawyers are skeptical readers and demand *attribution* to show that legal authority supports an argument.

§23.1 When and Why to Cite Authority

Cite authority in two instances:

1. to identify an authority that effectively supports something you say, or
2. to identify the source of words you directly quote from the authority.

A reader needs specific information about each authority you cite to support your analysis. To meet those needs, essential information for each authority must be expressed precisely and succinctly in "citation language" that the reader can quickly skim and understand. A properly constructed citation conveys a large amount of information in a small space. It's like the box on the TV screen that shows information during a ball game. A quick glance can tell the viewer a lot.

Lawyers follow unique citation rules. Think of citation format as a professional code you must learn to communicate efficiently with other lawyers. If your citation form is faulty, readers quickly notice. A lawyer who uses faulty citation form fails to meet the expectations of the reader, who can lose confidence in the quality of the writer's work in other ways.

From a citation, a reader expects to learn what authority supports the legal assertion and where that authority can be found. When the authority is a statute, the citation tells the reader which jurisdiction enacted the statute. For a court opinion, the reader wants to know which court decided the case, the date of the decision, and other basic facts affecting the authority's value. These are communicated through a specialized citation code consisting of words, abbreviations, and numbers that convey a precise meaning to the reader when they are expressed in a particular order, properly capitalized, and properly punctuated.

How do you learn this specialized code? Your professor has probably assigned one of two citation reference books that cover the conventional rules of citation—the *ALWD Guide to Legal Citation* or the *Bluebook*. Both address the same citation issues and produce nearly identical citations.[1]

Don't imitate the citation forms you see in judicial opinions. Most are not consistent with the citation rules you will learn in this course. The reason is that many courts and publishers follow their own unique citation rules that are inconsistent with the rules in the *ALWD Guide* and the *Bluebook*. And many citation rules have changed over the years, so citations in older cases and law review articles may be in a format no longer considered acceptable.

§23.2   Rules Governing All Citations

Readers expect to see a citation for *every* statement in a memo or brief that recites, explains, or illustrates a rule. Your readers are skeptical, and they rely on citations to authority to gain confidence in your analysis and arguments.

When you first read a judicial opinion or a legal memo, you may be surprised how often you see citations. At first, the writing may seem choppy because citations interrupt the flow of the writing. But to lawyers and judges who read your writing, those citations are essential. They demonstrate, in the context of your analysis, how well your argument is supported with authority and how convincing those authorities will be to the decision maker. When writing each sentence in your Discussion or Argument, *assume that your reader will not believe what you say.* Then find a good legal authority to cite in support of your statement to convince the skeptical reader that you are right.

Full citations and short-form citations.   Any authority can be cited using a full citation or a short-form citation. Short-form citations may take different forms depending on the circumstances. For example:

full citation	*Apple Computer, Inc. v. Microsoft Corp.*, 513 U.S. 1184 (1995).
short-form citation	*Apple Computer, Inc.*, 513 U.S. at 1199.
short-form citation	*Id.* at 1199.

Statutes and other kinds of authorities also have full citation formats and short-form citation formats, which are explained in detail in your citation guide.

---

1. The verb "bluebooking" does *not* mean using the *Bluebook* instead of the *ALWD Guide to Legal Citation*. When a senior lawyer asks whether you have "bluebooked your citations," she just wants to make sure your cites are in proper form.

Use a full citation when you mention an authority for the first time in your memo or brief. At any later point in the same document, use one of the short-form citations when citing the same authority. Use *id.* only when the same authority appears alone (without any other authorities) in the immediately preceding citation.

Citation sentences and clauses.   A *citation sentence* includes one or more citations and nothing else, ending with a period. A *citation clause* is a citation that supports only part of a *textual sentence*, separated from the rest of the text with commas. A textual sentence is made up of words like the sentence you are reading now. An *embedded citation* is a citation used as a part of speech within the textual sentence itself.

citation sentence	*Apple Computer, Inc. v. Microsoft Corp.*, 513 U.S. 1184, 1199 (1995).
citation clause	The Supreme Court held in favor of the plaintiff, *Apple Computer, Inc. v. Microsoft Corp.*, 513 U.S. 1184 (1995), and the trial court entered judgment for Apple on remand.
embedded citation	In *Apple Computer, Inc. v. Microsoft Corp.*, 513 U.S. 1184, 1199 (1995), the Supreme Court held . . .

Citation placement.   When a cited authority supports an entire textual sentence, place the citation in a separate citation sentence immediately after the textual sentence:

A defamation defendant enjoys an absolute privilege for expressions of mere opinion. *Gertz v. Robert Welch, Inc.*, 418 U.S. 323, 339-40 (1974).

When an authority supports only part of a textual sentence, you can insert the citation directly into your sentence as a citation clause, setting off the citation clause from the rest of the sentence with commas. For example, the following textual sentence includes two citations:

A defamation defendant enjoys an absolute privilege for expressions of mere opinion, *Gertz v. Robert Welch, Inc.*, 418 U.S. 323, 339-40 (1974), and whether a statement expresses a fact or opinion is a question of law to be determined by the court and not the jury, *Info. Control Corp. v. Genesis One Computer Corp.*, 611 F.2d 781, 783 (9th Cir. 1980).

While the sentence above is technically correct, it is hard to read because of citation clutter. When reading it, you probably found it hard to climb over the full citation to *Gertz* so you could get to the rest of the sentence. For that reason, avoid writing sentences with citation clauses. Instead, when a citation supports only part of a textual sentence, try breaking up the sentence into two shorter ones, so you can use a citation sentence to support each one in turn:

> A defamation defendant enjoys an absolute privilege for expressions of mere opinion. *Gertz v. Robert Welch, Inc.*, 418 U.S. 323, 339-40 (1974). Whether a statement expresses fact or opinion is a question of law to be determined by the court and not the jury. *Info. Control Corp. v. Genesis One Computer Corp.*, 611 F.2d 781, 783 (9th Cir. 1980).

Readers usually have no problem when a single citation clause appears in a textual sentence. But readers can be distracted when a full citation appears inside a textual sentence, or when a writer includes too many citation clauses in a single textual sentence.

Pinpoint citations.   Pinpoint citations allow your reader to trust your writing, to look up the idea faster, and sometimes both. A pinpoint citation directs a reader to the specific page in a case, treatise, or law review article that supports the statement in the writer's memo or brief. In this example, the pinpoint directs the reader to page 1201 in a case that begins on page 1184:

> *Apple Computer, Inc. v. Microsoft Corp.*, 513 U.S. 1184, 1201 (1995).

Most citations to cases, law review articles, or treatises require pinpoint citations to convince your reader that you have specific support for the statements in your memo or brief. When paraphrasing a rule or set of facts, the pinpoint page number refers to the page or pages from which you gleaned the information to support your assertion of the rule or facts.

Other kinds of authority also require pinpoint citations to the smallest subsection or subdivision that supports your statement. For example, if a defendant has been accused of violating a federal statute, don't cite the statute just by its popular name, title, or section number. Almost every statute is subdivided into subsections (and sometimes subparagraphs), usually designated with letters or numbers in parentheses. Cite to the smallest subdivision relevant to the statement for which you are citing the authority to help your reader focus her attention on that part of the statute.

Pinpoint citations are also essential when quoting from authority. For *every* direct quotation you must include a pinpoint citation so your reader can check its accuracy against the original source.

String citations.   A string citation is a list of authorities, all cited for the same purpose. If you have found eight cases, all holding that a minor in your state can void a contract for lack of legal capacity, you might be tempted to use all eight cases in one string citation to impress your reader that you have found them all. But usually that would be a mistake because your reader relies on you to filter out all but the *best* cases to cite.

The ideal case would be issued by the highest court in the controlling jurisdiction, and it would settle the law definitively on whether a minor can void a contract. It would explain the rule's policy and how the rule applies to facts like yours. If one of the eight cases you have found does *all* that, cite that one case alone, explain it thoroughly for your reader, and ignore all the others. But much more often, you might have to use more than one case to convince the reader that the law is well settled and to show how the rule works. Rather than cite several cases without much explanation, cite the few cases that will really matter to your reader, and explain them thoroughly.

In rare situations, a string citation can be helpful. For example, assume your state has no common law rule on an issue, and your state's courts could adopt either the majority rule from other states or the minority rule. You might use one or two string citations in your brief to show which states have adopted the majority rule and which ones have adopted the minority rule. But also explain a few cases illustrating the majority rule and a few others illustrating the minority rule to show how each one works. A string citation hardly ever does an effective job by itself, and most lawyers and judges aren't impressed by lengthy string citations. They usually skip over them.

Explanatory parentheticals. Two types of parenthetical notes appear in legal citations. One is an integral part of the citation itself, such as the parenthetical reference in a case citation to the court and year. The other type is an *explanatory parenthetical* that provides information about the authority. That same information could be given outside the citation. But to save space, lawyers sometimes compress that information into a parenthetical phrase immediately following the citation itself.

Some kinds of explanatory parentheticals denote something important about the authority itself. For example, you *must* add a parenthetical to show when you are citing to a dissenting or concurring opinion rather than the majority opinion.

Most lawyers use explanatory parentheticals when a full discussion of a case is not necessary. This kind of explanatory parenthetical generally begins with a gerund form of a verb, such as "holding" or "reversing." For example,

> *Riley v. California*, 134 S. Ct. 2473, 2485 (2014) (holding that police officer must generally secure warrant before searching contents of cell phone incident to warrantless arrest).

If the authority is complicated and important to the issue in your memo or brief, explain it in your text and then cite the authority. Use explanatory parentheticals only for simple information that is not an important part of your discussion or argument.

Section and paragraph symbols. In a citation, generally use a section symbol (§) and not the word *section*. Some citations to cases and treatises require a paragraph symbol (¶), which should be used instead of the word *paragraph*. Add a space between either symbol and the number that follows it. But when you begin a textual sentence with a reference to a section or paragraph, use the words and not the symbols ("Section 2-201 provides . . .").

Signals. Sometimes your purpose in citing an authority can be communicated most efficiently by using a *citation signal*. In legal writing, a signal is an italicized code word or abbreviation that introduces the citation and conveys a particular meaning about how the authority supports the statement that precedes the citation. Examples are *See*, *Accord*, and *Contra*. No signal is used when the authority you cite directly supports the statement that immediately precedes it, or when the authority identifies the source of a direct quotation or a legal rule. Your citation guide explains each signal and how to use it in more detail.

Signals can help compress information and clarify relationships among authorities cited in law review footnotes and in other kinds of scholarly writing, including the seminar papers you might write in the second or third year of law school. But in memos and briefs, use signals sparingly when truly necessary or helpful to reduce space. A person who must make a decision based in part on your writing needs to know not only what an authority stands for, but also exactly how the authority is relevant to the issue to be decided. Generally your own discussion of the authorities does that much better than signals can.

Typeface. Citations in memos and briefs use two typefaces, roman and italics. In a citation clause or sentence, both case names and signals appear in italics. So do Latin terms like *id., supra, infra,* and other terms specified by your citation guide.

Other typefaces, such as large-and-small caps, are used only in scholarly legal writing to designate certain kinds of authority. You may see them in the footnotes of law review articles as you research the issues for your legal writing assignments. But other typefaces aren't used in memos or briefs written by practicing lawyers or in judicial opinions.

If you use the *Bluebook*, be careful when using the examples in the Bluepages. Before computers were in common use, writers used underlining for emphasis because typewriters could not produce italics. The examples in the Bluepages at the front of the *Bluebook* allow the use of underlining, even though computers are now used for virtually all legal writing. You can easily use your computer for italics, which look more professional than underlining in legal writing.

§23.3   Notes on Quotes

Quoting can be useful occasionally. But if you aren't careful, quotations can consume your writing. This section explains when (and when not) to use a direct quotation and how to satisfy the format requirements for quoting.

§23.3.1   When to Quote

Quotations help when they express *exactly* the idea you want to communicate to your reader. And the citation after a direct quote tells your reader that the idea has authority behind it. Especially when your issue would be resolved by interpreting certain words, quote those words. With statutory issues, for example, quote the most essential words in the statute.

There is less reason to quote from a case. The language of a case resolves the issues in that case, so it might not directly apply to facts in a different case. In some instances, using phrases or words from a case may be the best way to communicate the case's meaning. But your reader doesn't always need to know factual details from the precedent case if they are irrelevant to the current problem.

§23.3.2   Quote Sparingly or Not at All

Quotations can eat up large chunks of your writing and your reader's attention. When that happens, many readers will simply skip over them. Your reader needs and expects your own analysis of the authorities and how they apply to the unique facts of your case. Just quoting from authorities is not legal analysis.

When you do quote, keep it limited to small, *essential* passages. Edit out words that don't apply or details that aren't meaningful in the context of your case. For example, although a statute or a case might set out the test that governs your facts, some of the elements might not be in dispute in your case. You can summarize or note the elements not in dispute, and then emphasize the contested ones by directly quoting those parts of the test. To illustrate, if a criminal defendant's only argument is that she lacked purposeful intent, the other elements of the crime are much less important. The only part of the statute or case worth quoting might be the part that requires purposeful intent for conviction.

Accuracy in quoting is essential. When you directly quote, check to be sure you have not inadvertently misquoted the authority. And be careful when you edit a quote. Make sure that your edited version accurately reflects the meaning of the original. Sloppy editing might cost you credibility with your reader.

Block quotations are especially troublesome. A block quote is a long quotation (50 words or more) separated from the rest of your text, indented on both the left and right sides, and single-spaced. Busy readers will often skim or refuse to read large block quotations because they know from experience that only a few of the quoted words will really matter, and it may take too much effort to find them. The more block quotes you use, the more quickly a reader will refuse to read any of them. Judges and supervising attorneys expect you to find the essential words, isolate them, and concisely paraphrase the rest. When you throw many block quotations at a reader, you are asking the reader to do some of your work.

On rare occasions, quoting an extended passage from a source of law helps the reader. But that is seldom true. Experienced and effective writers quote less often, and their quotes tend to be shorter.

§23.3.3   The Mechanics of Quoting

Readers look not only at the content of what you quote, but also at how you follow the format rules for quotations. Citation manuals set out rules governing the format of quotations. Here are the most essential requirements.

Quotation marks.   Enclose any words directly quoted from your source in double quotation marks. If the quoted material includes an internal quotation from another source, you must retain those quotation marks, but change them to *single* quotation marks within the double quotation marks surrounding the entire direct quotation. Your citation identifying the source of the quotation must include a parenthetical citing the source of the internal quotation.

Block quotations.   Citation manuals require placing quotations of 50 words or more in block-quote form. A block quote is single-spaced and indented one tab on both the right and left margins. It does not begin or end with quotation marks. Blocking a passage tells the reader that it is a quote. If the block quote has internal quotations, retain the double quotation marks inside the block quote. Its citation should include a parenthetical identifying the source of the internal quotation.

The citation identifying the source of the quotation doesn't appear inside the quotation block. Instead, it belongs at the beginning of the *next line of your text following the block quote*, which will generally be double-spaced. Here's how it works.

An example of an employer's control over creative work comes from the world of Marvel comics:

> In the 1950s and 1960s, [Stan] Lee supervised the creation of Marvel's comic books from conception to publication. . . . Lee assigned writers and artists to work on comic books and reviewed all work before it was published. . . . Lee also had authority to ask artists to revise or edit their work before publication and frequently exercised that authority.

> *Marvel Worldwide, Inc. v. Kirby*, 777 F. Supp. 2d 720, 740 (S.D.N.Y. 2011). Similarly, control over musical work has been held . . .

§23.3.4 How to Test Your Quotations for Effectiveness

While rewriting, ask the following questions.

1. Have you quoted and cited every time you use the words of others? The words of others must have quotation marks around them and a citation to the source. If not, you have plagiarized from your source, even if you did it out of sloppiness without intending to deceive your reader.

2. Have you quoted sparingly and only the essential words? Most readers dislike overquoting. Avoid using lengthy block quotations, which many readers skip over entirely. Generally speaking, quoted words should appear in your work *only* when they fit into one of the following categories:

- words that must be interpreted to resolve the legal issue;
- words that communicate the thinking of a court, legislature, or expert in the field with remarkable economy or clarity; or
- words that eloquently and succinctly express an important idea.

The most convincing descriptions of authority are written almost entirely in your own words, with very few and very short quotations.

3. Have you followed the mechanical rules for direct and internal quotations? Check your citation manual. There are rules for almost everything!

4. Have you placed quotation marks exactly where they belong? Make sure each quotation has marks to show where it begins and ends. And know where to change double marks to single marks for quotes inside another quote.

5. Have you quoted accurately? Cutting and pasting is a great way to ensure accuracy, but be sure the source makes it into your draft as well. Even an accidental failure to cite is plagiarism.

Exercise 23-A. Quoting the First Amendment

You are writing a memorandum involving the freedom of the press clause of the U.S. Constitution's first amendment. You intend to quote the words that the court must interpret. The entire first amendment reads as follows:

> Congress shall make no law respecting an establishment of religion, or prohibiting the free exercise thereof; or abridging the freedom of speech, or of the press; or the right of the people peaceably to assemble, and to petition the government for a redress of grievances.

Write a properly punctuated sentence for your memo that accurately quotes the relevant words from the amendment, without including more than your reader needs. Include a properly formatted pinpoint citation.

Part 6

Informal Analytical Writing

24 Advising and Counseling the Client

All clients expect counseling and advice. For the most part, lawyers do that in conversation, either in a meeting or over the telephone. But a significant portion is done in writing, typically in a client letter or an email.

This chapter explains advice and counseling as concepts. Chapter 25 explains how to communicate your analysis to a client in a letter. And Chapter 26 explains how to use email when communicating your analysis to clients and to other lawyers in your office.

§24.1 Advice and Counseling

Advice is explaining to a client how the law treats the client's situation. *Counseling* is guiding a client through the process of making a decision. Lawyers often use the words *advice* and *counseling* interchangeably, as synonyms. That's fine in the everyday practice of law. But to help you learn how to advise and counsel in writing, we'll distinguish between the two concepts.

A client tells you many facts, shows you a contract she has signed, and asks, "Do I have to sell my fishing boat to Spano? What happens if I don't sell it to him?" You read the contract carefully and check the law. Then you advise the client that yes, she is legally obligated to sell her boat to Spano, and if she doesn't sell it, she will have to pay damages. You explain how a court would calculate the damages.

"O.K. I'll sell it to him," she says. "I just wanted to know whether I can get out of this deal." "You can't get out of it," you say. You have provided only advice. The client wanted to know how the law treats her situation, and you explained it. Many lawyers do this at least a dozen times in a week.

After hearing your advice, a client will typically decide to do or not to do something. For example, your client decided to sell the boat. But this client's decision was not complicated. Once the client understood that she had no grounds to escape the contract, she felt she has only one (good) option.

Counseling includes advice, but it is much more. Advising necessarily shifts into counseling when the client struggles to make a complicated decision. The lawyer counsels by developing different options, evaluating them, explaining the strengths and weaknesses of each, and helping the client choose the one that will most effectively accomplish the client's goals.

Counseling first requires preparation. Throughout the client counseling process, a lawyer will help identify the client's goals, develop options that might accomplish those goals, and work with the client to evaluate each option for its advantages and disadvantages. As part of her preparation, a lawyer conducts the legal research and factual investigation necessary to assist the client. Factual investigation may include speaking with witnesses, discussions with opposing counsel, reviewing documents, and interviewing experts.

The lawyer communicates with the client. In counseling a client, the lawyer starts by working with the client to identify the goals the client would like to achieve through the representation (see §24.3). Some of these goals will be legal; others will be economic, social, or emotional. For instance, a client might wish to avoid paying a large fine, but also want to avoid time away from family or the stress of litigation. The lawyer will explain the different options to achieve those goals and then assist the client through the process of evaluating each option. During this conversation, the lawyer answers the client's questions until the client understands enough to choose among them. Often this becomes brainstorming as the client might mention insights that had not occurred to the lawyer, and the lawyer and client might then talk about ways to improve the options. While the lawyer cannot determine the value of avoiding time away from family for the client, her role is to explain the client the legal consequences of each option and help the client choose the one that will most effectively accomplish the client's goals.

Effective advice and counseling combine empathy and detachment. Empathy helps you understand the client's goals and needs. Detachment helps you see the problem as it really is.

§24.2   The Role of Writing in Advice and Counseling

Advice.   Much advice is communicated orally, in the lawyer's office or over the telephone. Sometimes it's a good idea to follow up in writing, either in a client letter (Chapter 25) or by email (Chapter 26). A letter or an email is helpful when your analysis is so complicated that a client might not understand it from conversation alone or when the client needs to share the advice with others. The client can read, contemplate, and read again as needed.

Counseling. Communicating with the client in writing can be useful during counseling. For example, a lawyer might explain the options briefly over the telephone and schedule a meeting at which the lawyer and client can discuss them. Between the phone call and the meeting, the lawyer might send a letter or an email explaining each option's details so the client can think about them before the meeting.

§24.3 Who Decides What

Legally, the client defines the goals of the representation. The lawyer decides what the ABA Model Rules of Professional Conduct call "technical, legal, and tactical issues,"[1] such as where to sue, what theory of the case to rely on, what evidence to submit and witnesses to call, and what arguments to make. The case law allows a lawyer to make those litigation decisions alone, without consulting the client and even over the client's objections. But if you do such a thing, the case law won't stop the client from firing you and telling every other potential client never to hire you.

In other respects, however, the Model Rules require that a lawyer "abide by a client's decisions concerning the objectives of representation [and] consult with the client as to the means by which they are to be pursued."[2] And the Model Rules suggest that the lawyer should defer to the client when technical and tactical decisions raise "such questions as the expense to be incurred and concern for third persons who might be adversely affected."[3]

§24.4 Predicting

Karl Llewellyn had the leading role in creating Articles 1 and 2 of the Uniform Commercial Code. He wrote that law as practicing lawyers know it is "[w]hat officials," including judges, "do about disputes"[4]—and not what statutes and cases say they should do. He also wrote that "'rights' which cannot be realized are worse than useless; they are traps of delay, expense, and heartache."[5] Your client might appear to have rights under a literal reading of a statute, but if judges will find ways to rule otherwise, you will not help your client by counseling with false optimism. Your client needs a realistic prediction of what the court will actually do.

Both advice and counseling require you to predict what will happen to the client. How can you possibly assure a client that you know with 100% certainty what

---

1. MODEL RULES OF PROF'L CONDUCT R. 1.2(a) cmt. 2 (2013).
2. *Id.* R. 1.2(a).
3. *Id.* R. 1.2 cmt. 2.
4. KARL N. LLEWELLYN, THE BRAMBLE BUSH 3 (1930).
5. *Id.* at 9.

the future will bring? You cannot be that certain, but the client needs your prediction anyway. A little insecurity can be helpful if it motivates you to be thorough in your research and candid in your advice. What you cannot do is let that insecurity interfere with your ability to advise your client.

It might help to remember that every day billions of dollars are invested, lent, or otherwise committed based on predictions about whether customers will like a product or hate it, or whether stock prices or interest rates will rise or fall. Many of those predictions turn out to be wrong. The earth won't swallow you up if a prediction you make turns out to be inaccurate. But lawyers whose predictions are right most of the time gain the loyalty and respect of their clients.

Out of fear of being wrong, you might want to hedge. One form of hedging—waffling—makes your advice less useful to a client, who must make a decision and needs the most accurate prediction you can make. From the client's point of view, if you waffle, you aren't really predicting.

A different form of hedging—adding qualifications or conditions—makes your prediction *more* realistic because qualifications and conditions identify variables that might change your prediction. For more on this, see Chapter 16.

Often you will have to predict without complete knowledge of the facts or the law. Some facts might not become available to you until later (or never). And some parts of the law are unsettled, such as when courts haven't yet filled a gap (see §8.4). When you predict, you should identify for the client not only what you know, but also what you do *not* know. And when you identify something you don't know, tell the client exactly how it would influence your prediction.

Your predictions should be frank and objective. If you have bad news, the client needs to know it. Hiding bad news does neither the client nor you a favor, and it risks the kind of misunderstanding that can turn into an ethics complaint or a malpractice action.

Step back from what you are doing and test the result of your reasoning for realism. Talk to the other lawyers in your office to gauge their reaction to your reasoning. If your result would strike the judicial mind as unrealistic and unreasonable, a court will reject your reasoning no matter how sound it seems to you.

25 Client Letters

§25.1 Why and How Lawyers Write Client Advice Letters

In advising and counseling clients, lawyers use letters and email when they need to communicate in writing. This chapter explains client letters. Chapter 26 explains email.

Make the tone of your client letter professional, precise, and respectful. Client letters are midway between a conversation with the client and an office memo. They record the essence of what you would say to the client in a face-to-face meeting. And often they summarize an office memo. A sample client letter appears in Appendix B.

In choosing a tone, ask yourself these questions:

- What does this client want from a professional?
- What does the situation call for?
- What am I comfortable with in terms of my own style?
- And how do I want to present myself to clients?

The first of these questions—what this client would want from a professional—might be the most complex. Consider the client's level of sophistication (education, occupation, experience with lawyers). And consider the client's feelings. Is the client experiencing anxiety, grief, or anger? Even in positive situations, such as buying property, happiness can be mixed with anxiety. Or is this transaction pure business from the client's point of view? It may be all business if the client is an organization or an entrepreneur, or if the client considers the transaction or dispute to be routine.

§25.2 Client Letter Format

A typical structure for a client letter is set out below. If the letter is complex, you might use headings to make the text less daunting to read. But adapt the wording in the headings to the client and the situation. Contractions ("don't," "won't") are fine in a client letter, but not in a memo or brief.

1. The beginning formalities.   These include the letterhead, which is already printed on your law office stationery; the date; the client's name and address; and the salutation ("Dear Ms. Lopez:"—always with a colon, never a comma).

2. One or two opening paragraphs, stating the problem about which the client has sought your help and a brief summary of your conclusion.   These paragraphs correspond to the issue and brief answer in an office memo. If you have bad news, this is where the client learns that it is bad. Think long and hard about the words you use to convey that bad news. Reading words on a page can be a cold experience for the client. That doesn't mean you must cloud the bad news with flowery words or praise. Indeed, doing so risks confusing the client about your conclusion. Keep in mind that you can exercise legal judgment without using judgmental language that might cause the client to disengage with the rest of the letter.

3. One or more paragraphs reviewing the key facts on which your conclusions are based.   You might think it wastes words to summarize the client's own facts, but several good reasons support doing so.

First, if you have misunderstood any of the facts and the client knows better, the client can correct you. Many lawyers add a sentence asking the client to do that ("If I have described any of the facts inaccurately, please call me.").

Second, reviewing the facts limits your conclusions to the facts recited, which can be important if the facts change. A tenant who doesn't have a claim right now against the landlord for a filthy lobby might have one next week if the lobby ceiling caves in. Thus, often the factual discussion of a client letter will state that the facts are dependent upon what the lawyer understands at the time the letter was drafted.

Third, you might have learned recently of some facts the client doesn't yet know about. If so, describe the newly found facts in ways that tell the client they are new ("Since we last spoke, I have discovered that the 1986 deed was never properly recorded in the county clerk's office.").

And finally, a fact recitation transitions into a discussion of the law itself.

4. The advice, which can be structured in either of two ways.   If the client wants to know how the law treats a certain situation—"Would I win a lawsuit against the airline?" or "Would my company violate the law if it were to import this product?"—you predict how a court would rule, or you explain the client's or other people's rights and obligations.

But if the client must make a decision, you counsel in the letter by suggesting the options from which the client can choose and, for each option, explaining the factors that might make it attractive or unattractive. List the options and explain their *advantages, costs, risks, and chances of success.* When you estimate risks and chances of success, you are predicting. Costs are not limited to money. The cost of suing includes not only legal fees and other litigation expenses, but also the time and energy the client would have to invest in the lawsuit and the stress many litigants suffer while the suit is in progress. (See Chapter 24.)

Be especially careful about the words you use to communicate your degree of confidence in your prediction. When you write that "we have a reasonably good chance of winning at trial," you might mean that you believe the client will probably win, although the risk of loss is significant. But many clients would read those words to mean that victory is nearly assured. It is only human for a client who has suffered a wrong to assume that forces of justice will correct it. Vagueness on your part can imply unjustified optimism. Find ordinary, everyday words that the client will understand exactly as you mean them: "Based on the facts and law as currently understood, I believe we have a chance of winning at trial. However, the risk of loss is significant, and no one can predict what a jury will do."

If the news truly is bad, don't cushion it so much that the client won't appreciate it. Don't say, "our chances in litigation are problematic," if you really mean, "we would likely lose if the other side sues."

A good client letter can be understood by a layperson in one reading.[1] It takes much work on your part to accomplish that. Use as little lawyer talk as possible. If a legal term of art has a good equivalent in ordinary English, use the equivalent even if it doesn't convey 100% of the meaning of the term of art. Eighty percent is good enough, unless the missing 20% is relevant to the client's situation. If you do use a term of art, define it using plain English. (See §22.3.)

When you translate lawyer talk into ordinary English, do so respectfully. This is not just good communication. It is also good business. Clients often feel uncomfortable with a stereotyped lawyer who speaks in legalese, or a lawyer who talks down to them. On the other hand, they can like and trust a genuine human being who does a good job of communicating the law.

Write simply, but don't oversimplify. If the law is unclear, point that out and explain why it is unclear ("courts disagree with each other on what the statute means"). Discuss authority only when it is central to the issue, such as a recent case that changes everything you have told the client in the past.

Unlike a supervising lawyer or a judge, your client assumes that you know the law, which means that you need not recite rules of law or cite and explain authority as

---

1. An exception to this is when you are writing advice to a client who is also a lawyer.

thoroughly as you would in a memo or a brief. But you do have to know what you are talking about. Nobody is perfect at predicting. But if you are wrong because you don't understand the law, you will lose clients and learn a lot about the details of malpractice law.

Organize the material in any way that will help the client understand it. Sometimes clients are confused by the CREAC formula described in Chapters 17 through 20. Remember that you are writing for a layperson who probably won't understand a detailed and thorough explanation.

Avoid a cold or confusing recitation of the law ("In this state, tax must be paid by the property owner on each lien against real property recorded in the county clerk's office."). Instead, describe the law's effect on the client, which carries a warmer, more personal tone and often eliminates the need to recite the law ("If you refinance the mortgage on your home, you will have to pay $1,250 in mortgage tax."). Further, clients are more interested in their own legal entanglement than they are in the law itself. Thus, your letter should be more about the law's effect on the client than on expounding on legal principles.

5. One or two closure paragraphs.   Sum up in two or three sentences. Specify what can or should be done next, who should do it, and when it should be done. For instance, you might ask again that the client clarify any facts that you have misunderstood or provide you with any documents related to the case. If the client needs to make a decision, set the stage. Invite the client to telephone you or, if extended conversation is needed, suggest that the client make an appointment to see you. On the other hand, if the advice is negative ("although your competitors behaved badly, they did nothing illegal"), closure might be limited to an offer to answer questions if the client would like to call.

6. Closing formalities.   Sign the letter above your typed name and under a closing like "Sincerely yours," or whatever words are customary in your office. Most readers never notice the closing or care about it, unless you say something completely inappropriate.

7. Other kinds of client letters.   While this chapter has covered advice letters, there are many other kinds of letters a lawyer writes to a client. A cover letter could explain a draft of a document like a will, that a client will need to review. A letter can also confirm your understanding of a client's choice, particularly if you believe the client has made a poor choice and you want to encourage him to rethink it. All the considerations on tone and language choice that apply to advice letters apply to these letters as well.

26 Electronic Communication

While most of this book describes how lawyers write, we also need to address how lawyers transmit their writing to others. The mode of communication influences how lawyers write and how their readers read.

§26.1 Professionalism, Confidentiality

Professionalism. If a colleague texts you, do you respond with emojis?

Standards of professionalism should act always as your yardstick. When communicating with supervisors, colleagues, and clients, write courteously and formally. Write "Dear Ms. Adegbalola" rather than "Hey there!" And take time to edit. The speed of electronic communication is a great tool, but nothing requires us to use that speed without regard to quality.

Even though an email can be less formal than other documents lawyers write, it's still a communication between professionals and should use a professional tone and precise language.

Confidentiality. Different modes of communication require different protections. When you meet with a client in your office, you shut the door. When you use electronic means to communicate, you must take similar steps to ensure your client's confidentiality. Your email must be delivered safely to only the person you intend. The American Bar Association provides guidance on how to protect client information in electronic communication.[1] The opinion recommends assessing how sensitive the client's information is, the risk involved, and the cost of additional safeguards, among other factors.

---

1. ABA Standing Comm. on Ethics & Prof'l Responsibility, Formal Op. 477R* (2017).

The best choices for communication are usually restrained and always protect client information. The ease of electronic communication produces many benefits, but ethical standards on how we work with and for clients never take a holiday.

§26.2   Email Memos Between Lawyers

An email memo might be appropriate when a supervisor needs analysis faster and more concisely than an office memo could provide. The supervisor needs an answer fast. The email memo must be written quickly, and the supervisor needs to be able to read and understand it within moments of opening it.

As with every other kind of document, more time spent by the writer result in less time spent by the reader. Compare the writing and reading times for two email memos:

	Email memo A	Email memo B
writing time	45 minutes	55 minutes
reading time	15 minutes	5 minutes

Assuming that both memos contain the same quality of analysis and that the only difference is how long it takes a reader to understand that analysis, supervisors prefer memo B. While your time is valuable, and the question your are answering is important, your supervisor may be juggling three separate email memos on topics that all need to be answered quickly. Even though the total time spent on this issue may be the same, the option that allows the supervisor to spend less time reading and understanding your memo makes it a more valuable product.

Writing the memo inside your email system can actually be slower than writing it elsewhere and then copy-and-pasting it into an email message. Your word processor was designed to help you write and rewrite. It might be more efficient to draft the memo in your word processor and, when finished, copy and paste into the email.

Office memo format developed over decades, and lawyers generally agree on how an office memo should be structured. Email memos, on the other hand, have developed more recently, and there's no consensus about their format.[2] An email memo might be structured somewhat like an office memo, or it might follow an entirely different format.

Email memo format should be flexible. What works in one situation might not work in another. On Monday, a lawyer might send an email memo concerning a

---

2. Brad Desnoyer, *E-Memos 2.0: An Empirical Study of How Attorneys Write*, 25 The Journal of The Legal Writing Institute 213 (2021).

proposed jury instruction in case X. On Friday, the same lawyer might send an email memo to the same supervisor explaining the law concerning a discovery demand in case Y. These email memos might be structured in entirely different ways because the problems they address are different. The following is one way in which an email memo might be structured.

The email's subject line. Specify clearly and concisely what this memo is about ("Smith v. Jones, interrog. 6 in plaintiff's 2d set"). In the inbox on your supervisor's screen, it will appear with many other messages, and the subject line should identify the problem your memo addresses.

The memo's first sentence—or its statement of the issue. Say why you're sending the email memo. It will be read today, but it might be read again in a year's time. Both today's reader and next year's reader should be told exactly why you've written this memo. Here's an example:

> You've asked whether we're required to answer interrogatory 6 in the plaintiff's second set of interrogatories.

Worded this way, no heading is needed. But if you word it as an issue, use a heading:

> **Issue:**
> Are we required to answer interrogatory 6 in the plaintiff's second set of interrogatories?

The answer. State your answer, with the essence of why. One or two sentences will probably accomplish this. Use a heading like "Answer" or "Brief Answer."

> **Answer:**
> No. That interrogatory seeks material protected by the attorney-client privilege.

An alternative way of beginning the memo. Instead of writing the two components above—the Issue and the Answer—you might combine them under a heading like "Summary":

> **Summary:**
> We are not required to answer interrogatory 6 in the plaintiff's second set of interrogatories. That interrogatory seeks material protected by the attorney-client privilege.

The facts.   Recite only the few facts that are crucial to your analysis. Your supervisor is working on the case right now and knows the facts generally. Don't recite the entire case story. You've been asked for a fast answer to a specific and narrow question. The only facts that matter are the ones that are essential to answering that question.

Your analysis.   Explain why your answer is correct. This might take one paragraph or six paragraphs or something in between. You will need to determine what level of explanation will satisfy your supervisor's two needs: for speed and for confidence that you're right. Finding the right balance becomes easier with experience. If you're not sure how to do that now, err on the side of including more explanation. The heading for this part could be "Analysis," "Explanation," or "Discussion."

Typography.   In email, headings don't center well. You can place headings along the left margin or indent them five or ten spaces from the left margin. Indenting makes them a little more obvious. Headings should be in bold print.

In a printed document, the first line of a paragraph is indented. But that isn't true in emails, where a paragraph's first line starts at the left margin.

§26.3   The Dangerous "Send" Button

The dangerous "Send" button.   Email is so easy to send that it's a marvel of convenience, but it's also dangerous. If you accidentally put the wrong address into the "To" box, you might send confidential client information to someone who shouldn't have it. And even if you don't make that mistake, whatever you send can be forwarded to people whom you hadn't imagined would read it. When responding to a message, use "Forward" and type in the recipient's email address. Developing this habit may save you from inadvertently hitting "Reply All" on a message that should not be read by all.

Check everything before you hit "Send." Don't let the demand for speed trick you into a painful mistake. Take a long moment and be sure that every detail is exactly as it should be.

Part 7

The Shift to Persuasion

27 What Persuades a Court?

What could you write to persuade a judge to give you what you're asking for?

§27.1 A Compelling Theory and Theme Persuade

A *theory* is a way of looking at the controversy that makes your client the winner. A *theme* is a sentence or two—or even just a phrase—that summarizes the theory. You're already familiar with theories and themes in a commercial sense. Think of the businesses or products to which you're loyal. Each of them is marketed with a theory and theme—sometimes implied rather than stated openly—that persuade you to spend money. Here are a few examples:

- Amazon—stop driving to stores: just click, and it's delivered to you
- Nike—performance athletic wear—Just Do It.
- Mt. Dew—go wild, surf, skateboard!—Do the Dew

In law, a persuasive theory is a view of the facts and law—intertwined—that justifies a decision in your favor and that *motivates* a court to render that decision. A persuasive theory:

1. relies on the supportive facts;
2. explains why the adverse facts should not prevent a decision in your favor;
3. has a solid basis in law and overcomes your adversary's interpretation of the law;
4. appeals to a judge's sense of fairness and good policy; and
5. can be summarized in one or two sentences, or captured in a vivid image, a theme that a judge can easily remember.

Unfocused writing can make a judge feel as though she is drowning in detail without a clear idea how all the detail adds up to a coherent view of the case. Judges complain about lawyers who write that way. To be persuaded, a judge needs a clearly stated theory, and writing that is sharply focused on proving that theory.

§27.2 A Compelling Story Persuades

The client's story makes the theory *come alive*. Although we live in a scientific world where logic is expected to explain everything, we think in stories. Stories grab our attention and engage our imagination.

You probably know this from your own experience. Suppose you're in an audience. Someone is speaking from a podium in the front of the room. For half an hour, that person talks about the logical connection between the Heisenberg uncertainty principle and the invention of chocolate. Your eyelids grow heavy. Then the speaker stops talking about logic. To illustrate some point, he tells about a family of ducks who start crossing a busy highway at rush hour—the mother at the head of a line of ducklings, the father who-knows-where. Brakes are screeching. Officer O'Leary is rushing up, waving his arms in the air.

Suddenly you're sitting upright on the edge of your seat. Why are you listening differently now? It can't be that chocolate has bored you. Instead, the story's tension has gripped you. Never mind about Heisenberg and his uncertainty. Will the cars hit the ducklings? Will all that slamming of brakes cause a huge chain collision, followed by drivers standing on the pavement and swearing at each other? Will Officer O'Leary be able to prevent all this?[1]

All good stories have tension. The stories lawyers tell courts have tension because they involve conflict. When we start to hear or read a story like that—and if the story is told well—we naturally start asking questions like these: Who's the good person? Who's the bad person? What bad thing did the bad person do? How did it affect the good person? (We are worried.) What happens next? How will the story end?

Every lawsuit has a story. You've been reading them in your casebooks. Actually, every lawsuit has at least two stories, one for each side. The one you read in the court's opinion is the winning story. Sometimes you read the losing story in a dissenting opinion.

How do we know judges are persuaded by stories? The judges say so in the opinions they write. They tell us, by the way they explain the case's facts, *how* they have been influenced by a story. For example, here are the first three paragraphs of *BMW v. Gore*,[2] a U.S. Supreme Court case:

---

1. Yes he will; the ducklings are fine, see Robert McCloskey, *Make Way for Ducklings* (1941).
2. 517 U.S. 559 (1995).

The Due Process Clause of the Fourteenth Amendment prohibits a State from imposing a "grossly excessive" punishment on a tortfeasor. The wrongdoing involved in this case was the decision by a national distributor of automobiles not to advise its dealers, and hence their customers, of predelivery damage to new cars when the cost of repair amounted to less than 3 percent of the car's suggested retail price. The question presented is whether a $2 million punitive damages award to the purchaser of one of these cars exceeds the constitutional limit.

In January 1990, Dr. Ira Gore, Jr. (respondent), purchased a black BMW sports sedan for $40,750.88 from an authorized BMW dealer in Birmingham, Alabama. After driving the car for approximately nine months, and without noticing any flaws in its appearance, Dr. Gore took the car to "Slick Finish," an independent detailer, to make it look "snazzier than it normally would appear." Mr. Slick, the proprietor, detected evidence that the car had been repainted. Convinced that he had been cheated, Dr. Gore brought suit against petitioner BMW of North America (BMW), the American distributor of BMW automobiles. Dr. Gore alleged, *inter alia*, that the failure to disclose that the car had been repainted constituted suppression of a material fact. The complaint prayed for $500,000 in compensatory and punitive damages, and costs.

At trial, BMW acknowledged that it had adopted a nationwide policy in 1983 concerning cars that were damaged in the course of manufacture or transportation. If the cost of repairing the damage exceeded 3 percent of the car's suggested retail price, the car was placed in company service for a period of time and then sold as used. If the repair cost did not exceed 3 percent of the suggested retail price, however, the car was sold as new without advising the dealer that any repairs had been made. Because the $601.37 cost of repainting Dr. Gore's car was only about 1.5 percent of its suggested retail price, BMW did not disclose the damage or repair to the Birmingham dealer.[3]

Dr. Gore is going to lose this appeal. We know it already. Here are the clues from the way the court tells the story:

- Dr. Gore drove the car for nine months without noticing that it had been damaged and repaired. Only a specialist noticed it.
- He paid about $40,750 to buy the car, in 1995!
- The pre-purchase damage was so minor that the repair cost BMW only about $600.
- Dr. Gore sued for $500,000 in compensatory damages and was awarded $2 million in punitive damages.

The amounts claimed are so disproportionate to Dr. Gore's loss that he seems greedy, and the damages seem irrational. This is BMW's story. The Court adopted it and tells us so before even beginning to analyze the law.

---

3. *Id.* at 562-64 (citations deleted).

But Dr. Gore has a different story, which the Court rejected. We know about it only because a dissenting justice told the story in the following words near the beginning of her dissent:

> Dr. Gore's experience was not unprecedented among customers who bought BMW vehicles sold as flawless and brand-new. In addition to his own encounter, Gore showed . . . that on 983 other occasions . . . , BMW had shipped new vehicles to dealers without disclosing paint repairs costing at least $300, [and] at least 14 of the repainted vehicles . . . were sold as new and undamaged to consumers in Alabama.[4]

Which story do you find more persuasive?

§27.3   Compelling Arguments Persuade

Arguments provide the logical reasons to accept a writer's theory. They are based on interpretation of statutes and judicial precedent as well as public policy. In all your courses, you've been immersed in arguments since you started law school.

§27.4   How Arguments and Stories Work Together

Suppose you're asked to believe the following:[5] *A farmer in India can earn dramatically more income simply by owning a basic mobile phone capable of no more than voice calls and text messages.*

Assume that you're a government official with a budget. You're besieged by people and organizations asking you to spend money on projects they consider important. For every request you approve, you will have to turn down a hundred more. You must decide whether to spend several million dollars to subsidize construction of rural cellular transmitting towers and to get cell phones into the hands of Indian farmers and the rural merchants who buy food from them.

A logical argument in support of this plan appears in the left column. Read it and decide whether it persuades you and, if so, how deeply you're persuaded ("this might work," "it probably will work," or "it absolutely will work!").

---

4. *Id.* at 608 (Ginsburg, J., dissenting).

5. *See* World Bank Grp., *Poverty Headcount Ratio at $2 a Day (PPP) (% of Population)*, WORLD BANK, http://data .worldbank.org/indicator/SI.POV.2DAY/countries/IN?display=graph (last visited Nov. 15, 2014); India Ministry of Home Affairs, *2011 Census Data*, OFFICE OF THE REGISTRAR GEN. & CENSUS COMM'R, http://censusindia.gov.in/Census_ And_You/literacy_and_level_of_education.aspx (last visited Oct. 27, 2018); 60% of Rural India Lives on Less Than Rs 35 a Day, ECONOMIC TIMES (India), May 4, 2012; Kevin Sullivan, *For India's Traditional Fishermen, Cellphones Deliver a Sea Change*, WASH. POST, Oct. 15, 2006, http://www.washingtonpost.com/wp-dyn/content/article/2006/10/ 14/AR2006101400342.html; Kevin Sullivan, *Cell Phone Turns Out to Be Grocer's Best Buy*, WASH. POST, Oct. 14, 2006, http://www.washingtonpost.com/wp-dyn/content/article/2006/10/13/AR2006101301043.html.

Then read the stories in the right column.

A Logical Argument

In economics, a market is any system in which buyers and sellers can transact business with each other. In an efficient market, all information is available to everybody so that each buyer or seller can make rational decisions. If all information is available to everybody, each person gets the most value out of the market, and waste is minimized.

But developing countries are plagued by inefficient markets, where people do not have access to the information they need, and where buyers and sellers have a hard time even finding each other. These inefficiencies are one of the greatest burdens that developing countries must overcome to achieve widespread prosperity.

More than two-thirds of the people of India live on income of less than $2 a day, according to the World Bank. The situation is worse in rural areas, where three-fifths of the population survives on little more than half a dollar a day, according to Indian government statistics.

The smallest and cheapest medium for transmitting information instantly is a cell phone. It is cheaper than a laptop and does not require telephone wiring or wifi infrastructure. It does require cellular transmitting towers, which have been built in urban areas where cell phone users are concentrated. Too few towers are in the less populated countryside where almost 70% of Indians live.

A cell phone does not require any education. The adult literacy rate in India is about 65%. But a person who cannot read or write can place voice calls on a cell phone.

Two Stories

Suraj Chopra is a farmer in a small village some distance from New Delhi. He lives with his family in a two-room hut with a dirt floor and no running water. He can see no way to improve that situation.

Sometimes a rural merchant will buy some of what Chopra grows and transport it in an unrefrigerated truck to a wholesale market in New Delhi. But a significant amount of Chopra's crop never leaves his village. In a hot climate, produce must be harvested as it ripens and taken to market fast before it spoils.

He has no phone of any kind. No cell tower is nearby, and his village, like many in India, was never wired for landlines. He has no way of contacting the outside world when he needs to.

Devi Datt Joshi sells fruit and vegetables from a three-wheeled cart on the streets of New Delhi. He has no store and no refrigerator. Before dawn each day, he goes to a fruit and vegetable wholesale market and buys as much as he thinks he can sell that day. This is the same market where a rural merchant might take produce grown by Suraj Chopra.

Joshi's pre-dawn decision of how much to purchase is crucial to whether he will make any money that day and how hard he will have to work to make it. Without refrigeration in the Indian heat, if he buys more than he can sell, he will have to throw away most of the excess because it will spoil by the following day. If he buys too little, he will lose sales and risk losing frustrated customers to other sellers.

Making this kind of gamble, Joshi used to earn an average of $3 a day for more than twelve hours of work. Everything changed when he got a cell phone. Now

Although the U.S. cost of buying a cell phone and paying the monthly bills would consume much more than an average Indian worker's entire income, costs in India are lower. Cell phone air time charges in India are a fraction of what U.S. consumers pay.

"One element of poverty is the lack of information," according to C.K. Prahalad, a professor in the business school at the University of Michigan, who has studied how cell phones can help people escape poverty. "The cell phone gives poor people as much information as the middleman."

Therefore, if farmers in India have cell phones, their incomes can grow significantly. The food distribution chain from farmers to city populations can become more efficient, with less food spoilage. And that can lower food prices for consumers in all income groups.

customers call him the night before to place their orders. He knows how much to buy, and they can depend on him to supply what they need.

"The mobile phone has more than doubled my profits," Joshi told an American newspaper reporter. He now earns $8 a day for about eight hours of work. He still gets up before dawn, but his work day ends before lunch. He has hired an assistant and put his children into better schools. And the food he buys rarely goes to waste.

Meanwhile Suraj Chopra, the farmer, sometimes sees his crops go to waste because, without a phone, he cannot contact a merchant when his crops are ready to sell. And a merchant cannot quickly and easily contact him when the merchant is ready to buy.

Suppose you hear the stories *without* hearing the logical argument. The stories make you interested, even excited, about the idea. But you don't yet feel confident that you should commit money from your department's limited budget to fund this project. Then you hear the logical argument, which gives you the confidence you didn't have before. *The stories provided motivation, and the argument finished the job by justifying with logic.*

The story and the logical argument complement each other. Neither alone would be sufficient. A story touches us and motivates us to act. A logical argument explains why the story is valid and provides a justification that a decision maker can rely on to explain the decision to someone else. Persuading thus requires a good story *and* an argument that *work together.*

§27.5 Overcoming Your Weaknesses Persuades

Which cases and statutes favor your adversary? Which facts work to your adversary's advantage? What are your adversary's strongest arguments? And what will your adversary say to contradict your arguments? The answers to these questions identify your weaknesses.

Hiding from these problems won't make them slink away in the night. You must confront and defeat them. "Be truthful in exposing . . . the difficulties in your case," an appellate judge has written. "Tell us what they are and how you expect to deal with them."[6] If you fail to mention your weaknesses, and if you fail to explain why they don't undermine your case, your opponent will—and the court will probably hold that against you. Acknowledging your challenges can preserve your reader's trust in you.

§27.6 Solving Judges' Problems Persuades

See the world through the judge's eyes, and make it easy for the judge to rule in your favor.

Imagine an office with a desk, a side table, and bookshelves. On the desk and side table, many files are piled up. Each file is very thick and represents a motion or appeal the judge must decide. The judge behind the desk has a huge docket of cases. To decide each of them, the judge must read what the lawyers have submitted—page after page after page of reading—and for most judges there are too few hours in the day to read all that. Patrick Barry explains that this is a matter of empathy:

> Too often we . . . rush to cram as much information as possible into our arguments and explanations, forgetting that an overstuffed brief is not a user-friendly brief. Judges already have many other overstuffed things in their lives: dockets, calendars, email inboxes. Why tax their brains (and their time) even more? Why not instead begin by thinking about what kind of brief you would like to read if you were in their position? Why not start with empathy?
>
> You might even think of this use of empathy in strategic terms. It's goal-oriented compassion. The more accurately you imagine what it's like to be the judge you are trying to persuade, the more likely you'll be to craft a brief addressing that judge's particular concerns and preferences. . . .
>
> The best briefs are a kind of gift. They say to the judge, "Look, I know you have a really difficult job to do. So read me. I can help." They collect the relevant cases. They highlight the relevant facts. And they proceed with a rhythm and honesty that makes for easy reading . . . .[7]

Most writing read by judges has a high word-to-meaning ratio: Many words are used to express a given amount of meaning. If *your* writing has a low word-to-meaning ratio—no wasted words, every word carrying weight—your work will be more persuasive simply because for the judge it solves a problem instead of creating one. You may have spent days writing a motion memo or brief, but the judge needs to be able to read it—and *completely understand it*—in minutes. To persuade, you will spend more time writing so the judge can spend less time reading. Think about the

---

6. Roger J. Miner, *Twenty-five "Dos" for Appellate Brief Writers*, 3 Scribes J. Leg. Writing 19, 24 (1992).

7. Patrick Barry, *Editing and Empathy*, Mich. Bar J., May 2018, at 42-43.

other problems a judge might have with your memo or brief, and solve them too so that the judge finds your writing a pleasure.

§27.7   Professionalism Persuades

Professionalism generates trust. Judges respect lawyers who hold themselves to high professional standards. One mark of professionalism is to produce memos and briefs that are sharply focused on the issue, carefully reasoned, thoroughly researched, precisely written, and diligently proofread, with careful attention to details.

28 Writing a Motion Memorandum

§28.1 Persuasive Writing in Trial Courts

A *motion* is a request, usually in writing, asking the court to issue an *order*. A lawyer who wants the court to issue an order *files a motion* or *moves* for an order.

Motions can come at the beginning, middle, and end of a case. Common early motions are those requesting dismissal, a preliminary injunction, or summary judgment. Motions to suppress evidence, change venue, or compel additional discovery may come later. Even after a trial is over, motions can ask the court to reconsider the judgment or to reduce a jury award.

With your motion, you may submit a supporting memorandum arguing the legal and factual basis for the motion. For instance, a motion for summary judgment would include a memorandum arguing why the court should grant summary judgment to your client. The title of the document might be "Memorandum in Support of Motion for Summary Judgment." When you file your motion and memorandum, court rules require you to file a copy with your adversary's lawyer, who will most likely file a response with the court titled "Memorandum in Opposition to Motion for Summary Judgment." In that document, your opponent will argue that the action you want the court to take should not be granted.

Similar documents submitted to the trial court might be called *trial memoranda* or sometimes *trial briefs*. They all refer to the same thing—a written request for the court to act (or not act), supported by an argument explaining why (or why not).

The judge (and the judge's law clerk) may look at a motion memo more than once. The judge may read some of it to prepare for a hearing or oral argument on the motion (if time allows), a second time just before deciding the motion, and a third time while writing the court's order or opinion. You can't assume that a motion memo will be read from front to back, or even at one sitting.

And you can't assume that a long motion memo will be read in its entirety. Most trial judges have a heavy workload and have very little time to read your motion and supporting memo. If you don't make your point quickly, you risk losing your audience.

§28.2 Motion Memorandum Format

The format of a motion memo is often more flexible than the format for an office memo or appellate brief. Few court rules govern the content of motion memos, and customs among lawyers differ from one jurisdiction to another. A typical motion memo might include these parts:

1. a heading identifying the court, the name of the case, a case or docket number, and a document title, which, taken together, are called the case caption
2. a Preliminary Statement, sometimes called an Introduction
3. a Statement of Facts, sometimes called a Statement of the Case
4. an Argument, which can be divided by headings
5. a Conclusion
6. a closing, signature block, and proof of service

For an example of one typical format, see the motion memo in Appendix C.

Heading, Caption, and Docket Number. The court's name, case name, and docket number should all be copied from the document that started the case—a pleading in a civil case and a charging document in a criminal case.

Document Title. The document title identifies the type of motion or memorandum and its purpose. For example, a motion memo supporting a motion to dismiss a complaint might be titled "Memorandum in Support of Defendant's Motion to Dismiss."

Preliminary Statement or Introduction. The purpose of the Preliminary Statement is to tell the judge why the matter has come before the court and to identify the type of decision to be made. The Preliminary Statement briefly sets out the case's procedural posture; identifies the parties (by name and relationship, to the extent necessary); explains the nature of the litigation; and describes the motion and the relief it seeks. If it can be done concisely, the Preliminary Statement might also summarize the parties' contentions, emphasizing the writer's theory supporting the motion. The whole Preliminary Statement might be shorter than a half page.

For example, a Preliminary Statement might begin this way:

This motion seeks an order preliminarily enjoining the defendant from marketing its Thimble Camera, which fits over the end of the photographer's finger. The defendant's product infringes nineteen separate patents held by the plaintiff. This memorandum explains how the plaintiff will prove its patent infringement claims and why the defendant has no defense to them.

The next few sentences will identify each of the parties by name and supply other details to help the court understand why a decision is needed at this stage of the case. It might seem illogical to summarize the reason for filing the motion before introducing the parties, but the judge will want to know the reason for the motion before reading the rest of the details. The two sentences in the example above will quickly get a judge's attention.

Statement of Facts. The Statement of Facts corresponds to the facts in an office memo, but there are differences in substance and in drafting technique. Often a motion brings the case before the trial judge for the first time, and a concise summary of the facts is essential. See Chapters 29 through 31, which explain how to write a Statement of Facts. Include the facts that are relevant to your theory supporting the action you want the court to take. Don't make legal arguments in the Statement of Facts.

Argument. The Argument corresponds to the Discussion in an office memorandum, but once again the goal is to *persuade* the reader as well as to clearly explain the law and show how it applies to the facts. The Argument is the largest section of your motion memo because it presents your legal analysis, supported by citations to legal authority. It's divided up by point headings and subheadings. Chapters 32 through 34 explain how to write an Argument in a motion memo or appellate brief.

Conclusion. In a motion memo, the Conclusion reminds the judge what you want the court to do, together with a quick summary of your supporting legal theory. The Conclusion doesn't include citations to legal authority and should not be longer than one reasonably sized paragraph.

Closing and Signature. Following the Conclusion, add your signature, typed name, mailing address, proof of service on the opposing party, and anything else required by your court.

§28.3   Writing the Memorandum

Lawyers differ regarding the sequence they follow for drafting parts of a motion memo. Most lawyers modify the order somewhat from document to document because a practice that works well in one instance might not work well in another.

Many lawyers start with the Statement of Facts. Telling a story in a persuasive way can be a productive beginning to help the writer develop the Argument. Other lawyers write the Argument first because that helps them better understand which facts to include. Some lawyers write the Argument and Statement of Facts simultaneously. Still others outline the Statement of Facts while writing the Argument.

Sometimes the Argument takes shape more easily by drafting the point headings and subheadings first, serving as a rough outline. Or a lawyer might begin by writing a rough draft of the Argument, waiting to see how it flows before crafting persuasive point headings and subheadings. The Conclusion is usually done last because it summarizes the key points in your legal argument.

There is no one "right" place to start writing, and it helps to remain flexible. Write the parts of the motion memo in whatever order works best for you. But save time to rewrite the motion memo so all of the parts form a cohesive whole before submitting it to the court.

§28.4   Handling the Procedural Posture

Because most of your law school courses focus on the substantive law of Torts, Contracts, Property, and Criminal Law, you might view legal issues primarily from the standpoint of whether your client will win or lose on the merits of the case. But judges must also consider legal issues in terms of their *procedural posture*—the procedural step, often a motion, that places an issue before the court.

Each type of motion is governed by procedural rules that dictate how the motion is to be decided. If you move for summary judgment, for example, your motion will be granted only if you satisfy the legal test for summary judgment. The elements of the test for summary judgment are (1) whether the case raises a genuine dispute regarding a fact that is material to the outcome, and (2) whether the plaintiff is entitled to judgment as a matter of law.[1] The arguments in your motion memo should be designed to satisfy that legal test. The procedural posture also determines how you discuss the facts.

§28.4.1   Researching the Law Governing the Procedural Posture

Start your research by identifying the procedural posture. What kind of motion has been filed? What has the court been asked to do?

Next, find the *procedural* law that tells the court *how* to decide the motion. You are looking for—

- the test for granting the motion, such as:

---

1. Fed. R. Civ. P. 56.

Summary judgment is appropriate if there is no genuine issue of material fact and if the moving party is entitled to judgment as a matter of law.

- procedural rules on how to evaluate the record when deciding the motion, such as:

In deciding a motion for summary judgment, the court views the evidence in the light most favorable to the party opposing the motion.

You might find what you are looking for in court rules or statutes. Often, both the test and the procedural rules for deciding the motion are explained in court opinions deciding that kind of motion, just after the fact summary and before the legal analysis begins.

§28.4.2 Writing within the Procedural Posture

Because the procedural posture and the rules governing it control the way the judge will make the decision, your motion must show the judge how to decide it within those procedural rules.

First, remember that in deciding a motion, the court will first ask about the procedural rule.

Some of these procedural tests for motions include an element of the substantive legal standard for the case. For example, a summary judgment test requires the moving party to demonstrate that it is entitled to *judgment as a matter of law*. Similarly, the test that applies to a motion for preliminary injunction has an element requiring the moving party to demonstrate that it is likely to *succeed on the merits* of the case at trial. In these motions, the court makes a procedural decision on the motion, but one element of that test for deciding the motion requires the court to consider the underlying substantive law.

Second, use CREAC to organize the Argument section of your motion memo based on the procedural test. If the procedural test incorporates the substantive law, begin by organizing one CREAC structure for the procedural test, and then organize the substantive element of the test as a sub-section. (See Chapter 19.)

Finally, procedural questions can often be addressed concisely. Most judges know the procedural tests because they routinely decide these kinds of motions. While you must identify the controlling procedural test and cite the mandatory law that governs, a short explanation usually suffices.

Part 8

Telling the Client's Story

29 The Statement of the Case in a Motion Memo or Appellate Brief

§29.1 How a Statement of the Case Persuades

> It may sound paradoxical, but most contentions of law are won or lost on the facts.
>
> —*Justice Robert H. Jackson*

In a persuasive memorandum or brief, the judge learns about the facts in the Statement of the Case (also called a Statement of Facts or just Facts). In the Statement, you must include every fact that you mention elsewhere in your memo or brief. You must also include in the Statement all facts on which you anticipate your adversary will rely. This is the one place in the document where all the legally significant facts can be seen together in the context of your client's story. And you lose credibility if you omit unfavorable facts.

In the Statement, don't argue, analyze law, draw factual inferences, or even characterize the facts. It's called a *Statement* because the facts are *stated* there and analyzed elsewhere. Inferences and characterizations of facts belong in the Argument. But you may report the inferences witnesses drew and the characterizations they made while testifying.

If you can't argue in a Statement of the Case, how can you persuade there? Persuade by *telling the story in a way that emphasizes facts that support your theory, while saying nothing that the adversary could reasonably claim to be inaccurate.*

Often the order of the facts can have an impact on persuasion. If your client is a veteran, for example, you might gain an advantage by noting that close to the start of your motion memo. If, on the other hand, your client has a long felony record, you would probably present that fact later.

Consider the two examples below. Assume that the plaintiffs are suing a backcountry hiking guide for negligence after the guide led them into disaster. When you write your facts, each sentence will cite to the record of the case. (You can see how this is done in the sample appellate brief in Appendix D.)

Version A	Version B
On July 2, the plaintiffs asked in Stove Pipe Springs whether a backcountry guide might be available to lead them through certain parts of Death Valley. After some discussion, they hired the defendant to take them on a full-day hike.	The climate in Death Valley is one of the hottest and driest known. The highest temperature recorded each summer reaches at least 120° and in many years at least 125°. The highest temperature recorded in Death Valley—134°—is also the highest recorded anywhere on earth. Rainfall is only 1 ½ inches per year, the lowest in the Western Hemisphere, and in a few years no rain falls at all.
When they started out the next day, the defendant carried a compass and map. Each plaintiff carried sunglasses, a large-brim hat, and a quart of water.	In the summer sun in Death Valley, a person can lose, on average, about four gallons of perspiration per day. After losing about two gallons, that person can become delirious and die of dehydration if the lost water is not quickly replaced.
A climatologist testified about the climate in Death Valley. Occasionally, winter temperatures fall below freezing, but there is no water to freeze. Spring and fall temperatures approximate summer temperatures elsewhere. July is the hottest month, with an average high of about 116° and an average low of about 87°. The highest temperature ever recorded in Death Valley was 134°. Average annual rainfall is about 1 ½ inches, and precipitation falls on only eight days in an average year.	The defendant advertised that he was a professional and experienced backcountry guide. Relying on the advertisement, the plaintiffs hired him. He then took them into Death Valley for a full-day hike in July with one quart of water each.

After reading Version B, you can believe that this hike was madness and that the guide was responsible for it. But in early drafts, many beginners instinctively produce a Statement more like Version A, which tells the story but not in a compelling way. How does Version B persuade?

First, in Version B the writer selected the few facts that would illustrate the theory: You can lose four gallons of water a day in such a place. After losing two gallons, you can become delirious, and if the water is not replaced, your life will be in danger. This was a full-day hike. The plaintiffs had a quart of water each. The defendant claimed to be a professional and experienced guide. As each of these facts is added to the story, the logic of the theory unfolds.

Second, Version B is free of factual clutter—marginal facts, such as temperatures in other months, that obscure critical information. It focuses instead on the facts crucial to the persuasive story.

Finally, Version B provides the kind of vivid details that make a theory come alive—the delirium, for example.

But Version B appears to be only a description of the relevant facts. An adversary can't reasonably challenge anything in it as untrue. Each fact is objectively verifiable in the record. And—most importantly—the writer never expressed any inferences from the evidence. *You drew all the inferences yourself.*

Sometimes a reader can think, "I can't tell whether this Statement was written by the plaintiff's lawyer or by the defendant's." That confusion is the surest sign that the Statement fails to persuade. Is it true of either of the Death Valley excerpts? If so, which one?

§29.2   The Record

The record might include any or all of the following:

- the pleadings
- evidence in the form of testimony, affidavits, and exhibits
- prior court orders, judicial opinions in the same case, and the judgment below in an appeal

A Statement of the Case can describe *only* the facts that are in the record. Other facts must be ignored, a process called limiting the Statement to the record. But you can point to the *absence* from the record of a particular allegation or piece of evidence—for example, "no witness identified the defendant"—if the absence shows that the opposing party has failed to satisfy a relevant legal test or burden of production.

In the Statement, describe the facts in terms of the type of record where they can be found. If the record includes testimony, explain how the witnesses testified. But if the "facts" are allegations in a pleading,[1] don't describe those allegations as events that actually happened.

For every fact you mention, courts require you to cite a specific page or paragraph in the record—not only when you recite the fact in the Statement of the Case, but also when you analyze it in the Argument.[2] This provides an easy method for the court to check the accuracy of what you say. Cites to the record also have a persuasive effect of their own. Careful cites give the reader confidence that every fact on

---

1. Allegations are most often at issue when the pleading is challenged in a motion to dismiss for failure to state a claim. *See* Fed. R. Civ. P. 12(b)(6).

2. *See, e.g.,* Fed. R. App. P. 28(a)(6), (c).

which you rely is fully supported in the record. Spotty or missing cites arouse a court's skepticism. Both the *ALWD Guide to Legal Citation* and the *Bluebook* explain how to cite to the record.

§29.3   Fact Ethics

It's unethical for a lawyer to "knowingly . . . make a false statement of fact . . . to a tribunal."[3] Even if it were not unethical, misrepresenting the facts never fools a court and hurts only the misrepresenting lawyer and that lawyer's client. Misrepresentations are quickly spotted by opposing lawyers, and once a misrepresentation is pointed out to a court, the entire motion memo or brief will be treated with deep suspicion. And afterward the court will mistrust the misrepresenting lawyer. You and your clients can't afford to lose a court's trust.

---

3. MODEL RULES OF PROF'L CONDUCT R. 3.3(a)(1) (2013).

30 Developing a Persuasive Story

When I was an attorney . . . , I realized after much trial and error that in a courtroom whoever tells the best story wins.

—*John Quincy Adams (fictionally) in the movie* Amistad

§30.1 The Power of Stories

Robert McKee[1] has taught many of the best screenwriters in Hollywood how to write stories. So many screenwriters are in his debt that he was actually portrayed in that role in the movie *Adaptation*. Nicolas Cage plays a screenwriter who consults McKee about writer's block.

McKee also teaches business people how to persuade by telling stories. In a common business situation, a young start-up company has developed a valuable idea, such as a drug that will prevent heart attacks. The company needs investment bankers to lend money or buy stock so the company can finish the job and put the drug on the market.

This situation resembles the one lawyers face when asking a court for relief: A person who wants something (a lawyer or a company's executives) tries to persuade a decision maker (a judge or an investment banker) who has very rational criteria for making the decision (legal rules or the math that would predict whether an investment will make a profit).

If the company's chief executive officer meets with the investment bankers and makes only a logical presentation based on statistics and sales projections, the "bankers would nod politely and stifle yawns while thinking of all the other companies better positioned" to bring this drug to market. But suppose the CEO tells a compelling

---

1. The quotes from McKee and the material about him are from Bronwyn Fryer, *Storytelling that Moves People: A Conversation with Screenwriting Coach Robert McKee*, Harv. Bus. Rev., June 2003, at 51.

story about how the company overcame obstacles to develop the drug, get it patented, and get regulatory approval, and now must overcome one final hurdle—financing—to bring the drug to market. That causes "great suspense" and the possibility that "the story might not have a happy ending. The CEO has the bankers on the edges of their seats, and he says 'We won the race, we got the patent, we're poised to go public and save a quarter-million lives a year.' And the bankers just throw money at him."

Why? Nothing should be more rational than finance. If the numbers on the spreadsheets and PowerPoint slides show that this project will produce a profit without too much risk, the bankers should invest in it. But they will be more likely to invest if they have been captured by the story. If you challenge McKee on this, he will say, "I know the storytelling method works, because after I consulted with a dozen corporations whose principals told exciting stories to Wall Street, they all got their money."

§30.2   How Stories Persuade

In a law school classroom, making the best logical argument is everything. That is as it should be. Legal argumentation is difficult to master, and legal education devotes a lot of effort to teaching students how to argue.

But in the real world, when you make purely logical arguments to decision makers like judges, as McKee points out, "they are arguing with you in their heads"—because logic and argument naturally arouse skepticism—and "if you do persuade them, you've done so only on an intellectual basis. That's not good enough because people aren't inspired to act by reason alone." A story, he says, persuades "by uniting an idea with an emotion."

A story also persuades by letting the reader decide—on her own—to agree with you *before* you've asked her to agree. In an argument, you start by telling the reader what you want her to believe, and then you set out the steps of logic to prove that position. With a story, you tell what happened. If you develop a good story and if you tell it well, the reader's decision *comes from her* while reading the story, and she is therefore more committed to it. She is motivated to act for two reasons. First, she saw the point before you told her what it was. (If you tell her the point during the story, it's no longer a story. It's an argument.) And second, stories move us in ways that logic cannot.

The most powerful persuasion comes from combining a logical proof with a gripping and well-told story. For an example, see §27.4. In that example, the logical proof (in the left column) assures you that building more cell towers in India makes sense. The story (in the right column) motivates you to act. Next week you won't remember the numbers in the left column. But you will remember the two people in the right column. The family of one of them has a better life and a better future because of a cell phone. The other person's future remains economically bleak because no cell phone tower is nearby.

One note of caution: Some litigation stories are better suited to juries than judges. A story with too much emotion may insult a judge's sense of professionalism. A story told to a judge can succeed only by simultaneously addressing both the legal issues and the judge's basic human sense of right and wrong.

§30.3 Building the Story—Generally

A Statement of the Case should meet these four goals:

1. ignite action—motivate by making a judge care enough to act
2. communicate who you are—actually, communicate who your side is by defining your client and supporting witnesses favorably
3. communicate who the other side is by unfavorably defining the opposing party or the harmful witnesses or some combination of them
4   neutralize bad news by explaining why facts that at first seem bad for your case should not be held against you (more about this in Chapter 31)[2]

These are the four goals in storytelling.

Most stories have a simple, three-part structure:

1. The story starts in a state of equilibrium. Things might not be wonderful, but they are at least okay.

2. Bad things happen to disrupt the equilibrium. If you represent the plaintiff or the prosecution, the disruption is whatever the defendant did wrong. If you represent the defendant, the disruption is the wrongful lawsuit or prosecution itself, which puts the defendant under stress and at risk.

3. The protagonist struggles to restore equilibrium. Unless you're the prosecutor in a criminal case, the protagonist is probably your client. Because prosecutors have no client, they often cast the crime victim as a protagonist. If you represent a plaintiff, equilibrium could be restored by a judgment awarding your client an injunction or damages. If you represent the prosecution, equilibrium could be restored by convicting and sentencing the defendant. If you represent the defendant

---

2. Stephen Denning, Squirrel Inc.: A Fable of Leadership through Storytelling 44, 47 (2004). *See also* Stephen Denning, The Springboard: How Storytelling Ignites Action in Knowledge-Era Organizations (2001).

in either kind of case, equilibrium could be restored by dismissing the lawsuit or prosecution and freeing the defendant from the unjust burden of being an involuntary litigant in fear of losing.

Next time you watch a movie, ask yourself whether the plot in the movie has this structure—equilibrium, disruption, struggle to restore equilibrium. Most do. Sometimes you will tell your client's story in exactly this sequence, and sometimes you will tell it differently.

This structure also works when the issue isn't who should win in the end, but instead some smaller part of the litigation. For example, if you represent a party resisting discovery before trial in a civil case, the equilibrium is your client's possessing private information that your client reasonably wants to keep secret. Disruption is the other side's demand for this information through interrogatories or a deposition. The struggle to restore equilibrium is your attempt to persuade the judge to grant a protective order that would prevent discovery of this information.

The judge is a hidden character in the third phase of the story, the struggle to restore equilibrium. Will the plaintiff win an injunction? Will the defendant win a dismissal? Will the party resisting discovery win a protective order? That is all up to the judge. If you build a good story and tell it well, the judge should *want* to restore equilibrium.

Once you've determined the inner structure of the story, the most important components are characters and imagery.

§30.4   Characters

Character can't be described. You can't say, "My client is a really nice person, extremely conscientious and responsible." A legal reader will not believe you. You must imply character by reciting things your client has or has not done. You will do the same, if you can, with witnesses and with other parties.

> Take, for example, a rear-end collision that caused a lot of soft-tissue and nerve damage to the driver. At first glance, it seemed like a routine personal injury case. The at-fault driver was a business woman coming home from work who had been talking on her cell phone when the accident occurred. What really established her character was the fact that she continued talking during the accident and for another five minutes afterward [which defined her] as callous.[3]

---

3. Joel ben Izzy, *Character Development*, L.A. Daily J., Oct. 26, 1999, at 8.

§30.5 Imagery

If you want to win a case, paint the Judge a picture and keep it simple.

—John W. Davis

Imagery has a powerful effect in stories.

A truck runs off the highway, through a farmer's fence, and into the farmer's cow. The truck driver's insurance company wants to pay as little as possible for this cow, and the farmer, of course, wants more.

The insurance company's lawyer will tell a story in which the cow is "a unit of livestock" or "a farm asset," as though the issue is how much money the farmer should get to replace a machine-like object that consumes grass as fuel to produce milk and an occasional calf. This story will focus on numbers from the farmer's books that show the productivity of this object, its acquisition costs, depreciation, useful life remaining at the time of its destruction, etc. The insurance company's lawyer will use this story because the numbers show the cow to be an unexceptional object.

The farmer's lawyer looks for a different story to tell. "Tell me about the cow," she asks the farmer. "That wasn't just any cow," replies the farmer.

> That was Bessie! She was the only Guernsey cow left in this county. She didn't give that thin milk you get out of a Holstein that people buy in the grocery store. She gave the thickest, most flavorful milk you ever tasted. We didn't sell it to the dairy. They wouldn't pay a decent price for it anyway because dairies care about quantity, not quality. We drank it ourselves and made the best butter and cheese out of it. And Guernseys are smaller cows. They're friendly, like pets, and Bessie was part of our family.

Imagery you can see in your mind creates the persuasive weight of each of these stories. The farmer's lawyer wants us to see a big pair of eyes in a Guernsey head nudging the farmer with affection—a loss to the farmer's family that exceeds the loss of an animal functioning as a grass-to-milk machine. The insurance company's lawyer, on the other hand, wants us to see the farmer's balance sheet, where a certain item of livestock is carried as an asset valued at a certain number of dollars.

If you develop an eye for revealing detail, your stories will much more quickly come to life as vivid and compelling. Vividness not only helps the reader remember the story, but it makes the story more believable. Imagery makes a story real.

Word choice is critical. The right words help the judge see the image.

§30.6   Finding the Story

Facts aren't the story. They are the *raw materials* for the story.

A client sits in your office, describing in detail a problem that the client wants you to solve. The facts are these details. The client isn't telling you a persuasive story. Clients usually don't know how to do that. They hire lawyers to do it for them. The client can tell you only facts—"I got this letter in the mail," "Smith told me the company was going bankrupt," "I can't pay my bills." In a law school writing assignment, you might get these details as part of your assignment.

Regardless of how you get the facts, they aren't yet a story. The story is *hidden* in the facts. You must find it there. Look for the equilibrium, the disruption, and the struggle to restore equilibrium. Look for details that reveal character. Look for details that lend themselves to persuasive imagery. Assemble these into a story that fulfills the four purposes of storytelling—to motivate the judge to act, to communicate who your client and witnesses are, to communicate who the other side and its witnesses are, and to neutralize the unfavorable facts.

Try telling the story to a friend or relative whose intelligence and judgment you respect and who doesn't know the case you're working on. Telling the story orally helps you refine it and test it out before you start writing it. *Saying* it helps you understand it and how to improve it. Then ask how your friend or relative feels about the story. Does it motivate? Do the characters seem realistic? And so on.

§30.7   Two Last Questions

Suppose you've discovered the story you want to tell. Now step back and ask yourself two questions.

First, can you summarize the essence of it *persuasively* in one or two sentences? If you can do that, those sentences are your theme (see §27.1). If not, either the story is too complicated or you haven't identified the core facts. If the story is too complicated, your reader will get lost. If you don't know the core facts, you won't be able to focus on them when you tell the story. You will need to focus on them at the very beginning of the Statement of the Case. The Statement of the Case should begin with a paragraph that summarizes those very facts (see Chapter 31).

Second, will the judge care? If not, the story won't work because it won't motivate.

31 Telling the Story Persuasively

§31.1 Selecting Facts to Tell the Story

Selecting the facts is a four-step process, identifying facts that show how legal tests are met, identifying additional persuasive facts, identifying facts that hurt your case that your opponent will use, and eliminating factual clutter.

Step 1: Identify the facts that show how the relevant legal tests have or have not been satisfied. Make a list of the facts that show either how you have satisfied the governing legal tests or how your adversary has not. Some lawyers do this by making an elements-facts-witness/evidence chart. For example, you might make the chart on the next page if you represent the plaintiff and must show that you have satisfied the test for negligence concerning an auto accident witnessed by two pedestrians, Sha and Jeri, both of whom corroborate the plaintiff's story (π = plaintiff; Δ = defendant).

The chart helps you see what the dispute is all about. The elements of duty, injury, and proximate causation are easily satisfied. The real issue is breach. Three witnesses say the defendant ran the stop sign, and one says the defendant did not. The chart helps you realize that your factual theory should be that the two disinterested witnesses (Sha and Jeri), as well as the plaintiff, testified that the defendant ran the stop sign, and that only the defendant testified that he stopped before entering the intersection. Why is that a good theory? The plaintiff and defendant testified consistently with their own interests. But Sha and Jeri are credible because they are disinterested.

Elements, Facts, Witnesses/Evidence Chart			
Elements	Satisfied?	Facts	Witnesses/Evidence
1. duty owed by Δ to π	yes	π driving on street that has no stoplight or stop sign—Δ driving on cross street with stop sign	testimony of π, Δ, Sha, and Jeri
2. Δ's breach of that duty	probably yes	Δ drove through stop sign without stopping	testimony of π, Sha, and Jeri — contradicted only by Δ
3. injury to π	yes	π's medical injuries and damage to π's car	testimony of π, doctor, paramedic, mechanic, Sha, and Jeri; X-rays and photos
4. proximately caused by Δ's breach	yes (if Δ breached)	the front of Δ's car hit the side of π's car	testimony of police officer, mechanic, π, Sha, and Jeri; photos of damaged cars

When you write the Statement of the Case, include everything in the Facts column together with the supporting proof from the Witnesses/Evidence column. For example, find the duty element in the chart. Look at the facts that satisfy that element and the witnesses who testified to those facts. Now you know what to say in the Statement of the Case concerning that element:

> All the witnesses, including the defendant, testified that the intersection did not have a traffic light; that the plaintiff entered the intersection from the north on State Street, where there was no stop sign; and that the defendant entered from the east on Maple Lane, where a stop sign required him to stop.

In the Statement, you will *not* mention the duty element or say it was satisfied. That is legal analysis, which you will do in the Argument. In the Statement, you will mention only the substantiating facts and whatever proved them.

The defendant's lawyer might make her own version of this chart to identify the facts and proof she will need to mention in the Statement.

If several tests are involved, you might make a chart for each test. For example, suppose the defendant in the auto accident case has pleaded the affirmative defense of comparative negligence. Now two tests are in the case. The plaintiff must prove that the defendant was negligent. And the defendant must prove that the plaintiff was comparatively negligent. The facts relevant to each test can be identified by making a chart for that test.

Step 2: Identify additional facts that help tell your client's story persuasively. Include facts that accomplish the storytelling goals explained in §30.3, such as facts that communicate who your client and witnesses are, as well as similar facts about the other side. Who is an innocent victim, who is predatory, who is careless, and so forth? For example, let the reader know that Sha and Jeri have no stake in the case. Only by understanding what each fact *reveals* about people and events can you tell the client's story in a compelling way. Also include facts that a reader would need to understand the story, facts that hold the story together.

Step 3: Identify facts that hurt your case and facts on which your adversary will rely. If you do not include unfavorable facts, your Statement of the Case will lack credibility. Treat an unfavorable fact as an opportunity rather than a threat. If you include the unfavorable fact, you can try to neutralize it. The next section in this chapter explains how (see question 6 there). If you do not include the unfavorable fact in your Statement, you cannot neutralize it—and it really will be a threat.

Step 4: Eliminate factual clutter. Too much information distracts from the story. Identify a witness by name only if the reader really needs to know. In the example above, the names of Sha and Jeri are needed because they testify to so many different things, and because their testimony is crucial to the disputed element. But the doctor, paramedic, mechanic, and police officer can be identified by their roles instead ("the emergency room doctor who treated the plaintiff testified that . . .").

Specify dates, times, and places only if they are essential to the story or your theory. Specifics about them can be seductively concrete while you are writing. But to a reader they can also obscure what really happened. It is not necessary to say that the witnesses agree that the accident occurred at 1:25 p.m., that an ambulance arrived at 1:40, that at 1:53 the ambulance delivered the plaintiff to the emergency room at Highview Memorial Hospital, or that at 1:55 a doctor there began to treat the plaintiff. Just say, "Thirty minutes after the accident, the plaintiff was treated by a hospital emergency room physician." Unless the hospital is being sued or its identity is otherwise significant, naming it gets in the way of telling the story. The exact times also get in the way.

§31.2 How to Test a Statement of the Case for Persuasiveness

While rewriting, ask yourself the following questions.

1. Have you correctly decided which facts to include in the Statement? See the first section of this chapter.

2. Have you chosen a method of organization that tells the story persuasively? Set out the facts in a sequence that persuades and can easily be understood. Sometimes the most effective sequence is chronological. But often, a topical organization works better because you can use the way you organize the facts to imply the logical relationships between them. In some cases, you might try a topical organization that breaks into a chronological narrative where it is important for the reader to understand the sequence in which events happened. If the Statement is long, you can add headings to break it up and to show how you have organized it.

3. Have you started with a punch? Begin the Statement with a short passage—one or two paragraphs—summarizing your most compelling facts and perhaps neutralizing the most unfavorable facts so that the judge understands the heart of your theory. This functions as an introduction to the story, although you might not call it that. For example:

> The defendant drove through a stop sign and into the plaintiff's car, putting the plaintiff in the hospital for a week and disabling him from working for seven months. Every witness except the defendant testified that the defendant entered the intersection without stopping. Although the plaintiff was driving an uninsured car with an expired registration, there was no evidence that these infractions caused the accident or contributed to the plaintiff's injuries.

Then, in the rest of the Statement, tell the story—describing in detail the facts you summarized at the beginning.

The opening passage is the most important part of the Statement. If written well, it puts the judge in a receptive frame of mind, tells the judge what facts to look for later, and creates a lasting impression. The opening passage is also one of the hardest parts of the Statement to write. But the extra time and effort are worth it. Never begin the Statement with neutral facts or unimportant facts. You can include the most unfavorable facts to neutralize them (as in the last sentence of the example above), but the introductory paragraphs are not always the best place to do this.

4. Have you reflected your theory throughout the Statement? Tightly focus the Statement on facts that advance your theory. If the Statement wanders aimlessly through the facts, the reader will not grasp your theory and may not even understand the story. Throughout the Statement, the reader should be aware of who you represent from the way you tell the story. If the reader wonders about that, even for a paragraph or two, your Statement probably is unpersuasive. Every word should be selected to make the theory more clear. If you focus the Statement in this way, it can be surprisingly short.

5. Have you emphasized favorable facts? You can do that through organization. Readers tend to be most attentive at the beginning, least attentive in the middle, and attentive to a middling degree at the end. You can also describe the most favorable facts in detail while omitting marginal facts that would cloud the picture you want the reader to see. If a favorable fact is undisputed, you can point that out:

> Every witness, including the defendant, testified that the stop sign could easily be seen by a driver in the defendant's position. (T. at 14, 35, 62, 68, 97, 132.)

You can also point to things that are missing from the record, if that helps you:

> No evidence suggested an emergency or other situation that might have justified disregarding a stop sign.

6. Have you neutralized unfavorable facts? The most effective method is to juxtapose an unfavorable fact with one or more favorable facts that show why the unfavorable fact should not hurt you. Juxtaposition is placing two things side by side. Effective juxtapositions often use "although" or "even though" contrasts. For example:

> Although the plaintiff was driving an uninsured car with an expired registration, there was no evidence that these infractions caused the accident or contributed to the plaintiff's injuries.

An unfavorable fact cannot be neutralized by simply tucking it away in an obscure part of the Statement. Hiding it will not make it go away.

7. Have you humanized your client? Be careful about how you refer to the parties. You could write "the plaintiff" and "the defendant" in a civil case or, in a criminal case, "the defendant" and "the State" (or, in some courts, "the People," "the Government," or "the Commonwealth"). More still can be conveyed by using some generic factual designation related to the issues: "the buyer" and "the seller" in a commercial dispute or "the employer" and "the employee" in a discrimination case. All those are clear enough for a reader to understand.

But how you refer to the parties can also have a persuasive effect. Many lawyers try to humanize their clients by referring to them by name while depersonalizing the opposing party ("the insurance company" or "the university"). Sometimes that works, and sometimes it does not. If the parties are both people, for example, it can be confusing and look unfair to call one party "Ms. Falco" and the other "the defendant."

In an appellate brief, a reader will be confused if you refer to the parties continually as "appellant" and "appellee." These designations identify only who lost in the court below. In many appellate courts, you are not allowed to use these designations inside a brief, although they appear on the cover page.[1]

Exercise 31-A. Storytelling

Using a case you have read in another course, develop the facts of the case into a story. Do not change or embellish the facts. Stay strictly faithful to the *substance* of what you read in the case. But develop a story that would move a listener or reader to feel or think that one party or the other should win. Use the techniques described in this chapter and in Chapters 29 and 30. Then tell the story to another student and ask that student to suggest improvements.

Exercise 31-B. Factual Inferences

You work at the local prosecutor's office and need to determine whether to charge a defendant with both battery and domestic battery. A local resident, Victor Tyne, was punched in the face by A.A. Bragenkrantz, who is the boyfriend of Victor's cousin, Anna Canelli. You already know you can charge battery. Can you also charge domestic battery, which would require Bragenkrantz to be one of Tyne's "household members"?

Bragenkrantz and Canelli stayed overnight at Tyne's house every Sunday through Thursday during the summer so they could attend summer classes at the university. Bragenkrantz and Canelli slept on a fold-out futon in Tyne's spare bedroom. They each kept clothing in a drawer of a dresser in the spare bedroom. Bragenkrantz had registered for summer classes using Tyne's address as his home address in order to qualify for in-state tuition. Bragenkrantz and Canelli spent their weekends at Canelli's parents' home, about two hours' drive away. Bragenkrantz has kept most of his possessions in a storage locker since his recent divorce.

Create a diagram like the one below to determine whether Bragenkrantz is a member of Tyne's household. Put your diagram on a piece of paper and leave space so you can add horizontal rows as you identify facts. Add facts from the paragraphs above this one if relevant inferences can be drawn from them. If a fact tends to show Bragenkrantz *was* a household member, add the inference you draw from that fact in the column on the far left. If a fact tends to show he *was not* a household member, add your inference in the column on the far right. If the fact could go either way, add

---

1. *See, e.g.,* Fed. R. App. P. 28(d), 32(a)(2)(E).

Facts and Inferences				
Inference?	Fact tending to show he **was** a household member	Facts that could go **either way**	Fact tending to show he **was not** a household member	Inference?
clothes indicate a permanent con- nection to the household	—	clothes in the drawer	—	not many clothes—so this is probably not his household
(add additional horizontal rows as needed)				

inferences in both columns. (To help you get started, we have inserted a fact that could go either way.)

If the clothes in the drawer tended to show *only* that Bragenkrantz was a member of the household, the inference on the left would appear in the diagram, and no inference would appear on the right. If, on the other hand, the clothes tended to show only that he was *not* a household member, the only inference would be on the right. Both inferences appear here because the clothes can be used to support each of them.

Exercise 31-C. Evaluating a Story

This chapter explains how to tell a story. Chapter 30 explains how to develop one. Chapter 29 explains how stories persuade. Using what you learned in all three chapters, read and evaluate only the "Factual and Procedural Background" portion of the Appendix C motion memo. If you were the judge, how would that portion of the memo affect you? What outcome do you expect the court to reach just from reading this section? Why? What are its strengths and weaknesses?

Part 9

Making the Client's Arguments

32 The Argument in a Motion Memo or Appellate Brief

§32.1 Arguments

A man walks into an office and announces that he's looking for a good argument. A second man, sitting at a desk, contradicts everything the first man says. After several minutes of this, the first man complains that what's happening is not an argument. "Yes, it is," replies the man at the desk.

"An *argument isn't just contradiction*," says the first man. "*An argument is a connected series of statements intended to establish a proposition*."

"No, it isn't," contradicts the man at the desk. And things go downhill from there in this skit performed by Monty Python's Flying Circus.

In a motion memo or appellate brief, an argument—a connected series of statements intended to establish a proposition—is expressed in the document's Argument section. An Argument section can contain several arguments. Often, you need to establish a series of propositions. For example, you might need to show that

- the words of a controlling statute support your position,
- the courts have interpreted that statute consistently with its wording, and
- the court's interpretation is consistent with the reasons the legislature enacted the statute (the legislative purpose and the policy behind the statute).

Each of these propositions must be supported by its own argument or arguments. Sometimes it takes several arguments to prove a proposition.

Writing the Argument is a process of (1) identifying the propositions you must prove, (2) developing persuasive arguments to support each of them, and (3) finding the words to articulate those arguments.

§32.2   Understanding the Judicial Audience

Ask yourself, "What will make the court *want* to agree with me?"

Proving that you're right is not enough.   Learning how to justify your own beliefs starts long before law school. But laying out a case for why you want to stay on your parents' phone contract isn't the same as getting inside their thinking and persuading them to *want* to keep you on their contract. To motivate, you must learn not only a new argument style but also a new process of creating arguments. The process of justifying your own position differs from *the process of persuading others to agree with you.* Here is how one student began to learn the difference:

> [In a college course, Kathleen wrote a paper on the] question "Is American Sign language (ASL) a 'foreign language' for purposes of meeting the university's foreign language requirement?" Kathleen had taken two years of ASL at a community college. When she transferred to a four-year college, the chair of the foreign languages department at her new college would not allow her ASL proficiency to count for the foreign language requirement. ASL isn't a "language," the chair said summarily. "It's not equivalent to learning French, German, or Japanese."[1]

Is this really why the department chair rejected Kathleen's request? If it is, Kathleen will be able to change his mind if she can prove that ASL is a real language, equivalent to French, German, or Japanese. But it might be only a rationalization for his decision—a statement he can use to justify saying no. If it is only his rationalization, then his motivation—the true cause of the refusal—remains hidden. If he is rationalizing, he might not even be aware of his own motives. In a moment we'll see whether what he has stated is a rationalization or his true motivation.

Kathleen was not satisfied with what the department chair had said, and in a different college course she decided to write a paper on this issue.

> While doing research, she focused almost entirely on subject matter, searching for what linguists, brain neurologists, cognitive psychologists, and sociologists had said about the language of deaf people. Immersed in her subject matter, she was [not] concerned with her audience, whom she thought of primarily as her classmates and the professor [who taught the class in which she was writing the paper. They] were friendly to her views and interested in her experiences with the deaf community. She wrote a well-documented paper, citing several scholarly articles that made a good case to her classmates (and the professor) that ASL was indeed a distinct language.

---

1. The quotes in this section are from JOHN D. RAMAGE & JOHN C. BEAN, WRITING ARGUMENTS: A RHETORIC WITH READINGS 10-11 (4th ed. 1998).

Proud of the big red A the professor had placed on her paper, Kathleen returned to the chair of the foreign language department with a new request to count ASL for her language requirement. The chair read her paper, congratulated her on her good writing, but said her argument was not persuasive. He disagreed with several of the linguists she cited and with the general definition of "language" that her paper assumed. He then gave her some additional (and to her fuzzy) reasons that the college would not accept ASL as a foreign language.

Now Kathleen has addressed the concerns the department chair expressed before. But rather than agree with her argument, he nitpicked it and offered new reasons that he had not mentioned before. Something else—which he has not specified— must be motivating him. Because Kathleen has not discovered the real cause of his refusal, she inadvertently made an argument that only challenged his rationalizations instead of one that addressed his true motivations.

What has happened to Kathleen is a common experience when *an advocate justifies a position rather than trying to influence the person making the decision*. The decision maker ignores ideas that made perfect sense to Kathleen and everybody else—except the decision maker. It makes no difference whether that person is a college administrator (as here) or a judge.

To persuade, figure out how a judge would react to the issues. Proving you are right and persuading the judge sound like the same thing, but they are not. Think about the person you are trying to persuade and what would matter to *that person*.

Kathleen could easily dismiss the chair of the foreign language department as a numskull, but for two reasons she cannot and should not. First, like a judge, he has the power of decision. The only way she can get her ASL work to count for the foreign language requirement is to *change his mind*.

Second, he might have sincere concerns that deserve attention. Does Kathleen know what they might be? At this point, she doesn't. Imagining only a friendly audience, she hadn't considered how a skeptical audience might react. But that audience—the department chair—has the power to decide. If Kathleen wants action, she must *concentrate* on that audience, no matter how frustrated she might feel.

How can Kathleen find out what the department chair's concerns might be? How can she address them?

Spurred by what she considered the chair's too-easy dismissal of her argument, Kathleen . . . once again immersed herself in research, but this time it focused not on subject matter (whether ASL is a distinct language) but on audience[, the department chair]. She researched the history of the foreign language requirement at her college and discovered some of the politics behind it (an old foreign language requirement had been dropped in the 1970's and reinstituted in the 1990's, partly—a math professor told her—to boost enrollments in foreign language courses). She also interviewed foreign language teachers to find out what they knew and didn't know about ASL. She discovered that many teachers [inaccurately] thought ASL was "easy to learn," so that accepting ASL would allow students . . . to avoid the rigors of a real foreign language class. Additionally, she learned that foreign language teachers valued immersing students in a foreign culture; in fact, the foreign language requirement was part of her college's effort to create a multicultural curriculum.

Now Kathleen has begun to understand what's *really* going on. She has gained insights into what the department chair is worried about, and she can write arguments that might genuinely influence him.

> This new understanding of her target audience helped Kathleen totally reconceptualize her argument. She condensed and abridged her original paper. . . . She added sections showing the difficulty of learning ASL (to counter her audience's belief that learning ASL was easy), and literature (to show how ASL met the goals of multiculturalism), and showing that the number of transfer students with ASL credits would be negligibly small (to allay fears that accepting ASL would threaten enrollments in language classes). She ended her argument with an appeal to her college's public emphasis (declared boldly in its mission statement) on eradicating social injustice and reaching out to the oppressed. She described the isolation of deaf people in a world where almost no hearing people learn ASL and argued that the deaf community on her campus could be integrated more fully into campus life if more students could "talk" with them [in their own language]. Thus, the ideas included in her new argument, the reasons selected, the evidence used, the arrangement and tone all were determined by her primary focus on persuasion.

Kathleen's second paper was good lawyering. She got inside the decision maker's thinking and showed him that what he cared about would actually benefit from doing what she wanted. This is how lawyers win cases.

Judges tend to be skeptical, but they know less about your case than you do. *Audience sense* is a writer's ability to understand a reader's thoughts. How do judges think?

Judges are *skeptical*. They will not believe a proposition until you have proved it. Their job requires that frame of mind. You earn a favorable decision only by proving—with persuasive arguments and good storytelling—that your client deserves it.

Judges *know less about your case than you do*. In most courts, judges are generalists rather than specialists. Although they know a great deal about rules of procedure (which they use constantly), they usually know much less about individual rules of substantive law (which come up less often). Thus, you will know more than the judge does about the *details* of the substantive law governing your case.

Judges want you to *teach* them your case. Think of a motion memo or brief's Argument as a *manual on how to make a particular decision*. If you show the court how the decision should be made, laying out all the steps of logic, you stand a much better chance of winning. If done in a respectful tone, this is not as presumptuous as you might think. A good Argument shows the court how to write the judicial opinion in your favor.

Truly persuasive writing speaks to each reader directly. How can you do that if you will meet judges for the first time when you appear in court for oral argument—*after* you have written and submitted your trial court memo or appellate brief?

An experienced lawyer has usually developed an instinct for how judges generally make decisions and view their responsibilities. And to some extent, the lawyer can research an individual judge by reading the judge's past opinions and talking to other lawyers who have appeared before the judge in past cases.

As a student, you might write to an imagined judge. Think of someone whose intelligence, wisdom, and judgment you deeply respect. Write to persuade this person, as though she or he were a judge with the power to decide for or against your client. Do that in your first draft. In later drafts, continue to write to this person. Rework your writing to improve its capacity to persuade your imagined judge and to satisfy the professional standards expected in your legal writing course.

§32.3   How to Test Your Arguments for Effectiveness

While rewriting, ask yourself the following questions.

1. Have you tried to persuade the court rather than just prove that you are right? Judges have the difficult responsibility of deciding. To them, a lawyer who doesn't help can seem like Calvin (the boy in the comic strip), who takes positions without worrying about others' needs.

2. Have you focused on what is most likely to persuade, and have you summarized or cut out the rest? A child opens the door to his bedroom and finds it filled from floor to ceiling with manure. With a shout of joy, the child gets a shovel and starts cleaning out the room. When asked about the shout of joy, the child exclaims, "With all that manure, there must be a pony in there somewhere!"

On its website, the North Dakota Supreme Court warns that judges "don't like to have to look for the pony."[2] Your most persuasive arguments might be *somewhere* in your writing. But unlike the boy, judges do not have time to dig around until they can find them.

Start by asking the question asked earlier in this chapter—"What will make the court want to agree with me?" Focus on your strongest contentions. Develop them fully. Leave out the weak ones. That creates a more compact document that explores more deeply the ideas that will most influence the court.

You might be tempted to throw in every good thing you can think of about your side of the case and every bad thing about your adversary's side. But don't hide the pony. Include only contentions that have a reasonable chance to persuade.

3. Have you organized persuasively? First, present the issues on which you are most likely to win. Within each issue, make your strongest arguments first, and use your best authority first.

Early impressions tend to color how later material is read, and, like most people, a judge might read most carefully at the beginning. In addition, because judges are so busy, they expect the strongest material first. If they find themselves reading weak material early, they assume that nothing better follows and might stop reading altogether. Sometimes, however, the logic of the dispute requires that the strongest material be delayed to avoid confusing the court. Some arguments are simply hard to understand unless preceded by less punchy material. In these situations, weigh your need for clarity against your need to show merit from the start.

In the Argument, the CREAC formula can be varied for persuasive reasons. For example, lawyers sometimes summarize the most compelling facts for a given issue before stating the rule. Normally, the CREAC formula puts the facts almost entirely in rule application (see Chapter 17). But if the most compelling facts are summarized before the rule, a judge can read the legal analysis in a frame of mind aroused by the story. Those same compelling facts would appear again in rule application to show how they combine with the rule to produce the conclusion.

4. Does your discussion of each issue begin with a roadmap briefly summarizing your argument? Insert the roadmap at the beginning of your analysis of the issue. For example,

> The defendant is subject to the jurisdiction of this state. Courts in other states have generally held that a defendant who maintains a website is subject to a court's jurisdiction when residents of the jurisdiction (1) have access to the website, and (2) can interact with it. The defendant maintains a website that meets this test.

---

2. *Appellate Practice Tips*, N.D. Sup. Ct., https://www.ndcourts.gov/supreme-court/filing/appellate-practice-tips (last updated Oct. 8, 2014).

This paragraph lays out a roadmap, showing the reader that in the following pages you will prove each of these propositions. To find where you prove a particular proposition, a reader can look at your point headings and subheadings (Chapter 33), which should reflect what you promise in the roadmap.

5. Have you given the court a precise statement of the rule or rules on which the case turns? In an appellate court, a judge might ask, "Counselor, what rule would you have us enforce?" The judge might be wondering how—if you win—the court should word the rule component of the CREAC formula when it writes the opinion. If the court will be making law, it wants to know exactly what rule you want it to adopt, and exactly how to phrase that rule for maximum clarity. In your brief, state the rule in the words that most precisely express it.

6. Have you handled authority well? Use the hierarchy of authority (Chapter 8) to choose the best authority. Focus on the cases and statutes that really matter. A judge does not have time to read an exhaustive explanation of every case you found. But if you cite and explain too little, the judge will not be persuaded. How do you steer a middle course between underciting and overciting and between underexplaining and overexplaining?

Predict the amount of citation and explanation a skeptical but busy judge would need. Then carefully study the available authorities. Place in a "major authority" category those that will probably *influence* the court and in a "peripheral" category those that are merely related to the issue. If you had to make the judge's decision, which authorities would be most likely to have an effect on you (including those adverse to your position)? The potentially influential authorities are the ones you must discuss. Peripheral authorities can be discarded unless they would fill holes in your argument not settled by the major authorities.

With case law, choose the few cases that most clearly make your argument. Concentrate on them and explain them thoroughly. Use other cases to settle odds and ends related to the issue. For a given issue, don't be afraid to spend 75% of your words on a few cases (for example, three) and 25% on the other cases (for example, ten). Taking a judge deeply into a compelling precedent can be very persuasive. Two, three, or four cases, thoroughly explained, can fill a judge with confidence in your argument. Thirty cases, each with no more than a sentence of explanation, are background noise.

Your goal is to give the court confidence that you are right without trying the court's patience.

7. Have you made persuasive policy arguments? Have you explained the benefits of a decision in your favor and the harm that would result from a decision in your adversary's favor? Explain how the parties have been affected by the dispute, how they would be affected by the relief you seek, or how in some other way what you seek is fundamentally fair. And go further to show that what you want will produce the best result in future cases as well, remembering that the decision could become precedent. If a court must choose between competing rules, for example, explain how the rule you urge is better than others. If you win, the decision will stand for that rule. Lawyers often introduce policy-based arguments with wording like the following:

> This court should reject the rule urged by the defendant because it would cause . . .

> Automobile rental companies [or some other category of litigants] should bear the risk of loss because . . .

> Not only is the order requested by the plaintiff not authorized by this state's case law, but such an order would also violate public policy because . . .

To learn how to make policy arguments in appellate briefs, see Chapter 38.

8. Have you attacked your adversary's authority and arguments? Hiding from your weaknesses and your adversary's strengths does not work. Your odds of winning are greatly increased if you confront them openly and boldly. Is a statute or case inconsistent with your argument in a troubling way? Adverse authority will not go away just because you ignore it. The court will know about it, and if you fail to argue against it, the court can assume that you have no defense to it.

If the adverse authority is a statute, show that the provision was not intended to govern the controversy, or that it was intended to govern it but without harm to your client. Use the canons of statutory interpretation explained in Chapter 9.

If the adverse authority is precedent, distinguish it or use other techniques explained in Chapter 10. If none of those techniques will work, you might need to attack the precedent head-on, challenging its validity on the ground that it is poorly reasoned or that changes in society or in public policy have made it unworkable. But in general, do not ask a court to overrule mandatory authority if you can win through distinguishing, reconciling, or some other skill of precedent analysis. Our legal system values precedent, and judges prefer distinguishing and reconciling precedent to overruling it.

Make your own arguments first. You will win more readily if the court's dominant impression is that you deserve to win, rather than that your adversary deserves to lose. A defensive tone can undermine an otherwise worthwhile argument. And your theory will be more easily understood if you argue it before you attack opposing arguments.

How much should you emphasize an attack on an adverse argument or authority? Give it as much emphasis as necessary to convince the judge not to rule against you. Little treatment is necessary if the point is minor and if the argument or authority is easily refuted. Say more if the point is significant or if your counteranalysis is complex.

Students sometimes have difficulty writing the transition and thesis sentences that introduce attacks on opposing arguments. Begin your counterargument in the very sentence in which you introduce the other side's argument:

> The plaintiff misconstrues § 401(d)(1). Four other circuits have already decided that § 401(d)(1) provides only for compensatory damages and not, as the plaintiff contends, for punitive damages as well. *[Follow with an analysis of the circuit cases.]*

Argue affirmatively and not defensively. These are much weaker than the example above:

> The plaintiff has argued that § 401(d)(1) provides for punitive damages, but . . .

> The plaintiff might argue that § 401(d)(1) provides for punitive damages, but . . .

A dependent clause can be useful in thesis and transition sentences:

> Although the House Judiciary Committee report notes that its bill would have provided for punitive damages, § 401(d)(1) more closely tracks the bill drafted in the Senate Judiciary Committee. Both that committee's report and the conference committee report flatly state that § 401(d)(1) does not provide for punitive damages.

9. Will a judge be able to understand your Argument quickly and easily? Think about the judge's limited time and heavy caseload. Have you written the Argument so that a busy judge will not have to struggle to understand what you are trying to say?

§32.4 Argumentation Ethics and Professionalism

The law of professional ethics—which in nearly all states includes the Model Rules of Professional Conduct—places limits on what you are permitted to do in argument.

First, and most importantly, you may not "knowingly . . . make a false statement of fact or law" to a court.[3] Judges rely on receiving well-researched and accurate information from lawyers. Without that foundation, our legal system could fail.

Second, a lawyer must inform a court of "legal authority in the *controlling jurisdiction* known to the lawyer to be *directly adverse* to the position of the [lawyer's] client and not disclosed by opposing counsel."[4] As lawyers we are *required* to present

---

3. MODEL RULES OF PROF'L CONDUCT R. 3.3(a)(1) (2013).

4. *Id.* R. 3.3(a)(2) (emphasis added).

that controlling, adverse authority to the court, but we have incentives beyond just complying with the rules. Presenting that authority to the court is an opportunity to challenge, minimize, or distinguish that authority.

Third, you may not advance a "frivolous" theory or argument, although you may make a "good faith argument for an extension, modification or reversal of existing law."[5] In a legal system like ours, where "the law is not always clear and never is static," the rules of ethics permit a lawyer to advance theories and arguments that take advantage "of the law's ambiguities and potential for change."[6] But a frivolous theory or argument—one that stands little chance of being adopted by a court—is unfair to courts and to opposing parties because it wastes their time, effort, and resources.

Exercise 32-A. Organizing Arguments

Read the motion memo in Appendix C. How well is the Argument portion of the memo organized? Explain your answer. What makes the organization effective? Are there weaknesses in the organization? Would you change the organization? If so, how?

In doing this exercise, use the following criteria (which are explained in §32.3, question 3):

- Did the logic of the situation require that certain arguments be made before others?
- Wherever possible, were the strongest arguments made first?
- Was the CREAC formula adapted effectively to persuasion?

---

5. *Id.* R. 3.1; *see also* Rule 11 of the Federal Rules of Civil Procedure and Rule 38 of the Federal Rules of Appellate Procedure. Both are printed in the rules supplement used in most Civil Procedure courses.

6. Model Rules of Prof'l Conduct R. 3.1 cmt 1.

33 Point Headings and Subheadings

Megan McCallister: You're not at all worried that something might happen to Kevin?

Buzz McCallister: No, for three reasons:
   A. I'm not that lucky,
   2. We have smoke detectors, and
   D. We live on the most boring street in the United States of America.

— Home Alone

§33.1   What Point Headings Do

Without titles, chapter names, or headings, a book would just be a sea of words from the first page to the end. Rather than leave readers adrift in a sea of words, most books include titles and headings that help readers navigate through text. Readers appreciate these tools because readers want to know what they are reading. Titles tell the reader the general subject matter; chapter names and headings indicate the specific topic of that section. Further, headings break up long blocks of text, which makes the material more reader friendly.

Written legal arguments use a similar structure to help readers focus on the topic and to make the argument text more inviting. Similar to titles and chapter names in books, point headings and subheadings in a legal argument guide readers to what they will read next. More important, in a legal argument, headings and subheading structure and strengthen your Argument.

In persuasive writing, a *point* is an independent unit within your Argument. Your reader will be better able to understand a lengthy Argument when you divide it into logical parts. Each point represents an alternative way your client can win the Argument, assuming the court agrees with that point.

For example, suppose your client is sued for breach of contract and wants to escape the contractual obligation. You might argue two alternative points: first, that the contract is void for lack of mental capacity, and second, that the contract is unenforceable for lack of consideration. Either point would persuade the court that your client should win the breach of contract claim. If the court disagrees with one point but agrees with the other, your client will still win.

Note that the number of point headings may depend upon which side of the case your client is on. For instance, in this contract dispute, the party seeking to enforce the contract would have one point heading because she would need to prevail on both the issue of mental capacity and lack of consideration to enforce the contract. Mental capacity and consideration would then be subheadings to a main heading asserting the enforceability of the contract.

Point headings (or subheadings under one main point) can also to enumerate the elements of a claim your client must prove to win—for example, each element of a criminal offense the prosecutor must prove to establish the defendant's guilt. The point heading might be a general statement that the prosecution has established each required element of the offense, and subheadings would address each of the specific elements that must be established beyond a reasonable doubt.

An effective argument must strike a balance between too many and too few points. Too many separate points can make it challenging for a reader to connect the points into an integrated and coherent whole. On the other hand, collapsing a complex argument into just one point can make your reader work too hard to sort out each step of the argument. Effective point headings unpack the argument into its logical parts that add up to support the overall legal conclusion you seek for your client.

Indeed, crafting your point headings is a good way to check for an effective structure for your Argument. If two point headings resemble each other too closely, you might really have just one point to make. And if a point heading seems impossibly complicated or difficult to understand, you might be attempting to cover too much at once. Consider dividing the single point heading into two or more point headings or subheadings.

Most important, effective point headings help persuade your reader. The point heading plants an idea in the reader's mind that you hope the reader will embrace as her own after reading that section of your Argument. Avoid overstating the point. Strive for *forceful reasonableness*—somewhere between neutral, which does nothing for your client, and too aggressive, which could harm your credibility with the court. Taking the middle ground demonstrates why the judge should have confidence that your Argument is not only legally correct but also achieves a just result.

§33.2 What Each Point Heading Should Include

An effective point heading is a *complete declaratory sentence*. A declaratory sentence is a *statement*, not a question. A point heading isn't the same as an issue statement or a question presented, which are structured as questions. Think of each point heading as the Conclusion at the beginning of the CREAC formula you follow to write the supporting legal argument for that point heading. In short, a point heading should state the legal conclusion you wish the court to reach on the particular legal issue and identify the key factual basis for that conclusion.

A point heading should include each of the following components:

- the conclusion you want the court to draw or the ruling you want the court to make
- a reference to the relevant legal rule or legal issue
- the essential fact or facts showing why the legal issue should be resolved for your client

First, identify the legal conclusion you want the court to reach or the specific ruling you want for your client.

For example, a point heading that refers to the client's desired *legal conclusion* in a contract dispute might look like this:

The Complaint Is Legally Insufficient Because It Fails to Allege Any Facts That Could Be Construed as an Offer.

The legal conclusion you want the court to reach for your client is a holding that the complaint is insufficient.

In the alternative, your point heading can refer to the *specific ruling* you want the court to make, like this:

The Court Should Dismiss the Complaint Because It Fails to Allege Any Facts That Could Be Construed as an Offer.

This alternative specifically refers the court to the procedural posture (a pending motion to dismiss the claim) and suggests the specific action you want the court to take.

Each of these point headings could be followed by identical legal arguments. The two differ only in that the first specifically asks the court to draw a legal conclusion (the complaint is legally insufficient to support a breach of contract action) and implies the result the writer wants from the court (dismissal of the complaint), while the second specifically asks for the desired result (dismissal) and implies the desired legal conclusion (the complaint is legally insufficient).

Second, be sure your point heading identifies the legal rule or issue you need the court to resolve. In the example above, the point headings allude to the legal issue by referring to an offer as an essential element in contract formation. Identifying the relevant legal rule or issue resembles the analysis you use to find the applicable legal rule when reading a case for your other classes.

Third, include the essential fact or facts that support the conclusion or result you seek. It isn't necessary to list every detailed fact supporting your argument in the heading. Instead, summarize the facts relevant to the essential point that particular section of your Argument will address. Finding those facts resembles identifying determinative facts in a judicial opinion. What specific facts make your client's case unique or especially difficult to decide? What facts make your client a winner in this part of your Argument? What facts, if changed, would result in a different conclusion? In the example above, the point heading relates the essential facts by noting the *absence* of allegations in the complaint that are necessary for an enforceable contract.

Don't go too far in defining the action you want the court to take in one point heading. Sometimes a single point heading can appropriately ask for all the relief your client desires. If this section of your Argument, standing alone, justifies granting or denying a motion, or justifies reversing a trial court decision, ask for that result. For example, if you represent a criminal defendant charged with burglary, you can win an acquittal if you defeat just one element of the criminal offense. A single point heading might challenge the sufficiency of the evidence to prove that your client had the intent to commit a felony before breaking and entering a dwelling. Because specific intent to commit a felony is an essential element of the offense, your client can win if you defeat just that one element of the prosecution's case.

But often the point you are working on will be just one of several building blocks in your Argument and would not be enough on its own for your client to win the entire motion or appeal. For that kind of argument, you may need multiple point headings or a point heading that is further divided into subheadings.

§33.3   Subheadings

While a point heading may state a dispositive point of your Argument, subheadings often identify logical steps necessary to support the main point heading. Unless an argument point is relatively short or straightforward, you can clarify each argument point by subdividing it with subheadings. Then, under each subheading, develop the reasons to support that logical step in reaching the legal conclusion or result you have identified in the point heading.

For example, assume you want to convince the court that your client deserves compensatory damages after a law student smashed into the back end of your client's new Lexus after a late night of studying before final exams. Your main point heading would refer to your client's negligence claim and state that your client is entitled to an award of compensatory damages.

You would then craft four subheadings, each addressing one element of negligence and the key facts supporting a favorable result on each element: (A) the student owed a duty of care to your client; (B) the student breached that duty by carelessly smashing into your client's car; (C) the collision was the cause-in-fact and proximate cause of her harm; and (D) she sustained property damage to her car. If the court agrees with you on every subheading, those elements add up to the legal conclusion you want.

None of the subheadings *standing alone* will result in a winning claim for your client because negligence requires a finding in her favor on *all four* elements. For that reason, the main point heading focuses on the overall negligence claim for compensatory damages. Each subheading demonstrates how she can meet every essential element of that claim, adding up to a winning case for compensatory damages for the defendant's negligence.

But avoid going overboard with subheadings. Too many subheadings, with only two or three paragraphs under each one, can result in a choppy, ineffective Argument that fails to persuade.

§33.4 Organizing Your Point Headings and Subheadings

Organize your point headings and subheadings in traditional outline format, using Roman numerals for main point headings, capital letters for subheadings, and Arabic numbers (if necessary) for sub-subheadings. Be sure your headings are worded, punctuated, and indented *identically* in the body of your brief as well as your table of contents. The following diagram shows how to designate and organize your headings:

I.   Point Heading. . . .
     A.   *Subheading.* . . .
     B.   *Subheading.* . . .
         1. Sub-subheading. . . .
         2. Sub-subheading. . . .
     C.   *Subheading.* . . .
II.   Point Heading. . . .
III.   Point Heading. . . .
     A.   *Subheading.* . . .
     B.   *Subheading.* . . .

The emphasis (bold or italics) and indentation differ for each level of heading, which helps the reader follow each division and sub-division of your argument. The table of contents, which includes these headings, reveals the overall structure and organization of your Argument for your reader's benefit—an important tool for your reader, and a valuable opportunity for you to start persuading.

§33.5   How to Test Your Point Headings for Effectiveness

While rewriting, ask the following questions.

1. Do your headings and subheadings lay out a complete, logically sequenced, and persuasive outline of your Argument?   Many judges read the point headings *before reading any other part* of a memo or brief. In an appellate brief, a judge generally reads them all at once in the table of contents because they form an outline of the Argument. In a motion memo, a judge often reads the headings first by leafing through the Argument section. Consequently, well-crafted point headings and subheadings introduce and outline your case's legal theory, making them important persuasive tools. Your goal in crafting headings and subheadings is to persuade the judge to rule in your client's favor by the time the judge finishes reading *only* your Argument headings. The rest of your Argument should reinforce the headings' conclusions.

Some lawyers draft the headings before writing the full Argument. Others write the headings and the supporting Argument at the same time. Either approach is acceptable. Just remember that revision is key to good drafting. Once you compile the headings and subheadings in the table of contents of an appellate brief, you might find you need to redraft them to fill in gaps or resolve inconsistencies that aren't apparent when the headings are scattered around in the Argument. Even in a motion memo without a table of contents, you might find it helpful to copy and paste your headings into a separate document (without the supporting argument) so you can review and revise them for effectiveness. Chances are the court will read your headings first, even if they aren't compiled in a separate table of contents. Take every opportunity to persuade the court by redrafting and polishing your headings to summarize your Argument step by step.

2. Do you have an appropriate number of point headings and subheadings—neither too many nor too few?   Too many headings overwhelm the reader with complexity and interrupt the flow of your Argument. Too few weaken your Argument by insufficiently breaking down your legal reasoning and by failing to accurately outline your Argument. Use subheadings to subdivide the argument when a point heading requires separate logical steps in reasoning to persuade the court to reach the result you seek.

3. Is each heading or subheading a single sentence that a reader can immediately understand? Readers simply ignore headings that are too long or dense. Because an effective point heading includes a request for relief, a reference to the legal rule or issue, and at least one essential fact, a single heading can easily become unreadable. Edit your headings to convey the point as clearly and concisely as possible. A single heading cannot fully develop the argument. Instead, it summarizes the essence of the argument and introduces what comes next: the supporting rule explanation and detailed rule application. If too long, a heading discourages your audience from reading further. Effective point headings are short, complete, and case-specific, priming your reader for persuasion.

4. Does each point heading identify the legal conclusion or judicial decision you want? Point headings should not leave the judge wondering what you want the court to do. Each point heading *must* clearly state your client's desired result or legal conclusion for that part of your Argument. Because subheadings divide up the argument supporting and reinforcing each point heading, they only need to address any conclusion stemming from *just* that sub-point.

5. Does each point heading allude to the relevant legal rule? A point heading need not state the legal rule completely. Often it is enough to allude to the legal concept involved. But be specific. For example, assume your brief or motion memo challenges whether the parties entered into an enforceable contract, and this part addresses whether an offer was ever made. Your point heading should use the more specific word "offer" rather than a broader term like "contract formation," which could include other legal concepts like "acceptance" and "meeting of the minds."

6. Does each point heading include at least one essential fact? Beginning lawyers often write point headings that simply restate the applicable legal rule. An effective point heading isolates the key facts that *persuade* the court to reach the desired legal conclusion *given the particular facts of this unique case*. The court may agree with your statement of the applicable legal rule, but that alone is not sufficient to persuade the court to rule in your client's favor. Identify the persuasive facts favoring your client's position, and deliver them on a silver platter to the court by clearly and concisely integrating them with the relevant legal rule in the point headings. They must show the court how the legal rule applies to the determinative facts to support the legal conclusion you seek.

7. Are your headings appropriately numbered and subdivided? Use Roman numerals, letters, and numbers as you would in a formal outline. Under a point heading, never use just one subheading. Remember that subheadings *divide* the argument on that point to show each of its supporting logical steps, which implies more than one step in the legal reasoning. If you find yourself with just one subheading under a point heading, look again at the legal rule and reconsider whether you need any subheadings. If you have trouble coming up with at least two subheadings, try to figure out whether it helps your reader to subdivide that section. Avoid subdividing the flow of your argument without good reason.

8. Are your headings appropriately typeset? Traditionally, lawyers used ALL CAPITAL LETTERS to add emphasis to point headings when typewriters were used for preparing legal briefs. Now that computers allow lawyers to emphasize point headings in other ways, all-caps have fallen out of favor,[1] and practitioners more typically use bold type instead of all-caps.[2] Similarly, subheadings were once <u>underlined</u> because typewriters weren't capable of adding any other kind of emphasis. Today, most lawyers use either *italics* or underlining (but never both) for subheadings.

In subheadings, and in headings that aren't all-capped, many lawyers capitalize the first letter of each significant word, as you would in the title of a book. Some lawyers capitalize only the first word of the sentence. Always single-space point headings so they stand out on the page.

Exercise 33-A. Evaluating Point Headings

The U.S. Supreme Court ruled in *Riley v. California*[3] that as a general rule, police officers may not search the digital contents of an arrestee's cell phone without first securing a search warrant. Point headings from the petitioner's and respondent's Supreme Court briefs are reprinted below as they appeared in each brief's table of contents.

Critique each set of point headings in light of what you have read in this chapter. How could the brief writers have improved them? Did the writers make the right choices in balancing completeness against brevity? If you had been on the Court when the case was decided, which side of the case would you have found more persuasive based *solely* on the point headings and subheadings? Which party's headings are easier to read? What other changes would you make. Explain your answers.

---

1. An additional reason to avoid all capital letters is because, in the age of social media, all caps is deemed shouting. You would not want to shout at a judge in court or in a brief.

2. *See* Ruth Anne Robbins, *Painting with Print: Incorporating Concepts of Typographic and Layout Design into the Text of Legal Writing Documents*, 2 J. ALWD 108, 115-16 (2004) (making the case that the use of all-caps in brief headings slows down reading speed); PRACTITIONER'S HANDBOOK FOR APPEALS TO THE UNITED STATES COURT OF APPEALS FOR THE SEVENTH CIRCUIT 133, 141, 145 (2017), http://www.ca7.uscourts.gov/forms/Handbook.pdf.

3. 573 U.S. 373 (2014). The petitioner's opening brief is available on Westlaw at 2014 WL 844599. The respondent's brief is available at 2014 WL 1348466.

Petitioner's Brief:

I. The Search of the Digital Contents of Petitioner's Smart Phone Exceeded The Bounds of a Legitimate Search Incident to Arrest.
   A. The Search Was Unnecessary to Serve Any Legitimate Governmental Interest.
      1. Digital Data Does Not Threaten Officer Safety.
      2. Once Seized, It Is Unnecessary to Search A Smart Phone Without a Warrant to Preserve Evidence.
   B. The Degree of Intrusiveness of the Search of Petitioner's Phone Rendered the Search Unreasonable.
      1. Smart Phones Hold Extraordinary Amounts of Sensitive Personal Information.
      2. Smart Phones Hold Information That Implicates First Amendment Concerns.
   C. Limiting Searches of Smart Phones to Situations in Which Officers Believe Such Phones Contain Evidence of the Crime of Arrest Would Not Solve the Constitutional Problems Inherent in Such Searches.
II. The Search of Petitioner's Phone At The Stationhouse Was Too Remote from His Arrest to Qualify as a Search Incident to Arrest.

Respondent's Brief:

I. Under Existing Law, the Police Were Entitled to Search Photos and Videos on Petitioner's Phone as an Incident to His Lawful Arrest.
   A. The Law Has Long Allowed Police to Search Objects Found on the Person of an Individual Who Is Lawfully Arrested.
   B. Cases Addressing Searches of the Area of an Arrest Have Not Questioned the Categorical Rule Applicable to the Arrestee's Person and Effects.
   C. The Evidence at Issue Here Was Properly Obtained Under Any Standard.
      1. The Photos and Videos Were Found in Searches of an Object Recovered from Petitioner's Person During His Arrest.
      2. The Searches Here Were Reasonably Related to the Crime of Arrest.
      3. A Cell Phone Such as Petitioner's Presents Safety, Identification, and Evidentiary Issues at Least as Powerful as Those Relating to Other Items Routinely Seized and Searched Incident to Arrest.
         a. Safety and Identification
         b. Preservation of Evidence

II. The Technological Advances That Petitioner Highlights Do Not Warrant the Adoption of Special Rules for Cell Phones in This Case.
    A. The Information Taken from Petitioner's Phone Is Not Fundamentally Different from That Found in Other Searches Incident to Arrest.
    B. The Circumstances of This Case Suggest No Basis for Specially Limiting Cell Phone Searches Incident to Arrests.

Exercise 33-B. Creating a Point Heading

Part 1. For a motion memo or brief that your professor has assigned, select one point you have written about or will be writing about. Before writing the heading for that point, identify words or phrases for each entry in the following chart:

Relief or conclusion requested

Relevant legal rule or issue

Essential determinative fact(s)

Part 2. Now combine these words and phrases in several alternative configurations to see which produces the most effective point heading.

Part 3. Write persuasive subheadings as needed to subdivide the argument into the logical steps in reasoning the court must follow to grant the requested relief or to reach the desired legal conclusion.

Exercise 33-C. Revising Point Headings

The point headings below were drafted by first-year law students based upon the following facts and legal issues. First, revise each point heading for completeness to be sure it includes all necessary components. Second, revise the headings for persuasiveness. Finally, edit them for clarity and conciseness.

Facts: A California Highway Patrol officer spotted Megan Goering driving her copper red 2007 Mazda Miata just outside the city limits of Los Angeles. While driving, Ms. Goering was wearing Google Glass, an eyeglass-like device that allows a wearer to view a small video display in the upper-right corner of her field of vision. After the officer stopped her car, he asked Ms. Goering whether she was viewing a video display while driving. She responded that she was, but only to follow directions to her ultimate destination using the Google Maps website. Her Miata convertible doesn't have an installed GPS navigation system. The officer cited her for violating the following statute. Should the court dismiss the charge?

California Vehicle Code § 27602

(a) A person shall not drive a motor vehicle if a television receiver, a video monitor, or a television or video screen, or any other similar means of visually displaying a television broadcast or video signal that produces entertainment or business applications, is operating and is located in the motor vehicle at a point forward of the back of the driver's seat, or is operating and the monitor, screen, or display is visible to the driver while driving the motor vehicle.

(b) Subdivision (a) does not apply to the following equipment when installed in a vehicle:

(1) A vehicle information display.

(2) A global positioning display.

(3) A mapping display.

(4) A visual display used to enhance or supplement the driver's view forward, behind, or to the sides of a motor vehicle for the purpose of maneuvering the vehicle.

(5) A television receiver, video monitor, television or video screen, or any other similar means of visually displaying a television broadcast or video signal, if that equipment satisfies one of the following requirements:

(A) The equipment has an interlock device that, when the motor vehicle is driven, disables the equipment for all uses except as a visual display as described in paragraphs (1) to (4), inclusive.

(B) The equipment is designed, operated, and configured in a manner that prevents the driver of the motor vehicle from viewing the television broadcast or video signal while operating the vehicle in a safe and reasonable manner.

Student A (representing the defendant)

I.   The court should dismiss the count alleging a violation of California Vehicle Code § 27602 because the defendant was using Google Glass as a mapping display, which is one of the exceptions within the statute.

Student B (representing the state)

I.   The court should deny the defendant's motion to dismiss the traffic citation because the product used by the defendant, Google Glass, is a means of visually displaying a television broadcast or video signal, which is prohibited by the traffic statute.

II. The court should deny the defendant's motion to dismiss the traffic citation because the Google Glass product was being operated at the time of the traffic stop and was located at a point forward of the back of the driver's seat.

III. The court should deny the defendant's motion to dismiss the traffic citation because the Google Glass product was not installed in the vehicle while the defendant was using the mapping display.

Student C (representing the state)

I.   The California court should deny defendant driver's Motion to Dismiss because she violated a California traffic statute by viewing a monitor or video display while driving.

     A. The court should deny defendant driver's Motion to Dismiss because the visual display that her use of Google Glass provided was at a point forward of the back of the driver's seat.

     B. The court should deny defendant driver's Motion to Dismiss because her use of Google Glass provided a display visible to defendant driver while she was operating her Miata.

     C. The court should deny defendant driver's Motion to Dismiss because the visual display that Google Glass provided her was not one that has been installed in Miata.

Part 10

Appellate Briefs and Oral Argument

34 Appellate Practice

§34.1   Introduction to Appeals

When a lower court makes its final judgment, decree, or order, that final action can be appealed. In some limited cases a court's action before a final judgment can also be appealed. This chapter explains the process for appeals from final decisions.

The appellate process performs two functions. One is correcting errors made by trial courts. The other is making new law and clarifying existing law through the precedents created by appellate decisions. A lower appellate court tends to view its job largely as error correction, although it necessarily engages in some law formation and clarification because appellate decisions are precedents. Higher appellate courts, on the other hand, generally view their work primarily as making and clarifying law.

The party who appeals is the *appellant* or the *petitioner*, and the opposing party is the *appellee* or *respondent*, depending on local court rules and the type of appeal. Before writing a brief, check the court's rules for the terms appropriate to your type of appeal. If you cannot find the answer, see how the court referred to parties in a reported case that *procedurally* resembles your own.

§34.2   The Roles of the Brief and the Oral Argument

The brief and oral argument perform different functions. Each is crucial, but in a different way.

In a brief, you can tell the client's story and make the client's arguments in persuasive detail. A successful brief not only persuades the judge that your client should win, but it also explains to the judge why to make the decision and how to justify it in an opinion. A judge may use the brief when preparing for oral argument, deciding whether to reverse or affirm, preparing for the conference with other judges, and writing the opinion.

The oral argument can do two things better than the brief: First, in oral argument you can more immediately motivate the court by focusing on the most important ideas—the few facts, rules, and policies that most make your case compelling. Second, in oral argument you can try to discover, through the bench's questions, each judge's doubts. And, on the spot, you can explain exactly why those doubts should not prevent a ruling in your favor. Oral argument, in fact, is your only opportunity to learn directly from the judges the problems they have with your arguments.

But oral argument also has a significant disadvantage: It lasts only a few minutes, and memories of it can fade. The brief, on the other hand, has permanence. It is always among the judge's working materials, and it "speaks from the time it is filed and continues through oral argument, conference, and opinion writing."[1]

The brief and oral argument differ in another important way. Detail is communicated best in writing, which can be studied. But the spontaneity of conversation during oral argument encourages dialogue and lends itself to the broad sweep of underlying ideas.

§34.3   How Judges Read Appellate Briefs

In a single month, an appellate judge might hear oral arguments and confer with colleagues on several dozen appeals. For each appeal, the judge will read at least two briefs or, in multiparty cases or public interest cases, perhaps a half-dozen briefs or more, together with portions of the record. The judge and her clerks will also draft memoranda to her colleagues summarizing the facts, explaining the legal issues, and proposing a resolution. The judge will write majority opinions in a portion of the appeals. In addition, the judge may write several concurring or dissenting opinions. The judge will also read opinions drafted by other judges and at times will write memoranda to colleagues suggesting changes in those opinions. And the judge will spend a fair amount of time reading some of the cases and statutes cited in all these briefs and draft opinions.

With all this work, the typical appellate judge would find it a luxury to spend as much as an hour reading the average brief. The time available is often no more than half an hour. That is why briefs, although sometimes lengthy, must be written carefully to persuade with the least possible time and effort from the reader.

---

1. Herbert Funk Goodrich, *A Case on Appeal—A Judge's View* (1952), *reprinted in* A CASE ON APPEAL 10-11 (Joint Comm. on Continuing Legal Educ. of A.L.I. & A.B.A., 4th ed. 1967).

How does a judge read a brief? The answer varies from judge to judge, but the following is not unusual:

> Usually I first read both parties' statements of the questions presented; then I read the appellant's statement of the general nature of the controversy. Then I look at his outline of argument to see what points he makes. Then I look at the appellee's outline of argument to see what he is going to do in reply. . . . Then I read the appellant's statement of the facts and the appellee's statement. Thereafter I examine the two briefs one point at a time, first the appellant's and then the appellee's, on the first point; then both briefs on the second point, etc. If the point is an obvious one, or if one side or the other seems to be wholly without strength on it, I do not spend too much time on that point in my first study. On the really contested points I study both sides, read the cases, and, if facts are critical check the record references.[2]

Other judges might read the parts of a brief in a different sequence—perhaps reading the point headings before anything else—and a given judge might vary the sequence from case to case. But several things are true regardless of the judge's work habits.

First, you write for several different readers. Depending on the court, an appeal might be decided by a bench of from three to nine judges. Briefs are also read by law clerks or research attorneys who assist the judges by studying the briefs and recommending decisions.

Second, briefs—like memos—are not necessarily read from beginning to end at a single sitting. They are read in chunks, at different times, depending on the needs of the reader. You probably read an appliance or automobile owner's manual in pretty much the same way, and a good brief is a manual for making a decision.

Finally, a brief is read for different reasons at different times, depending on who is reading and when. The judges will read or at least scan it in preparation for oral argument. Afterward, they will read the brief again to decide how to vote. One judge will be assigned to write the court's opinion, and that judge will reread various portions of the brief several times, looking for the detail needed to justify and explain the decision. And all along the way, the judges will be assisted by law clerks who check the details of the brief while the judges focus on the broader principles. Each segment of the brief must be written to satisfy all of these purposes.

---

2. E. Barrett Prettyman, *Some Observations Concerning Appellate Advocacy*, 39 Va. L. Rev. 285, 296 (1953).

35 Writing the Appellate Brief

§35.1 Appellate Brief Format

Although rules on format differ from court to court, the required structure commonly includes the following. Some courts require additional material, such as a statement specifying how the court acquired jurisdiction over the appeal in question.

1. a cover page
2. a Table of Contents (sometimes called an Index)
3. a Table of Authorities
4. the words of a constitutional provision, statute, administrative regulation, or court rule—if the appeal rests on interpreting those words
5. a Preliminary Statement (also called Proceedings Below or Nature of the Proceedings)
6. a Question Presented or Questions Presented (also called Statement of the Issues)
7. a Statement of the Case
8. a Summary of Argument
9. an Argument, broken up with point headings and subheadings
10. a Conclusion

See the brief in Appendix D.

The **cover page** includes the caption, followed by the document's title—such as "BRIEF FOR APPELLANT"—and the name, address, and telephone number of the lawyer submitting the brief. The caption includes the name of the appellate court, the appellate court's docket number, the court from where the appeal originated, and the names of the parties and their procedural designations (appellant, appellee, etc.) in the appellate court. The cover page doesn't use a page number.

The **Table of Contents** begins on the page after the cover page. It lists all of the components of the brief (except the cover page and the Table of Contents itself); reproduces the point headings and subheadings from the Argument; and sets out the page number on which each component, point, or subpoint begins.

The **Table of Authorities** appears on the first page after the Table of Contents. It lists the cases, statutes, and other authorities cited in the Argument together with every page number in the brief where each listed authority is cited.

The **Constitutional Provisions, Statutes, Regulations, and Court Rules Involved** specifies any enacted law crucial to the appeal and quotes the sections at issue. If a brief does not involve a crucial provision, omit this section. A provision is crucial to the appeal if the parties disagree about its meaning and *if the court cannot dispose of the appeal without resolving the disagreement.* A court rule that merely provides for the type of motion made below is not critical to the appeal unless the parties disagree about the rule's meaning and the appellate court has been asked to resolve the disagreement. Phrase the heading of this section of the brief to fit its content. If, for example, the First Amendment—and nothing else—is at issue, the heading would read "Constitutional Provision Involved" with no mention of statutes, regulations, or court rules.

The **Preliminary Statement** briefly sets out the appeal's procedural posture by explaining who the parties are, listing the relevant procedural events, and describing the judgment or order appealed from. (If a party is a government or a large, well-known organization, you don't need to explain who that party is.) The Preliminary Statement can also describe the reasoning of the court below and identify the grounds on which that court's judgment or order is challenged on appeal. The Preliminary Statement should tell the court why the appeal is before it and specify the type of decision you want the court to make. You can usually accomplish this in less than a page. Many lawyers add a paragraph summarizing their own arguments.

This portion of the brief goes by different names in different courts. If it isn't titled "Preliminary Statement," the heading might read "Proceedings Below," "Nature of the Proceedings," or the like. In some courts, the Preliminary Statement is called the "Statement of the Case" (and the client's story is told elsewhere in the brief in a "Statement of Facts").

A persuasive **Question Presented** is explained in Chapter 37.

The **Statement of the Case** is explained in Chapters 29 through 31.

A **Summary of the Argument** is what its name implies. The point headings and subheadings, as they appear in the Table of Contents, *outline* the Argument. The Summary, on the other hand, *condenses* the Argument into a few paragraphs—perhaps one paragraph per issue—with more explanation than will fit into headings. The Summary should not merely repeat the point headings, and it should not include citations to legal authority. This is the first place in the brief where you can purely argue why your client should prevail. Seize this opportunity to use the case's facts to explain to the court the legal conclusion it should reach.

The **Argument** and its point headings are explained in Chapters 32 and 33.

Although some lawyers use the **Conclusion** to reargue and resummarize the theory of the appeal, it is better to limit the conclusion to a one- to three-sentence reiteration of the relief you want together with the ground on which that relief would be based. For example:

> For all the foregoing reasons, the Circuit Court's order dismissing the complaint should be affirmed because the complaint does not state a cause of action.

The primary purpose of the Conclusion is to remind judges exactly what you want them to do.

Every court has rules governing the contents of briefs and other submitted documents. The rules are designed to make briefs easier for judges to use, and judges understandably become exasperated when the rules are ignored. Egregious violations of court rules can result in the court's striking the brief, in financial penalties imposed on the lawyer, and even in dismissal of the appeal. Ignore these rules at your—and your client's—peril.

§35.2   Three Brief-Writing Suggestions

1. Start writing before you finish the research. "I can't start writing yet," you might say. "I haven't found *all* the cases." But waiting until you find all the cases can feed procrastination. Until you start writing, you can't know for sure what kind of cases you should be looking for.

Certainly in the beginning you must cast a wide net in researching. But at some point researching like a vacuum cleaner becomes inefficient. Starting to write helps you identify that point because writing and thinking are inseparable. The act of writing will help you focus on what really matters to the arguments you must make and thus show you where you need more authority.

Start writing as soon as you have enough research to know roughly what your theory will be. When you go back into research after doing some writing, you can focus on what you really need. Research will take less time and effort if you know what you're looking for.

2. Start practicing oral argument before you finish writing the brief. It might seem illogical to spend time on oral argument when you're up against a deadline with the brief. But many students discover that when they *talk* about a complicated subject, they say surprisingly interesting and perceptive things—and come to valuable insights—because talking helps them understand more deeply. Many people learn not just by reading and listening, but also by talking and doing. The best reason for practicing oral argument early is to help you write a better brief.

Suppose you disregard this advice. You submit your final draft brief, rest for a few days, and then start developing an oral argument. As you practice, you come up with some terrific wording and wish you could put it in the brief—but by then it is too late.

3. Think of brief writing as a collection of small tasks rather than as one huge task.   A huge task can be intimidating and cause procrastination. But a collection of smaller tasks can be done one by one.

"The secret to good brief writing is to write small pieces."[1] You haven't been given one big assignment. You have been given several smaller ones: a Question Presented, a Statement of the Case, and so on. You can write all these things separately—as separate word processing files, if you prefer—and then stitch them together into a single document. Even the Argument can become two or more smaller jobs. If you have two points, writing each of them is a separate task. But be careful to coordinate all these smaller tasks so that the resulting brief is coherent and internally consistent.

§35.3   What Part of the Brief to Write First

Just as a judge doesn't read a brief from beginning to end, neither does a lawyer write it that way. The Table of Contents and Table of Authorities are always done last (see the last section in this chapter for why). The order in which the other parts are written differs from lawyer to lawyer and from appeal to appeal because one lawyer's work habits aren't necessarily effective for someone else, and because an effective lawyer adapts to the individual task at hand. Eventually, you will settle into a range of work habits that work for you. Your first brief is an opportunity to begin to understand yourself in that way.

To help you start, consider two very different methods of writing a brief.

Model I	Model II
1. point headings	1. Questions Presented
2. Argument	2. Statement of the Case
3. Statement of the Case	3. point headings
4. Questions Presented	4. Argument
5. rest of brief	5. rest of brief

A lawyer who uses Model I writes point headings and subheadings first as a way of outlining the Argument. This lawyer might draft the Statement of the Case after writing the Argument on the theory that writing the Argument reveals which facts have the most legal significance. The Questions Presented would be written

---

1. John T. Gaubatz & Taylor Mattis, The Moot Court Book: A Student Guide to Appellate Advocacy 41 (3d ed. 1994).

afterward because the lawyer identifies the most essential facts—the ones recited in the Questions—while working out the Argument and the Statement of the Case.

But a lawyer using Model II would begin the first draft by writing the Questions Presented in the belief that the other parts of the brief will be more focused if the issues are first precisely defined. A lawyer who uses this model writes the Statement of the Case next, using it to work out the details of the theory of the appeal (which the Model I lawyer does while writing the Argument). Both lawyers draft the point headings before the Argument because the Argument is easier to write in segments (which the headings create).

A lawyer with flexible work habits might use Model I in an appeal with difficult and complex legal issues and authority and Model II in a more fact-sensitive appeal. Some lawyers write the Question Presented and the Statement of the Case (and sometimes even the Argument) simultaneously.

§35.4 The Last Step: Creating the Table of Contents and the Table of Authorities

Why you should create the Tables last. For pagination purposes, a brief is broken down into two parts. The two Tables (sometimes called the "front matter") are paginated in lowercase roman numerals ("i," "ii," "iii," and so on). The rest of the brief (the "body") is paginated separately in arabic numbers, beginning with "1," on the first page immediately following the Tables.

This might seem odd. But it has a very practical purpose. Because the Tables must include page references to the body, *any* change in the body—even a change of only a few words—can alter the page breaks and require changes in the Tables. And because you can't know how many pages the Tables will occupy until you're ready to print them, the body must begin on page 1. The only efficient solution is to use two separate paginations: lowercase roman numbers for the Tables and Arabic numbers for the body. (The same thing is done for the same reasons in your textbooks, including this one. Look at the pages *preceding* Chapter 1.)

What the Table of Authorities should look like. Although the Table of Contents is easy to visualize and put together, the Table of Authorities is more complicated. In the Table of Authorities, list a complete cite for every authority together with the page number for every place in the brief where the authority is cited or discussed. If you rely very heavily on certain authorities, place an asterisk to the left of the citations and in a footnote identify them as "authorities chiefly relied on" or similar words to the same effect. Plan plenty of time to create the Table of Authorities as it takes more effort than you might imagine.[2]

---

2. Resist the urge to use word-processing macros or tools to generate either a Table of Authorities or Table of Contents. Doing so can introduce coding into the text that might not appear properly in the final submitted document.

The Table of Authorities is usually broken down into sections headed "Cases," "Statutes," and perhaps "Other Authorities." List cases in alphabetical order. If constitutional provisions, court rules, administrative regulations, or legislative histories are cited in the brief, you can add one or more extra sections for them. Sometimes legislative histories are included with statutes. Some lawyers include constitutional provisions with statutes. Others put them in a separate section. The heading should reflect where they are. "Other Authorities" is reserved for secondary authorities, such as restatements, treatises, and law review articles.

36 Handling Standards of Review

Appellate judges aren't allowed to reverse merely because they disagree with what a lower court did. Instead, they can reverse only when the relevant standard of review allows them to do so. The standard of review controls the appellate court's decision. For that reason, it's essential to craft your arguments with the appropriate standard of review in mind. Arguing with the wrong standard of review can render much of your argument superfluous or unhelpful to the court. Appellate judges become annoyed when lawyers write and speak as though standards of review don't exist.

§36.1 The Three Main Standards of Review

The type of ruling made by a trial court determines the standard of review on appeal. The three main standards of review are:

- *de novo* review for issues of law
- *clear error* review for issues of fact
- *abuse of discretion* review for discretionary issues

Other standards of review exist, but these are the most important ones.

Issues of law—de novo review. A trial court decides an issue of law when it interprets the law or decides what the law is. For example, when a trial judge instructs the jury at the end of a trial, the judge explains the law the jury must follow in reaching a verdict. When deciding what to say to the jury, the judge decides a pure issue of law. If the jury instruction accurately states the law, the trial judge has not committed error. But if the instruction is wrong, the judge has erroneously decided an issue of law and could be reversed on appeal.

In reviewing a trial court's ruling on an issue of law, an appellate court measures error simply by asking whether it would have interpreted the law in the same way the trial court did. *De novo* is the term used in federal courts for this standard of review. In Latin, it means to do "from the beginning" or "as though new." Some states use other phrases, such as "independent and nondeferential review." These terms mean the same thing. If the trial court interpreted the law incorrectly, an appellate court can reverse.

When you're assigned to write an appellate brief, look first for the type of decision the trial court made. If it is one of the following, you have an issue of law subject to de novo review:

- an order dismissing a plaintiff's complaint or other pleading
- a summary judgment
- a directed verdict
- a jury instruction
- a judgment notwithstanding the verdict
- a decision denying a motion or request for any of the above

Many other trial court decisions resolve issues of law, but these are the big ones.

Most law school appellate brief assignments involve de novo standards of review. If that's true of your assignment, you probably won't have much difficulty arguing within the standard. A de novo standard is neutral, like a pane of clear glass through which light passes without distortion. The other standards (explained below) are like filters and lenses that modify the image because they defer to the trial court, which a de novo standard does not.

With a question of law there's no reason to defer in any way to the trial court. An appellate court can decide an issue of law at least as well as a trial court can, and the appellate court might do a better job because an appeal is decided by several judges as opposed to a single judge in the trial court.

Issues of fact—review for clear error. An issue of fact is a question about what happened factually between the parties. For example, was the defendant's gun loaded or unloaded at the time of the crime? Which witness should be believed: the one who testified that the defendant loaded the gun with bullets just before the crime, or the one who testified that the defendant instead emptied the gun of bullets?

Although these fact issues and many others would typically be decided by a jury, some fact issues are decided by a trial court judge. When a law school appellate brief assignment includes a fact issue, it usually involves a bench trial or a pretrial motion. A bench trial is one in which a judge decides the facts without a jury.

Decisions on pretrial motions are also decided by the judge without a jury. A pretrial motion asks the judge to make a procedural decision before the trial begins. For example, if a criminal defendant moves to suppress his confession, the defendant is asking the judge to exclude the confession from the evidence admitted at trial. If the defendant claims that he confessed only because a police officer threatened to beat him up, the judge would decide whether the police officer really did that—which is a fact issue.

Don't confuse a fact issue with a law issue. An issue of fact arises when there is a dispute whether a fact occurred. An issue of law arises when the dispute is over the legal significance of that fact. For example, suppose a defendant claims that the police officer bragged that he is an amateur boxer who is so good at punching opponents that he almost qualified for the U.S. boxing team at the last Olympics.

fact issue: Did the police officer brag in the defendant's presence?

law issue: Does that kind of bragging violate the defendant's Fifth Amendment right against forced confessions?

When a trial judge's findings of fact are challenged on appeal, the appellate court will reverse only if the trial judge's decision was "clearly erroneous."[1] It's not enough that the trial court was wrong. A deeper level of error is required for reversal. The error must be one a reasonable fact finder could not have reached.

Typically, courts say that they will reverse only if they "are left with a definite and firm conviction that a mistake has been made."[2] The Seventh Circuit has put it more bluntly: "To be clearly erroneous, a decision must strike us as more than just maybe or probably wrong; it must . . . strike us as wrong with the force of a five-week-old, unrefrigerated, dead fish."[3] Other courts use less vivid language to express the same idea.

However you express it, this is a very difficult standard for an appellant to satisfy. Appellate courts defer to the trial court's factual determinations because the trial judge saw and heard the witnesses testify while appellate courts can only read the trial court's transcript, which appellate judges describe as a "cold record."

Discretionary issues—review for abuse of discretion. Many procedural issues permit a trial judge to exercise discretion. Here is a typical appellate court formulation of what that means:

When we say that . . . a district court has discretion to grant or deny a motion, we do not mean that the district court may do whatever pleases it. The phrase means instead that *the court has a range of choice, and that its decision will not be disturbed as*

---

1. *See, e.g.,* Fed. R. Civ. P. 52(a).
2. *United States v. Brown,* 156 F.3d 813, 816 (8th Cir. 1998).
3. *Parts & Elec. Motors, Inc. v. Sterling Elec., Inc.,* 866 F.2d 228, 233 (7th Cir. 1988).

long as it stays within that range . . . . An abuse of discretion, on the other hand, can occur . . . when a relevant factor that should have been given significant weight is not considered; when an irrelevant or improper factor is considered and given significant weight; and when all proper factors, and no improper ones, are considered, but the court, in weighing those factors, commits a clear error of judgment.[4]

Notice the italicized words. How do you know what the "range of choice" is? You must read your jurisdiction's case law, where you'll find general definitions that might (or might not) resemble the one above.

The abuse-of-discretion standard—like the clear-error standard for fact decisions—reflects appellate deference to the trial court. Appellate courts reason that the trial judge is closer to the problem and might have a better view of how to solve it. As long as the trial judge chooses a decision within the permissible range, that decision will be affirmed.

Some decisions involve a combination of discretionary and other types of issues. For example, suppose a plaintiff moves for a preliminary injunction alleging that the defendant is infringing the plaintiff's trademark by selling a product called a Hyper Blob Blaster. (A preliminary injunction is a court's command to a party to do or not do certain things before trial.)

In this situation, some appellate courts will divide up the issues like this:

fact issue: Is the defendant selling a product called a Hyper Blob Blaster?

law issue: What rules of trademark law govern this dispute?

discretionary issue: Is a preliminary injunction an appropriate remedy in this situation?

With this view of the issues, an appellate court will reverse for clear error in fact-finding, or for an erroneous interpretation of the law (de novo), or for abuse of discretion in choosing or rejecting a preliminary injunction as a remedy.

Mixed issues of law and fact. Sometimes a fact issue can't be separated from a law issue. For example,

fact issue: What factually happened between the parties?

law issue: What's the governing legal test?

mixed issue: How does the legal test apply to these facts?

---

4. *Kern v. TXO Prod. Corp.*, 738 F.2d 968, 970 (8th Cir. 1984) (italics added).

It's hard to generalize about how courts handle mixed issues of law and fact on appeal. If you have a mixed issue, find the case law on issues like the one in your assignment and read carefully to see how the courts in your jurisdiction analyze the issue.

§36.2 How to Figure Out Which Standards of Review Govern Your Issues

First, look at what the appellate court is being asked to decide (i.e., look at the lower court decision and/or the statement of the issue(s) in the notice of appeal). Suppose the trial court determined what the facts are, decided what the law is, and chose a discretionary remedy. Suppose also that the losing party appeals only on the ground that the trial court misinterpreted the law.

In this example only the trial court's decision of law has been appealed. The fact and discretion issues have been left behind and are not before the appellate court. (Most law school assignments are pure issues of law.)

Law issues usually don't have labels on them that say "Law Issue Right Here." Instead, you might be told something like this: "The appellant contends that the trial court misinterpreted § 1331." That's an issue of law, which can be resolved entirely by deciding what the law is and how it should be applied to the facts.

Second, look also at how the analogous case law discusses your issue. Standards of review are usually found in case law, although they might partially be addressed in court rules. Look for cases that tell you not only what the standard is, but also what it means and how it works. When a court mentions the standard of review in a decision, it usually does so right after reciting the facts and just before beginning the legal analysis. Here's an example of the type of language you'll find:

> We review *de novo* the district court's dismissal of a complaint for failure to state a claim under Rule 12(b)(6). In reviewing such a motion, we accept all material allegations of fact as true and construe the complaint in a light most favorable to the non-moving party. We have consistently emphasized, however, that "conclusory allegations of law and unwarranted inferences" will not defeat an otherwise proper motion to dismiss. Dismissal for failure to state a claim is appropriate only "if it appears beyond doubt that the [non-moving party] can prove no set of facts in support of his claim which would entitle him to relief."[5]

Here we learn what the standard of review is (de novo). The court explains how the standard works by describing how the lower court should have made its decision ("Dismissal for failure to state a claim is appropriate only . . .").

---

5. *Vasquez v. L.A. Cty.*, 487 F.3d 1246, 1249 (9th Cir. 2007) (citations omitted).

Occasionally, you'll come across an issue that is subject to more than one standard of review. Each portion of this test for laches has a different standard of review:

> Our standard of review on the laches issue has various components. We review factual findings such as length of delay and prejudice under the clearly erroneous standard; we review the district court's balancing of the equities for abuse of discretion; and our review of legal precepts applied by the district court in determining that the delay was excusable is plenary [meaning de novo].[6]

§36.3   How to Use Standards of Review in a Brief

In federal appeals, the appellant's argument "must contain . . . for each issue a concise statement of the applicable standard of review (which may appear in the discussion of each issue or under a separate heading placed before the discussion of the issues)."[7] The appellee can omit this statement "unless the appellee is dissatisfied with the statement of the appellant."[8]

When you tell the court the standard of review, it often helps to explain, at the same time, the procedural posture below and the procedural test that governs it. And—if it can be done succinctly—tell the court how the standard justifies reversal (if you're the appellant) or how it doesn't (if you're the appellee). For example, from an appellant's brief:

> The plaintiff appeals from a summary judgment, which is reviewed de novo in this court. [*Citation.*] Summary judgment should be granted only where there is no genuine issue as to any material fact and the movant is entitled to judgment as a matter of law. [*Citation.*] In this case, the defendant should not have been granted summary judgment because he was not entitled to judgment as a matter of law.

This passage tells the court that the standard is de novo and that appellant will argue that the second element of the test for summary judgment was not satisfied. In the paragraphs that follow, the writer will have to explain thoroughly why the appellee was not entitled to judgment as a matter of law.

Set out the relevant standard of review at or near the beginning of the Argument section of the brief. Or, if you have more than one point, each with a different standard of review, a point's standard can be set out shortly after the point heading. Cite to authority to prove the standard of review. A conclusory rule explanation

---

6. *Bermuda Express, N.V. v. M/V Litsa*, 872 F.2d 554, 557 (3d Cir. 1989) (citation omitted).

7. Fed. R. App. P. 28(a)(9)(B).

8. Fed. R. App. P. 28(b).

(Chapter 18) is usually sufficient because appellate courts are generally familiar with the applicable standards of view.

If the standard is de novo, you can state it at the beginning and ignore it afterward because it's a neutral standard. But if the standard is one of the deferential ones—clear error or abuse of discretion—you must argue in terms of the standard. For example, if you're appealing from a decision involving the trial court's discretion, show exactly how the trial court abused its discretion. If you're the appellee in such a case, show the opposite. With any deferential standard, weave it into your argument.

If you're unsure of how to do any of these things, take a look at several opinions in which the court to which you're writing has handled the same standard of review in appeals involving the same procedural posture as in your case. Look for a definition of the standard. Try to learn its relationship to other procedural rules. And get a feel for the court's expectations about how the standard should be used.

37 Questions Presented

§37.1 The Purpose of a Question Presented

An effective Question Presented does two things. First, it *defines the legal issue* the court is being asked to resolve. Second, it *persuades* by framing the legal issue in the context of the determinative facts that support your theory.

If the Question Presented defines the legal issue objectively, it fails to persuade. And if it argues the case, it fails to credibly articulate the legal issue. The solution is to persuade through juxtaposition and careful word choice, just as you do in a Statement of the Case—but much more concisely.

The "question presented" by the situation includes not only the legal issue but also a reference to the governing legal test or concept and the key determinative facts. Asking "Is a manufacturer liable to a purchaser?" is a question, but it is not a *Question Presented* that frames the exact issue before the court.

A Question Presented combines:

- the legal issue to be resolved,
- a reference to the legal test or concept that governs the result, and
- the most important determinative facts.

§37.2 Two Generally Effective Formats

The three ingredients listed above can be put together in either of two ways. The format you use will depend upon your approach to the case.

The Verb/Concept/Facts format. Here the inquiry begins with a verb and subject:

Is the manufacturer of an electronic keyboard <u>liable</u> . . .?
<u>Does</u> a manufacturer <u>violate</u> a duty to the purchaser . . .?
<u>Can</u> the purchaser of an electronic keyboard <u>recover</u> . . .?

After beginning this way, add the legal concept. Then attach the most determinative facts in a *when* clause.

Here's an example, with its component parts identified:

Question Presented	Is the manufacturer of an electronic keyboard liable to a purchaser for violating an implied warranty of fitness for a particular purpose, when the keyboard exploded in the purchaser's hands the first time it was plugged in?
inquiry	is an electronic keyboard manufacturer liable to a purchaser?
legal concept	implied warranty of fitness for a particular purpose
facts	keyboard exploded in purchaser's hands when first plugged in

The Under/Does/When format. This format works particularly well when your reader needs to know what jurisdiction's law applies to the case. To structure a Question Presented this way, begin with the word *under*. Then specify the jurisdiction whose law governs the issue, together with a reference to the general nature of the legal rule:

Under § 51 of the New York Civil Rights Law, . . .
Under federal copyright law, . . .

Next, add the word *does* and introduce the basic inquiry and the legal issue or concept:

. . . does a professional model have a cause of action for invasion of privacy against an online vendor . . .

. . . does a music composer have a copyright claim against iTunes . . .

Finally, add the word *when* and the most determinative facts:

. . . when the defendant advertised the plaintiff's photograph for sale on its website without her consent?

. . . when iTunes sold the composer's recordings without paying her a royalty?